AIKIDO
IN AMERICA

AIKIDO
IN AMERICA

EDITED BY
JOHN STONE & RON MEYER

Frog, Ltd.
Berkeley, California

Published by Frog, Ltd.

Frog, Ltd. books are distributed by
North Atlantic Books
P.O. Box 12327
Berkeley, California 94712

This is issue #52 in the *Io* series.

Cover photo by Diane Evans
Cover and book design by Paula Morrison
Typeset by Catherine Campaigne
Printed in the United States of America

1 2 3 4 5 6 7 8 9 / 99 98 97 96 95

ACKNOWLEDGMENTS

We would like to extend our sincere thanks to the individuals presented in this book. We appreciate and honor their frankness and their dedication to aikido. Finally, we want to thank Kathy Glass, our copy editor, who made our manuscript flow.

I would like to thank my friend and partner, Ron, who kept a fire going under me when I needed it most. Without him this book would never have come into existence. I would also like to express my gratitude to all of my teachers, particularly Saotome Sensei, Ikeda Sensei, Peter Ralston and Bob Bryner, all of whom have had a profound effect on my understanding of aikido and the martial arts. Finally, I would like to thank my wife and fellow *aikidoka*, Robin Cooper, who has unfailingly supported me with love and encouragement wherever I have chosen to go.

John Stone
aikido *godan*

I especially wish to thank John, my first aikido teacher, and his wife Robin Cooper, who introduced me to a new life-long passion. Having moved to Boulder, my friend and aikido teacher, Hiroshi Ikeda Sensei, has gently pushed me to complete the book, "little by little." I also thank Diane Evans, my wife, who has encouraged me for more than ten years to keep practicing aikido. Finally, I want to thank Deborah O'Grady and Lisa Uzzilia Stauder for putting the manuscript together.

Ron Meyer
aikido *nidan*

TABLE OF CONTENTS

PREFACE

The idea for this book began over lunch in Boulder, Colorado, where we were training aikido at a seminar with one of our teachers, Hiroshi Ikeda Sensei. At one point in our meandering conversation one of us mentioned that it would be interesting to write a history of aikido in America. Even if nothing came of our efforts, at least it would be fun to travel around to other aikido schools and talk to some of the interesting people in the art. We consulted with Rick Fields, a friend of Ron's and a well-respected author in his own right, and after looking at samples of our writing, he thought we could make a go of it and extended his kind assistance in our search for a publisher.

Aikido was developed in Japan and brought to the United States by Japanese instructors. Much of the history of aikido in America concerns the meeting of our two cultures, and a complete history cannot exclude the Japanese students of the Founder who came here and introduced the art to Americans. But early in our research we decided to concentrate on the American side of the equation— with no disrespect to our Japanese teachers. Most of us who study aikido have or have had Japanese teachers, and we owe them an unpayable debt. They remain the exemplars of aikido. But for this book we were primarily interested in how Americans have responded to, changed and expanded aikido. Another equally interesting book could be written about how the Japanese instructors have responded to and been changed by America and Americans. But that, we felt, was someone else's job. So we began to interview interesting senior American instructors. It soon became apparent that we could not write the broad history that we envisioned, one that traced the development of the art in this country from the beginning to the present;

it was too large a topic. We decided therefore to limit the book to the people we had interviewed.

Our choice of people to interview was decidedly idiosyncratic, conditioned as it was by our own aikido history and our biases. We knew personally or by reputation many fine instructors, but we were mainly drawn to people who fell into one or more of the following categories: they had known or trained with the Founder of aikido, Morihei Ueshiba; they were well-known and influential in the post-war aikido styles we were both familiar with, or they had taken their art "off the mat," making serious efforts to apply aikido principles to non-martial situations. Not entirely coincidentally, most of the people we chose to interview live on the West Coast. More closely tied to the Far East than any other part of the U.S., the West Coast has the longest aikido history outside of Hawaii, the highest concentration of aikido schools in the continental United States, and is an area that does not have a dominant Japanese aikido instructor, as do the Midwest and the East Coast areas. Despite the inevitable narrowness of our choices, we feel that the people in this book, besides being fascinating in their own right, represent and embody many, though certainly not all, of the trends we wanted to examine.

We conducted the interviews over a period of several years, from 1990 to 1994. In one sense, then, the interviews are dated and show the concerns and attitudes of the people interviewed at a specific point in time. Their opinions and even the focus of this training may have changed by the time you read this book. But as you will see, that is just the point: for these people aikido training is evolutionary, a process of constant growth and of deepening insight and understanding. The stories these people tell bear eloquent witness to that fact and to the joy and difficulty of their life-long journeys of discovery and revelation.

We made one final change to our plan before completing the book. Instead of presenting verbatim interviews, we decided to edit out our own voices. Our aim was to make it seem that these people were talking directly to the reader, explaining themselves and their ideas.

The model we had was the one-act, one-actor play about an historical figure—Mark Twain, say—composed of words spoken or written by that person. We hoped as well to retain some of the oral flavor of the interview while editing, rearranging where necessary and occasionally rewriting for clarity or even adding a sentence or two for continuity. Since we could no longer call them "interviews," we refer to them as "conversational essays."

You are holding the result of our efforts. If you have never practiced aikido, we hope the words here will inspire you to investigate it further. If you are fortunate enough to live near one of the instructors in this book or to visit the areas in which they live, we urge you to check out their schools. If you have practiced or are practicing aikido, we hope that our book will provide fresh insights into the wonderful path we all follow, and that you will take any opportunity you have to train with the teachers featured here.

—John Stone
Ron Meyer

INTRODUCTION

Aikido, a modern Japanese martial art with a rich and fascinating philosophy, was first practiced on American* soil in the 1950s. Since then the aikido community has grown from a small group of predominantly Japanese-Americans in Hawaii to include schools in every state and major city. More importantly, and unlike most other martial arts, its influence extends to people who have never set foot in an aikido school. This book presents thirteen prominent American practitioners of the art in an effort to show how they embody some of the directions aikido has taken in America. The words of these intelligent and sincere people shed light on the history of aikido in this country and explain why they have chosen to dedicate themselves to the study of this particular martial art.

On first seeing aikido art, many people are surprised at how dance-like it looks. There are several reasons for this, but the most important is that aikido, like dance, involves blending with someone else's movement and energy. In aikido, the purpose of this blend is to use the attacker's force and intent as a means to subdue and

---

*We use the terms "America" and "Americans" in their common usage within the United States to refer to our country and its citizens. We acknowledge that "America" also encompasses Central and South America, and that all people in the Western Hemisphere are by some definitions "Americans." Given the awkwardness of making this distinction throughout, we have adopted the only practical option, which is the common use of "America" to refer to the U.S. Our apologies for this grammatical limitation.

control him or her. To accomplish this, aikido uses joint locks, hip throws, sweeps and projections. This description makes aikido sound a bit like judo, jujutsu or t'ai chi and it does share certain similarities with them. Its techniques are very much like those used in some forms of jujutsu, and aikido shares an emphasis on suppleness and "using the opponent's energy" with judo and t'ai chi. What makes aikido unique is its philosophical and spiritual claims. Practitioners will speak of "universal love," of "protecting the attacker" and of "becoming one with the universe." All of these claims, and indeed much of the appeal of the art to the first American practitioners, derive from one enigmatic and fascinating man, Morihei Ueshiba, the Founder of Aikido. In many ways Ueshiba was and still is synonymous with aikido. In his life are found all the elements that draw people to aikido as well as the seeming contradictions that bedevil its practitioners today.

Born in 1883 in Tanabe, Japan, Ueshiba was the son of a prosperous farmer and politician. As seems often to be the case with people who later develop great physical abilities, he was small and weak as a child. Spurred on by his concerned father, Ueshiba became obsessed with the desire to be strong—stronger than anyone else. The fact that he remained short, even for a Japanese (5 ft. 2 in), undoubtedly contributed to his obsession. He threw himself into all kinds of physical exertion, sumo wrestling, swimming and running. In the Japanese tradition of ascetic self-abuse, he doused himself daily with ice-cold water, encouraged his friends to throw chestnuts at him to toughen his skin, and hammered his head one hundred times a day against a stone slab to thicken his skull. By the time he was a young man, Ueshiba's strength was prodigious. He was often asked to carry sick children to the nearest doctor, who lived fifty miles away! He also liked to volunteer to make *mochi*, a rice paste, in local village festivals. This task required that the rice be pounded in a large wooden bowl for several hours, demanding endurance as well as strength. Usually, this was entrusted to several young men. Ueshiba was so strong that he pounded the *mochi* alone and often broke the bowl with the force of his blows. After word of the broken bowls spread, the local villages refused to allow Ueshiba to volunteer anymore.

Ueshiba left home at the age of eighteen to start a business in Tokyo. While there, he discovered he had an affinity for the martial arts and began studying several forms of jujutsu (empty-handed fighting) and kenjutsu (sword-fighting). After marrying in 1902, Ueshiba joined the army and served in Manchuria during the Russo-Japanese War. After his discharge, he tried his hand at several types of business but could not find any outlet for his considerable energy aside from his martial training. In 1912, encouraged by reports of the opportunities in the unsettled areas of the northern island of Hokkaido, Ueshiba moved there as the leader of a group of pioneer families. For the next eight years he threw himself into the task of clearing and farming the land, building up the community and developing local businesses. His restlessness remained, however.

Two men played a pivotal role in providing Ueshiba with a path on which he could profitably and meaningfully exploit his talents. Successful in his bouts with other martial artists, Ueshiba met a man in 1915 who easily defeated him. This man was Sokaku Takeda, master of an art called Daito-Ryu jujutsu. Ueshiba became Takeda's student, building a dojo on his own land so Takeda would have a place to instruct when he visited. Most of the physical techniques in aikido derive from this older school of jujutsu. But there was something about his teacher that troubled Ueshiba. Takeda had killed several men and as a result was incredibly wary and suspicious. He insisted that Ueshiba prepare all his food for him, was plagued by nightmares, and sometimes erroneously suspected that people were lying in wait for him outside the training hall. What was wrong with the martial arts if their foremost exponents were men like Takeda who, for all his prowess, was a suspicious and vain man?

The other influential man in Ueshiba's early life was Onisaburo Deguchi, the leader of a native Japanese religious sect called Omoto-Kyo. The founder of this sect was Nao Deguchi, an illiterate peasant woman who one night fell into a trance and dreamt that a god named Konji was speaking through her. Konji instructed the illiterate Nao to write down his words, which eventually became the 100,000-page central scripture of the sect. At first, the group that gathered around the humble Nao was small. But it began to grow quickly after the arrival of Onisaburo, who at that time (1898) was named Kisaburo Ueda. Independent of Nao he had experienced a vision in which he toured the cosmos and learned the secrets of the gods. But he was without followers or influence. One day he heard a voice while performing a ceremony at a shrine. The voice told him to go West where he would meet someone who was expecting him. Nao for her part had received a message from Konji that she should expect the arrival of someone from the East! When Ueda suddenly appeared, Nao and her people were at first suspicious, but eventually accepted Ueda as the messenger whose arrival had been foretold. Deguchi married Nao's daughter, adopted her last name and eventually became the leader of the sect. Handsome, charismatic, a gifted reader of other people and a superb artist, Deguchi soon attracted many followers to the sect, which took the name Omoto-Kyo, "The Great Origin."

Omoto-Kyo is a sect of Shinto, the native Japanese religion. It preaches that the god who spoke through Nao is the true God, the God who reveals Himself in all religions, the God who is in all things and all beings. He revealed Himself to Nao to enlist mankind's aid in the reconstruction of the world. Adherents of Omoto-Kyo believe that before Nao's revelation, mankind had wandered away from God. Nao's mission was to bring everyone back to the true path and to proclaim the message that only together can humanity build a paradise on earth.

Meanwhile, despite his success in Hokkaido and his discovery of the powerful art of Daito-Ryu, Ueshiba felt that something was missing in his life. Hearing stories of Deguchi, Ueshiba traveled to the Omoto-Kyo headquarters in Ayabe to investigate. Deeply impressed by the atmosphere surrounding the place and by Deguchi himself, Ueshiba moved his family to live there, abandoning his important and respected position in an impetuous act which understandably upset his wife and children. But Ueshiba felt impelled to go, sensing that Deguchi would open to him the dimension he knew was missing in his life. Once his family was established, Ueshiba threw himself into the study of Omoto-Kyo's doctrine and its spiritual practices. Deguchi taught Ueshiba various spiritual exercises whose aim was *misogi*, or spiritual cleansing, and initiated him into the mysteries of Kotodama medicine, which teaches that certain sounds have profound medicinal value. Much of the spiritual energy that inspired Ueshiba to transform the martial techniques of Daito-ryu aiki-jitsu into aikido derive from his devotion to Omoto-Kyo and his association with Deguchi. Many of the spiritual practices with which Ueshiba would begin aikido practice sessions were taught to him by Deguchi. And much of his sense that aikido has a mission in the world can be traced to Ueshiba's exposure to Omoto-Kyo's desire to "reconstruct the world." If Takeda provided Ueshiba with the shell of aikido, Deguchi showed him how to pour his soul into that shell, how to make it into a living thing capable of growth, development, wisdom and enlightenment.

Four years after arriving in Ayabe, Ueshiba accompanied his eccentric master on an ill-fated trip to Mongolia where Deguchi hoped to spread his message and establish a spiritual kingdom on earth. Naively unaware of the political situation in northern China where the Japanese were already setting the stage for their occupation of Manchuria, Deguchi and his companions fell into a trap. In an attempt to embarrass the Japanese government, the Chinese captured Deguchi and his group of "revolutionaries," bound them in leg irons and brought them before a firing squad. Fortunately, the authorities felt that killing the foreigners might be too provocative, although they did milk the situation for everything it was worth: the Chinese waited to inform their captives of the pardon until the soldiers had raised their guns and were about to fire. Several days later, Deguchi and company were released into the custody of the local Japanese officials. Although a total failure in most ways, the trip changed Ueshiba. On their wanderings, bandits had assaulted the group several times and Ueshiba found that he could actually dodge the bullets! "Before the opponent could pull the trigger, his intention to kill me would form into a ball of light and fly at me. If I evaded this ball of light, no bullet could touch me."[1] Through exposure to Deguchi, Ueshiba had discovered his spiritual vision and had begun a journey few of his later students were able fully to understand.

Several years after returning to Japan and starting to teach the followers of Omoto-Kyo martial skills, Ueshiba had an even more profound experience. Challenged to a fight by an officer who was an expert swordsman, Ueshiba easily evaded all attacks, even though he himself was unarmed. After the man had admitted defeat, Ueshiba went into his garden to wipe sweat off his body and rest. Suddenly he felt himself bathed in a golden light streaming down from the sky. In this exalted state he felt no separation between himself and the gods, between the sweat on his body and the evening mist, between his martial study and his spiritual quest. Suddenly able to understand the songs of the birds calling to one another in the garden, he knew that "I am the universe." If he moved in harmony with the universe and the laws of nature, how could there ever be any question of defeat? How could one overcome a hurricane? How could one attack the wind? In this one moment we can see much of what has appealed to Americans about aikido—the profound marriage of physical prowess and spiritual insight that Ueshiba demonstrated so clearly in the art he created.

Transformed by this experience, Ueshiba became truly invincible and capable of amazing feats. Two photos taken during that time give some idea of his abilities. In the first shot, Ueshiba is standing in the middle of a circle of young men armed with wooden swords and staffs. They are all attacking Ueshiba simultaneously, and the velocity of their strikes shows itself in the blurring of the weapons. Ueshiba is looking calmly at the camera, and there is no indication that he is about to move. In the next photo, the students have all just completed their attacks, and their weapons meet in the center of the circle where Ueshiba had just been standing. He is now outside of the circle, controlling the weapons of two of the students. The fact that he escaped is startling, even if physically comprehensible. What is truly amazing is that he escaped directly to his rear, in a direction he could not possibly have seen! "Regardless of how quickly an opponent attacks or how slowly I respond, I cannot be defeated.... As soon as the thought of attack crosses my opponent's mind, he shatters the harmony of the universe and is instantly defeated regardless of how quickly he attacks."[2]

Ueshiba even threw sumo wrestlers with ease. There is a famous story of how the sumo wrestler Tenryu became his student. Watching a demonstration of aikido in the 1930s, Tenryu was convinced it was staged. Sensitive to the mood of his audience, Ueshiba invited anyone to attack him. Tenryu was the first to volunteer. Ueshiba invited him to grab his arm and do anything he wanted. The giant Tenryu did so. "The moment I grasped his hand I felt overwhelmed, I was amazed. It felt like I was holding an iron bar."[3] He tried to push Ueshiba over, but couldn't budge him. Then he lunged at him and was sent flying. Finally Ueshiba pinned him with one finger. Now convinced of Ueshiba's ability, Tenryu asked to become his student.

As word of his abilities spread, Ueshiba began to attract students from outside the sect. Soon he was receiving numerous requests to conduct training sessions in other parts of the country. Realizing that his martial studies now provided him the arena in which to deepen his spiritual understanding, Ueshiba embraced his new calling as a martial arts instructor. By 1931, Ueshiba had left the Omoto-Kyo headquarters and built a dojo in Tokyo. Before leaving, Ueshiba received Deguchi's blessing: "Budo will be your practice to manifest the divine," Deguchi told him.[4]

Ueshiba was very careful about whom he admitted to his new school. He demanded two recommendations from prospective students, and most who joined were already proficient in at least one other martial art. Many other martial artists came to investigate Ueshiba. The art as Ueshiba practiced it then was much rougher than today's aikido. In fact, training in the Tokyo dojo, the Kobukan, was so severe that the school acquired the name of "Hell Dojo." Nonetheless, Ueshiba's *aiki-budo,* as it was called then, was still different enough from other martial arts that many people thought Ueshiba was a fake.

He would throw his students the instant they attacked him, and it was often difficult to see exactly what he had done. Not knowing what they were looking at, visitors with martial experience would often challenge Ueshiba or one of his students. Regardless of who they were or what their background, all the challengers were defeated.

One of the extraordinary abilities Ueshiba acquired was that he never had any *suki* (openings), moments when he was vulnerable to attack. In an effort to impress the importance of this ability on his students and to train himself, Ueshiba offered a reward to anyone who could sneak up on him without his knowing it. His students tried everything, including attacking him in his sleep. Once, while accompanying Ueshiba on a trip, a disciple was sure he had caught his master unawares. Ueshiba had stretched out for a nap and appeared to be fast asleep. The disciple reached over for Ueshiba's fan and was about to strike him on the head when Ueshiba's eyes opened: "My guardian deity tells me that you are thinking of hitting me over the head. You wouldn't do such a thing, would you?"[5] Having acquired the ability to intuit what his students were thinking, he was never caught off guard.

As World War II approached, Ueshiba was enlisted to train men at the Military Police Academy and at an "espionage college." In addition, he instructed some of the most important officials directing the war effort, including Prime Minister General Hideki Tojo, Admiral Yamato and the members of the Imperial family. But Ueshiba was disturbed by his country's movement toward war. "The military is dominated by reckless fools ignorant of statesmanship and religious ideals, who slaughter innocent citizens indiscriminately and destroy everything in their path. They act in total contradiction to God's will, and they will surely come to a sorry end."[6] Ueshiba's fears were strengthened when the government, worried about the popularity of Deguchi and his calls for a new age, crushed the Omoto-Kyo sect, burning its headquarters and imprisoning Deguchi. In 1942, despite his popularity and a new-found prosperity, Ueshiba retired from martial arts instruction and moved to the countryside. There, in Iwama, he constructed a shrine to "the spirit of aiki" and continued his meditations.

World War II and the defeat of Japan had a profound effect on Ueshiba, forcing him to reevaluate his art and his training. He became convinced that the art he had developed, which he now called Aikido, "the way of harmony with the energy (of the universe)," was a new kind of martial art. The purpose of the traditional martial arts was to fell an opponent. Even he had been concerned with that and had knowingly trained soldiers preparing for battle. The aim of aikido, he now saw, was to obliterate even the idea of an opponent from the minds of men. If he could do this, he could build the paradise on earth that Deguchi had envisioned.

> Martial arts are not means of felling the opponent by force or by lethal weapons. True martial arts call for bringing the inner energy of the universe in order, protecting the peace of the world, and molding as well as preserving everything in nature in its proper form. Training in martial arts is tantamount to strengthening, within body and soul, the love of God, the deity who begets, preserves and nurtures everything in nature."[7]

This message found fertile ground in America in the '60s and '70s when so many people were sickened by our experience in the Vietnam War.

In keeping with his new vision, Ueshiba modified his art, eliminating many of the strikes to anatomical weak points *(atemi)* and making the movements more circular and flowing. He even got rid of the idea of using the art to attack someone, making it into a purely defensive art. "In aikido there is absolutely no attack. To attack means that the spirit has already lost. We adhere to the principle of absolute non-resistance."[8] A number of Ueshiba's pre-war students could not understand their teacher's new form of the art with its more pronounced spiritual emphasis. They felt that he had become weak and formed their own schools, where they sought to preserve the harder, pre-war style. The proliferation of varying aikido styles accelerated dramatically after the Founder's death in 1969 and has affected American aikido as well. Indeed, we even have several home-grown aikido organizations.

Convinced of the importance of his new understanding, Ueshiba opened the study of aikido to a broader public. Soon, aikido spread overseas. In 1953, aikido was demonstrated on American soil for the first time when the head instructor of the new Tokyo dojo, Koichi Tohei, traveled to Hawaii. During the demonstration Tohei easily handled an attack by a group of local judo black belts and aikido soon acquired an enthusiastic following. In 1957, Ueshiba—in his only trip outside Asia—visited Hawaii and put on an impressive demonstration. Soon thereafter, people on the mainland began to hear about the art and some traveled to Japan to investigate or, like several people in our interviews, stumbled upon the art while traveling or living in Japan. What they saw amazed them. The sight of a tiny, white-bearded old man tossing around men fifty years his junior was astounding.

But what impressed many of them the most was the man's presence. Humble and unassuming off the mat, as soon as he donned his training uniform and started to lead a class, Ueshiba changed completely. He would often begin class with a ceremony in which he used a *jo* (or wooden staff) in a ceremony of ritual purification *(misogi)*. As he swung the *jo* around him in wide and ever-faster movements, he would seem to grow and his eyes would flash. It was as if he became a vehicle for a power much greater than himself, an incarnation of some divine being. Over the years, as Ueshiba's physical power waned, he was able to manifest his spiritual understanding more and more clearly. Terry Dobson, one of the people interviewed in this book relates that Ueshiba never taught technique. "He was not a tennis pro. For him, aikido was not a technical exercise at all. It was part of a play of spirit, a movement of the universe." A story has it that a famous Zen master, Yasotani Roshi, once met Ueshiba and spent some time talking with him. Afterwards, Yasotani remarked to one of his disciples, Philip Kapleau, "This man is deeply enlightened." No wonder his students called him O-Sensei, "Great Teacher."

Ueshiba's life and the art he founded are filled with paradoxes and seeming contradictions. As a martial artist, Ueshiba was invincible. Without this fact, aikido would undoubtedly never have become famous. But Ueshiba said that his invincibility came from transcending the idea of winning and losing; moreover, he was not invincible—it was the universe embodied in him that could not be defeated. Aikido is firmly rooted in physical reality. Students spend their time grabbing and striking each other; they sweat, pant, feel pain and sometimes experience injuries. Many years are required to master the numerous and complicated techniques. But for Ueshiba, technique and the physical practice were the means to and an expression of a deep spiritual understanding: "Aikido is the path which joins all paths of the universe throughout eternity; it is the Universal Mind which contains all things and unifies all things."[9] Aikido seems in many ways to be the most traditional of the popular Japanese martial arts. Participants wear a skirt-like garment called the *hakama* which has no utilitarian function; there is no competition; some of the attacks and techniques are based on situations which could only arise in a society where people spend much of their time kneeling and carry swords for self-defense. Yet Ueshiba, as we have seen, tried to fashion aikido into a completely new kind of martial art, with the professed aim of self-perfection, not martial effectiveness.

These paradoxes and the example set by the Founder's own life have, on the one hand, made aikido deeply appealing to Americans and, on the other, had a lasting impact on development of the art in America. Naturally enough, many students are drawn by the idea that aikido may be the ultimate martial art, i.e., the most martially effective. Students who begin with this idea often concentrate on one of the older forms of aikido and tend to downplay the decidedly religious overtones of Ueshiba's later years. Others are intrigued by the combination of a physical art with a spiritual center. Sometimes the emphasis on the non-physical side has resulted in a gentle and soft version of the art with none of the physical roughness of pre-war aikido. Practitioners of this version of aikido have clearly been fascinated with the image Ueshiba projected in his later years of a wise and gentle sage who could effortlessly and gently control any attacker. And in a time that questioned all tradition and paradoxically yearned for something to replace it, aikido's unique blend of traditionalism and innovation proved particularly enticing to Americans in the '70s. The image of a continually growing and experimenting Founder has even inspired some Americans to devise versions of aikido that seem to have little relationship to the more orthodox styles.

Two other factors directly related to the life of the Founder have helped draw Americans to aikido. For most Americans, any intensely physical practice belongs to the young. We have no traditions of physical arts in which one's understanding and practice continually expand and deepen throughout one's life. The Founder's life and the art he created have provided Americans with a model of a new kind of physical practice, one which enriches all of one's life and in which true understanding only comes with long practice. Moreover, Ueshiba's life directly contradicts the widely held belief that old age only means a lessening of one's powers, insight and abilities.

The spiritual nature of Ueshiba's art has also proven to be very inspiring. In the '60s and '70s, during an age of moral relativism, when many people saw the flaws of the established religions and searched in vain for heroes whose lives could stand up to close scrutiny, many Americans looked to the spiritual traditions and leaders of the East for inspiration. Ueshiba's life and art grew out of these traditions and held out to Americans the hope of the kind of deep spiritual enlightenment that Americans sought but did not find in their own religious leaders. Today, as the spiritual awakening which began in the '60s continues to grow, the spiritually rich and deeply moral life Ueshiba led, the amazing and seemingly miraculous feats he performed, combined with the very physical art he created, continue to prove intensely attractive to Americans.

Unfortunately, the spiritual side of aikido is the least understood part of the art, primarily because Ueshiba's spiritual talks are devilishly difficult to understand. He often expressed his ideas in terms

12

of an idiosyncratic and virtually impenetrable interpretation of Shinto mythology: "*Nagi* and *Nami* gave birth to Oyashima, in other words, *odo no kanzawa*, which was accomplished through *shimaumi*, and *shimaumi* is aikido."[10] He would sometimes say, "Whatever wisdom you may have, you cannot understand my lectures because even I cannot understand what I mean."[11] He apparently felt that his words came to him from the *kami*, the world of the gods, much as Nao Deguchi's words came to her. No wonder his Japanese students found it difficult to follow his rambling talks. This, coupled with the fact that his *deshi* were usually hot-blooded young men more interested in bashing heads than in deepening their spiritual insight, has meant that aikido has no consistent esoteric teaching. Nor, since Ueshiba was on a constant voyage of discovery and little interested himself in developing a teaching methodology, has aikido any generally accepted means of transmitting Ueshiba's profound enlightenment beyond the idea that "in training, all things become clear."

For Westerners, the difficulty in understanding Ueshiba is compounded by the fact that so few people approach life as did Ueshiba, for whom all activities were part of a continual prayer. In our secular world, many of the people intensely involved in spiritual exploration and experimentation—the followers of Bhagwan Rajneesh and other gurus, the believers in the power of crystals, channelers of ancient Egyptians, soul-travelers—are often viewed as self-deluded fools or even lunatics. Yet Ueshiba has much more in common with them than with the average Westerner. What, after all, is one to say of a man who once claimed to have fought a sword-wielding ghost for three nights running, after which his sword-work became peerless! Even more foreign is the idea that a martial art can have anything to do with a life of prayer. For us the juxtaposition is ludicrous. We have no St. Francis of Assisi of the boxing ring! But this very unfamiliarity and the tantalizing hints of what Ueshiba was trying to show his followers are what draw so many to begin the journey of aikido.

In fact, without this intriguing spiritual dimension, aikido would be little known outside the world of martial arts. Ueshiba's assertion that the principles of aikido are universally applicable—indeed, that the physical art of aikido is only one expression of a universal truth—has attracted many people to aikido who have little interest in the more combat-oriented martial arts. Inspired by what they have learned, many of them have applied their new insights to their own lives and to the other "arts" they know. Dance, massage therapy, psychology, business management—all the disciplines involving social interaction have felt the influence of aikido. It is now possible for someone to be exposed to the principles of aikido without even knowing its name or practicing one of its physical techniques.

Aikido came to this country as a Japanese art; the earliest teachers here were Japanese; and high-ranking Japanese instructors continue to play an important role in the growth and spread of aikido in America. But the Japanese could not do what the earliest American practitioners have been able to do: make aikido an American art, and interpret the message of aikido in a way that makes sense to Americans without distorting or watering-down that message. Four of the people we interviewed were fortunate enough to have met and begun their training with the Founder himself: Terry Dobson, Robert Nadeau, Robert Frager and Mary Heiny. Terry Dobson carries the added distinction of being the only American to be a personal student of Ueshiba. We call these people the Disciples. They represent the elite of the first generation of American *aikidoka*, those who began their practice in Japan during Ueshiba's lifetime. In their non-doctrinaire approach to technique and their search for the spiritual heart of aikido, we can catch glimpses of the fire which burned so brightly in Ueshiba. For each of the Disciples, meeting Ueshiba irrevocably altered his or her life. Dobson, who died in 1992, was convinced that aikido and Ueshiba had rescued him from becoming a murderer or a suicide. The first time he saw aikido, Dobson knew he had to study the art. Instinctively he knew that aikido was the antidote for the violence within him. Dobson spent the rest of his life working out the problem of how to turn violence and conflict into something constructive. He became an influential, respected and controversial spokesperson for aikido and the first American to write about aikido's role "off the mat."

A dedicated student of the martial arts, Robert Nadeau had long been interested in mind-body connections and what he would later call "energy work" at a time when few others seemed to be exploring that realm. Training with Ueshiba was a relief for Nadeau. All Ueshiba talked about was energy. All his demonstrations were embodiments of *ki,* universal energy. Ueshiba was living proof for Nadeau that he was not insane: the strange things he had been examining were at the heart of an entire art. After returning to the United States Nadeau became one of the most important explorers of "energy work" on the West Coast, and for many years led seminars at the Esalen Institute.

Robert Frager was an ambitious graduate student of psychology at the time he trained under the Founder. Seeing that Ueshiba was able to perform seeming "miracles" anytime he felt like it forced Frager to completely revamp his view of what was humanly possible. He eventually founded his own institute for the training of psychologists and included aikido as a required part of the curriculum.

Mary Heiny was in Japan studying Japanese when she was persuaded by Frager, her friend and fellow student, to come watch an aikido demonstration. While watching Ueshiba perform his art, Heiny had an extraordinary experience that she describes fully in her interview. Because of that experience, Heiny knew immediately that she would devote the rest of her life to the study of Ueshiba's art. Now she is the highest-ranking woman instructor in North America and is widely respected for her abilities as a teacher and for her deep commitment to aikido.

Those who began their practice in the United States in the early years of aikido are represented by a group we call the Teachers: Frank Doran, Rod Kobayashi and George Simcox. All three of these men actually met or saw the Founder, but of much more importance to them was the influence of the most prominent and charismatic of Ueshiba's post-war students, Koichi Tohei. Everyone who started aikido in the United States before Ueshiba's death was in some way a student of Tohei, who introduced aikido to the United States and who was in charge of American aikido until he left the parent organization in Japan in 1972. Tohei developed his own style of aikido, what he would later call *Ki Aikido,* in which he attempted to present in a rational and (he felt) more understandable way what Ueshiba clothed in Shinto terms. Where Ueshiba talked about "the bridge between life and death," Tohei talked about the "four principles: keep one-point, relax completely, extend *ki* and weight underside." Where Ueshiba was spiritual, abstruse, non-systematic and undogmatic, Tohei was down-to-earth, easy to comprehend, systematic and very specific about how to perform techniques.

Despite these seeming differences, Tohei was Ueshiba's heir-apparent and chief instructor at World Aikido Headquarters. But after Ueshiba's death when, in traditional fashion, Ueshiba's son Kishomaru became the new head of aikido, Tohei felt that limits were being placed on his ability to explore and teach aikido as he saw fit. So in 1974 he split with the Founder's son and started his own system of aikido. Ueshiba was a charismatic and powerful figure and while he lived, everyone acknowledged him as the head of aikido: he had, after all, taught them all. After his death, fissures in the organization, old rivalries, and differences about the direction aikido should take began to surface. Tohei's departure was the first of several splits within the aikido world. Now there are numerous world-wide organizations and many distinct styles, sometimes even within the same organization. This disunity is taken as a matter of course by new students of aikido, but those who practiced at the time of Tohei's departure experienced a great shock. Friendships were destroyed as people faced the agonizing choice between following their teacher or staying loyal to the Founder's designated heir. When the split came, Rod Kobayashi stayed with Tohei. Kobayashi had a deep connection to Tohei, having spent some time with him in Japan.

Doran's connection was less strong, partly because he too had been to Japan and had seen the many different styles of aikido taught by Ueshiba's other students. There was more than one way to perform even the most basic of techniques. A military man, Doran felt his loyalty must lie with the parent organization, not just with one of its teachers.

Starting in Hawaii under teachers trained by Tohei, Simcox chose to follow him because he felt an affinity for Tohei's approach. Those who had stayed with World Headquarters seemed less interested than he was in explicitly presenting and exploring what he saw as the principles of aikido and in applying them to everyday situations.

Kobayashi, Doran and Simcox share one other connection which in some ways derives from Tohei: their dedication to teaching the art. As Doran states in his interview, Tohei was a master teacher. His entire system is a deeply considered attempt to teach the art in a rational way. Simcox even feels that Tohei's method of instruction would not exist without America: here Tohei could not rely on the traditional Japanese method of instruction, which eschews verbal explanation and relies on unquestioning imitation by the students and hours and hours of sweaty repetition. Tohei's American students asked, "Why?" Kobayashi, Doran and Simcox are dedicated instructors who have trained countless students. Kobayashi is the head of his own aikido organization and devotes much of his time to training instructors. Frank Doran is known for the precision and power of his technique and for the clarity of his teaching. Many of the prominent instructors in the San Francisco Bay Area are or have been his students. And Simcox devotes a great deal of energy elucidating the principles of Ki Aikido and showing his students how they can apply them to their own lives.

The first generation of completely American aikidoists, those whose primary teachers have been American, is represented in part by the last group in our book. In fact, several of them are or have been students of the Disciples or the Teachers. But this group, which we call the Innovators, by no means reflects all of the trends within their generation. None of them, for example, are primarily concerned with aikido's martial effectiveness. We have chosen them because they are all first and foremost interested in aikido as a *do*, a path or way, a means of increasing self-understanding and a life practice. Most of them have distinguished themselves further by applying what they learned in aikido to other realms. They have taken aikido "off the mat" and made their lives an arena of practice and refinement as well.

George Leonard has written extensively of his involvement with and ideas about aikido in numerous books, such as *The Ultimate Athlete* and *Mastery*. Inspired in part by his training with Robert Nadeau, he has also created a series of exercises which he teaches in something called "Leonard Energy Training."

Richard Heckler has applied aikido principles to his work as a psychologist and bodyworker. Aikido is taught as part of the curriculum at The Lomi School, which he co-founded with Robert Hall. Heckler is the author of three books about aikido and his own approach to psychology: *In Search of the Warrior Spirit, The Anatomy of Change* and *Aikido and the New Warrior.*

Wendy Palmer developed her own system of body and energy training which she calls "Conscious Embodiment," in which people examine explicitly many of the personal and inter-personal issues that are usually only implied in standard aikido practice.

Tom Crum is probably the most prominent aikido proselytizer in this group. Through his work with John Denver and the Windstar Foundation, he has acquainted thousands of people here and abroad with "the principles of *aiki.*" He has also written a popular book, *The Magic of Conflict.*

Danielle Evans, another northern California *aikidoka*, applied aikido to Model Mugging, which started out as an intense women's self-defense course and has, under Evan's influence, become a means of empowering people to confront violence and co-dependency issues in their lives.

The final member of this group is Koichi Barrish. The art he teaches does not descend directly from Ueshiba. He inherited a traditional Japanese family martial art, a form of *aiki-jitsu,* one which grew from the same roots as Ueshiba's aikido. Although not of Ueshiba's line, Barrish professes a spiritual affinity with Ueshiba, having trained in Japan at Tsubaki Grand Shrine and been authorized to instruct some of the esoteric spiritual practices that Ueshiba learned through his association with Omoto-Kyo. Because Barrish has allowed that spiritual connection to suffuse and transform the art he inherited, he feels that he no longer teaches aiki-jitsu but aikido.

Barrish is certainly the most controversial teacher we interviewed. Many view his claim to be an aikido instructor with skepticism. If aikido is only the physical art that Ueshiba originated, then by his own admission, Barrish does not teach it. But as the preceding pages have made clear, Ueshiba himself meant much more than the physical art when he talked of aikido. "I didn't create aikido. *Aiki* is the Way of the *Kami* [gods]. It is to be a part of the laws of the universe. It is the source of the principles of life. The history of aikido begins with the origin of the universe. Do you think a human being could possibly have created these laws?"[12] Does Barrish teach the aikido Ueshiba speaks of here? We don't know.

We make no claims that the individuals you read about in this book are "the best" or even necessarily the most important practitioners of aikido in America today. We have, for example, purposely overlooked all of the outstanding Japanese instructors in this country, without whom aikido would be unknown here. And we have inevitably overlooked many other fine and significant American instructors. But we do believe the people we call the disciples, the teachers and the innovators are worthy of your attention. They describe, discuss and reflect upon the most important trends in the history of aikido in America and are fascinating and impelling spokespeople for this rich and fascinating art.

Notes

1. Mitsugi Saotome, *Aikido and the Harmony of Nature,* (Boston, Shambala, 1993), p. 10

2. John Stevens, *Abundant Peace,* (Boston, Shambala, 1987), p. 112

3. "Doshu Interview: Tenryu and Aikido," *Aiki News* 23, p. 10

4. Stevens, *Abundant Peace,* p. 37

5. Stevens, *Abundant Peace,* p. 74

6. Stevens, *Abundant Peace,* p. 47. (See also Mitsugi Saotome, *Aikido*

and the Harmony of Nature, (Boston, Shambala, 1994), p.11

7. Kisshomaru Ueshiba, *The Spirit of Aikido,* trans. Taitetsu Unno, (Kodansha International, 1984), p. 9

8. "An Interview with O-Sensei and Kisshomaru Ueshiba," *Aiki News* 18, pp. 6–7.

9. Saotome, *Aikido and the Harmony of Nature,* p. 17.

10. "O-Sensei Radio Interview Transcript," *Aiki News,* p. 23

11. Koichi Tohei, *This is Aikido,* (Tokyo, Japan Publications, 1975), preface. We have read interviews with other students of Ueshiba which corroborate this.

12. Saotome, *Aikido and the Harmony of Nature,* p. 17

THE DISCIPLES

I

TERRY DOBSON

A large bearded man, Terry Dobson was a charismatic teacher, a fascinating raconteur and a passionate advocate for aikido. As he reveals in the following interview, he first encountered aikido in Japan in 1960. What he saw affected him so strongly that he resolved there and then to devote himself to the study of aikido. Within a year he had become the only American to be accepted as a personal student of the Founder. He vividly describes the wonderful case of "beginner's mind" that possessed him in his early years of training and paints a fascinating portrait of Ueshiba as a "polished being." After he came back to the United States in 1969, Dobson founded two dojos, one in Burlington, Vermont, and one in New York City.

In 1978 he published Giving in to Get Your Way, *the first book written by an American about the application of aikido principles to everyday life. He started conducting seminars based on his ideas, pioneering the interpersonal study of "conflict management." Around 1980 he moved to Northern California, partly with the hope of expanding his seminar activity and partly to join the large aikido community there. He became a regular teacher at Aikido of Tamalpais in Mill Valley and led aikido seminars and classes in many other places. He also met Robert Bly there, with whose "men's work" he became more and more involved, and about whom he speaks with affection and enthusiasm.*

Ill from a progressively-worsening case of a rare lung disease, he moved back East to live in Vermont in the late 1980s. He grew so ill

*he considered quitting aikido at one point but he found he could not
give it up. As he himself said, "Aikido has been my refuge, my excuse,
my living.... It has been a very good friend to me and a very harsh
teacher at the same time." Dobson's devotion to the truth as he saw it
and his emotional honesty emerge clearly from his words as he talks
candidly about his difficulty with his fellow* uchi deshi, *his struggles
as a teacher, his perceived failure to succeed in California and his sick-
ness, which he blames partly on his own conduct. His condition
improved somewhat and he began teaching aikido seminars again.
He died in 1992 in San Francisco shortly after teaching an aikido class.*

The first time I saw aikido was in 1960 when I was twenty-
three years old. I had spent two years in the Marines, from
1957 to 1959. I used every opportunity to beg them to send
me to Japan, because I was really interested in martial arts. But you
know how it is. If the only thing you're suited for is working on cars,
they'll make you into a typist. Anyway, I finally got to Japan after a
friend of my family had wangled me a job up in the mountains with
a kind of private peace corps, a non-profit project funded by the
Episcopal church in the States. I worked as a volunteer there. I got
$30 a month, plus room and board. After I got there I started look-
ing around for someone who could teach me about martial arts. I
thought, as a lot of people did then, that every Japanese did martial
arts and to be Japanese was to be, *ipso facto,* a master. There was
one guy who was pointed out to me as knowing martial arts. But
when I talked to him it turned out that he had had a year of judo
when he was in the seventh grade, or something like that. It was
really a very rude awakening.

So later on, when I happened to see a notice in a newspaper for
an aikido demonstration being given in Yokohama, I was immediately interested. Here was a chance to see a real martial art. The
place where the demo was to be held turned out to be a movie theater on the Yokohama army base, which had been sort of decom-
missioned. It was now 1960 and troops were no longer billeted there.
It had devolved into some sort of quasi-PX or something. I walked

into the theater and the demonstration was already in progress.

There was hardly anybody there. There were about eight people in the audience, Americans who were probably out shopping and didn't have anything better to do. Yamada [an *uchi deshi* or live-in student of aikido, now chief instructor of the New York Aikikai] was on the stage with his *ukes* [people who assist by taking falls], demonstrating *yokomen uchi shiho nage* [a basic aikido technique]. I saw that one movement and I immediately understood the significance of it. Even then I understood in some way that aikido was a tool of immense significance for people whose idea of power is skewed. And I mean that in a large sense, coming from, as I did, a culture where power is celebrated as being connected to large things, like strength and money, you know, the standard view of power that Americans as a race seem to hold. Aikido seemed the perfect antidote for that. And I knew right away that I would spend the rest of my life in some degree connected with what I had seen, trying to understand it at successively deeper levels.

That moment changed my life. Imagine that you have been on a boat and shipwrecked on this desert island. You are pretty resigned to the fact that there is nothing to eat and you're going to die. And all of a sudden, this beautiful white gleaming yacht heaves to and a boat is sent to fetch you. You are taken on board the yacht and the crew is very nice to you and, in fact, you always wanted to be a sailor. The boat has sails and masts you can climb and you can do all these things you had always wanted to. All around is nothing but the sea and this vessel and there are nooks and crannies and it would take you a year to really know that vessel, much less the people on it. The appearance of the yacht has not only saved your life, it has given you what you always dreamed about. Your eyes would be bright from morning to night with discovery. That's the way I was. It was a feast. Sometimes in your life you meet someone or you see something or you understand something on a deep level, and in that one moment your fate is decided. You decide that you want to be next to that woman or you want to be next to that device or whatever it is. It's an absolute, it's like a magnet meeting a piece of steel.

There's no temporizing, there's no way you can avoid the consequences of having met that piece of steel.

I went up to Yamada after the demonstration and said, "I want to practice aikido. What do I do?" He didn't know so he said, "Come with me." Then I went with him back to Hombu Dojo [the main aikido dojo or training hall in Japan], where I got a registration form and became a member of the dojo. Then I bought a book about aikido and went back to the mountains. Unfortunately there was no question of practicing in Tokyo. I had to work out my contract with the people in the mountains, which was a year. I think three or four months had passed by this time and I had another eight months or so to go before I could be released from the contract. So the only thing I could do was practice by myself. Outside of my room, there was this apple tree. You know how the boughs of an apple tree resemble the general curve of an arm? Well, I was doing *shiho nage* and *ikkyo* and *kote gaeshi* [basic aikido techniques] on apple boughs long before I touched a human being. It was really instructive, because after I broke a couple of boughs I realized that there are only so many boughs on a tree, and if I were to keep on breaking boughs, I wouldn't have anybody to practice with pretty soon. So I couldn't do *kote gaeshi* beyond a certain point. It had to be done gently.

When my contract finally ran out, I went to Tokyo, found an apartment and started going to the dojo all the time. Since I was there all the time—I mean, they had to throw me out at night to get me to go home—I started asking if I could live in the dojo. I'd say, "Can I live here? After you guys throw me out I spend the rest of the night thinking about it and then I've got to get up and come back here. Why can't I stay, is it possible? You guys have got room here. I won't take up much space. It'll save me train fare." I didn't think of becoming an *uchi deshi* or any of that stuff. I didn't know what an *uchi deshi* was, I didn't know anything. I was living one day at a time.

So I asked Tamura to ask O-Sensei if that would be possible. And he did and I know he caught a lot of shit for doing it, because there were a lot of people who didn't want me there, mega-didn't want me there. There was a lot of opposition to my becoming *uchi deshi*. Not that they disliked me particularly; it was just that they didn't want a foreigner there. There had been one other foreign *uchi deshi* before me, a Frenchman, and he had fallen into disfavor for some reason, and when I came along, some people in the organization cited his example as a reason for keeping me out.

But O-Sensei didn't care about that. He said, "Yeah, yeah, I like this guy, whoever he is. I want him." And they said, "Well, we don't think you ought to do it." And he said, I know this happened, he said, "I want him. Period." And if he hadn't wanted me, there's no way I would have become *uchi deshi*. But he wanted me. He wanted me because I was captivated by aikido, and when someone is captivated by something, they're an extremely enticing student. I was totally seized by my interest in the art. I had nothing else to live for, nothing else that I wished to do. I clung like a drowning man to aikido. That commended itself. I had a good beginner's mind. I had a case of beginner's mind that was absolutely irresistible because it was unforced and because aikido appeared to me to be an answer to all of my problems.

As long as I was in the dojo I was learning something. When I wasn't in the dojo, I was thinking about aikido. "So what happens if I do this?" And there was nobody from whom I couldn't learn. Even people who started after me, I figured maybe they understood something I hadn't. It was not because of my noble, virtuous character; that's just the way it was. I would pay everything, I would pay the rest of my life, if I could spend a month with that head now, if I could get beginner's mind and see aikido as I first saw it. I've been on the other side of that and I've seen people who've had the same hunger. I'll be thinking, "Shit, I've got to teach aikido class. Maybe I can get so-and-so. . . . No, she's out of town." That's the level of my jadedness. And here's somebody who says, "Are you going to teach tonight?" It's a rebuke in a sense. You wish to Christ you had that feeling. That's the most beautiful place that a person can get and that's where I was then. O-Sensei saw that and he wanted me. I mean, he really wanted me to be there. Nobody else did.

So I became an *uchi deshi*. The days began around 5:30 when we had to be up to clean the dojo. Then I'd go to the first couple of morning classes, which started at 6:30. After that I might teach English, that was how I supported myself. But I might also arrange to go carry somebody's bag, like Tohei Sensei [then chief instructor and later founder of his own style of aikido], follow him around, be his *uke* for the day. Or I would just go on my own and study with different teachers. Then at night there would be two or three more classes. Then I'd probably hang around working out until everybody had gone and then, maybe around ten o'clock, I'd go to sleep.

As time went on and I got more experienced, I started taking *ukemi* [falls] from O-Sensei and would go with him on his trips. If there's one thing people ask me about, it's what it was like to be thrown by him. Well, in many ways it was like taking *ukemi* from any of the other teachers: you were supposed to give the best that you had. If I was doing my job right, which I frequently did not, I would give 100 percent attention and commitment to whoever was throwing me. Nobody told me to do that. It took me a while to figure out that that was the name of the game. Still much longer to keep my attention from wandering. But one thing that distinguished O-Sensei was that he was extremely subtle in his call for an attack. Just by a tiny nod of the head, which never exceeded a quarter of an inch, he would tell you not only to attack but what attack to use. After a while it was easy enough to pick up those signals. But you had to be right there every single instant, which was often difficult. If your knees were killing you because you were sitting in *seiza* [kneeling] and it was a hot day out or something, your attention tended to wander. Sometimes he would talk for forty minutes or so between techniques and then all of a sudden he would make one of those movements and you had to be right there with him and attack him at once. If you didn't do that he would send you back to sit down. Not a good feeling, I can tell you. You just had to be out there. You had to give it to him. And if he called for something, you had to give it 100 percent, and then you had to worry about if you'd made a mistake. But that was his lookout. If he called for *shomen* and you gave him a *tsuki*, well, that was his lookout. And that's the way he wanted it. He could handle it, you just had to trust he could handle it.

The actual experience of being thrown by O-Sensei for the most part was pretty much like being thrown by anybody else. I mean, you'd leave your feet and land on your back. But in another way, the experience was very different. For one thing, he was always gentle. He was way beyond pile-driver technique. He was so far beyond that that I don't know where he was. For another thing, he could freeze you with a look. I fucking guarantee it. You've probably experienced something like that; I mean, your mother or somebody in your life could probably freeze you with a look whenever they damn well wanted. But I don't think that ability is so dependent upon your relationship. And I don't think it's something that's limited to white, middle-class people studying a martial art. It's something cosmic or organic and involves energies that all things share. In that way, taking *ukemi* for O-Sensei was very different.

I remember the first time I really, sincerely attacked O-Sensei. I had always been really respectful, but I had always wondered if I was letting him get away with it. I wasn't ready to go around clocking seventy-eight-year-old guys like Mike Tyson. But in the back of my mind was always the assumption that if push comes to shove, I'll fucking put his lights out. So one day I had enough spice or orneriness or enough general hatred to say, "Fuck it, I'll get down. If he calls for me today, I'm going to let him have it." I left "good little boy" behind and became a cynical teenager. I presented the side of myself that says, "Oh, fuck this shit! Let's go for it. I don't have to hang around getting beat up all the time by all these other clowns." I really felt liberated in the sense that if he couldn't handle it, I was out of there. I'd go and do something else. I'd go off and have some fun. So he called for me and I let him have it, and I arrived on the floor a lot quicker than I ever had before, with much less of an idea of how the hell I got there. I was shocked to the core of my being. I mean it. I had really smoked one in there. And it didn't bother him in the slightest. In fact, I'm 100 percent sure that even if he under-

stood the attitude or the basic spirit behind the attack, he never gave
it a second thought.

It totally blew my mind. If I had been a serious student up until
then, I was a doubly serious student from then on. Because it seemed
to me that the consequences of what he had just done were absolutely
tremendous in their implications. If might does not make right, if
this "turning the other cheek" bullshit really means something, if
power is not a function of strength, then my whole attitude about
this world and this life and this process was really put on the block.
I had to change something. That's why I felt so totally validated in
going after him.

O-Sensei was a nice man. He was a very deep man. He had these
huge hands, immense for his height. Even into very old age, they
were gorgeous; they were wonderful hands, very strong, very broad.
Of anything, I remember his hands much more than any other part
of his body, except for his eyes. I was gifted by the kindness of other
teachers, but there was nobody I had the kind of relationship with
that I did with O-Sensei, even though O-Sensei and I hardly ever
had a conversation about anything. I mean, here I was a twenty-
two-year-old American and he was a seventy-eight-year-old Japanese master. His interest was not in the world. His interest was in
other things. He was not interested in which baseball team was two
games out of first place or if the price of washing your clothes was
going up or down. His involvement with the world was very immediate and very there, he understood what was going on but he was
not interested in it.

And O-Sensei wasn't your father. I remember one time. I was living in the dojo. I didn't go out on dates and I hadn't gone out with
a woman for two years. Then I met this woman. All the guys in the
dojo knew her, she was a hostess in a bar. She lived right near the
dojo. So Saturday mornings I'd get up and do first and second class,
and then there would be a space of maybe an hour before I would
have a private lesson. I'd bow out—I'd be in my *gi* [uniform], see,
and I'd put on my *geta* [sandals] and run as fast as I could and go
jump in bed with her and have a fine old time. Then I would go back

to the dojo. I thought nobody would notice the sight of a foreigner in a *gi* running like a madman. I really did. You talk about stupidity, I thought nobody would figure it out! I'd go clomping up the stairs to her room and jump in the sack, and thirty minutes later I'd come running back to the dojo and put on this mask of real sincere "please teach me." One day O-Sensei caught me coming in five minutes late and putting that face on. It wasn't the lateness for class so much that was the issue, but I came in and tried to look very sanctimonious, as though I had just been on some very important errand for some other teacher. He just looked right through me. He sort of smiled a little bit. I had guilt written all over my face. He looked at me as if to say, "What the fuck are you doing? Everybody knows you're going down there and getting laid. Now, come on! Don't put that face on. If you want to go down and get laid, do that. But don't come back and put on this pious face." He just let me know in a very gentle way, just by that look, that I hadn't succeeded in fooling him at all. I couldn't help it, I had to smile. It was one of those unspoken things that passes between two people. It was really nice. He wasn't trying to tell me that I shouldn't be doing that kind of thing. I mean, he wasn't into that. He was not a critical person, at least not the person that I saw. I always saw him encouraging people. I would come to my own conclusions about whether that was appropriate or inappropriate. He had other things to worry about. He was not the social director, the moral warden or something. It's just that he didn't want me to get feeling that I was doing quite the job that I thought I was doing.

I remember another time, there was one teacher who liked to kick the living shit out of his *ukes*. I used to hate to go to his classes because he would always use me as an *uke*. He took particular delight in a good *shiho nage* where if you didn't know how he operated as a teacher, you'd get your shoulder broken. You had to know just exactly how to take his *ukemi* or you could be in really big trouble. I used to think it was really unfair and really stupid, really contrary to the spirit of aikido, what he was doing. Although he was many ranks above me, I still thought I had got the real essence and he had

31

missed it. So one night he was really torquing me around when all of sudden O-Sensei came into the dojo and immediately everyone dropped down on their knees and bowed to him and O-Sensei says, "Just keep practicing, carry on." So the teacher, now that O-Sensei was in the room, decided he was really going to show off and he called for me. I came out there and he cranked everything in my body totally wrong, smashed me down on the mat as hard as you can smash a person. As I was rolling to my feet, I glanced over at O-Sensei. I was sure he was going to say something, reprimand the guy for doing something that was obviously contrary to what the basic principle was. But instead he looked like he hadn't noticed at all. I still feel to this day that the teacher didn't know his ass from his elbow in terms of aikido, that while he was very proficient in the martial stuff, he hadn't understood the soul of the art. And whether or not I'm right is immaterial. What is important is that O-Sensei made no effort to intervene or correct him or anything, just said, "Very good, very good, carry on," and went about his business. He understood that if you just keep training, gradually the rough spots will be smoothed out. The answer to just about any aikido question is "just keep practicing and you'll find out." I expected him to criticize what was an obvious breach of common sense, let alone non-violence. But he never criticized. I only heard him criticize two or three times, and they were really flagrant breaches of decency—once when somebody hit a young boy and once when one of the *uchi deshi* beat a dog to death. O-Sensei heard about it and hit the roof. I still think he should have thrown that *uchi deshi* out, but that was not his way.

The hallmark of a very polished being is that he reflects back to you what lens you see through. I know one person who was far closer to O-Sensei than I ever was by a factor of 100 who maintains that to his way of thinking O-Sensei advocated non-violence simply because it was in vogue after the second World War. He thinks that O-Sensei simply adopted a convenient metaphor or philosophical stance to coincide with the current around him, whereas in truth O-Sensei's feelings were directly opposite to that. This man had a much more intimate relationship to O-Sensei than I ever did and I think he's out of his head. But this is his view. He needs to have a crafty, wily old man who was far more Machiavellian than my model. He could be right, but not by my lights.

I never saw him show anybody a technique. He was certainly not interested in whether you picked up the techniques of aikido, I'll guarantee you that. He was not a tennis pro. He was teaching non-violence. He would just watch people. There was a quality that he was after. I don't think he ever taught anybody anything, actually. He would just do something with you: if he wanted to throw you, he would call for an attack; you'd attack him and he would throw you. But for him it was not a technical exercise at all. It was a play of spirit, a movement of the universe.

I'm damned if I know if I ever got what he was showing us. That was part of the difficulty for Westerners, particularly for me any-way: it wasn't black and white. It was something that you practiced, not something you got. Nobody ever told you if what you were prac-ticing was what he was saying, although everybody who was prac-ticing felt he understood what O-Sensei was saying.

O-Sensei was very spiritual, but he never forced anyone to par-ticipate in his practice. In a sense he would include you in the same way that one might have watched Thomas à Becket pray at chapel. If you were in the chapel with him, you were included, but he didn't give a damn what you were doing: he was praying. In some ways it was like watching some guy taking his change out of his pocket at night and putting it on the dresser; it was an automatic movement, except that it wasn't taking change out of your pocket—it was a real spiritual essay.

He would come in every morning and teach, but his teaching was largely talking, and in the beginning and at the end, he would clap [as a way of opening and closing class]. Sometimes he would pray and you would sit there, and if you were like me and about 99 percent of the other people, you'd be thinking about chicks, the mun-dane world; you were not praying. But every once in a while, some-thing would move you, and for a moment there, you would really feel that you knew what he was feeling. But he certainly didn't look behind to see who was praying and who was thinking about chicks. He was totally uninterested in whether or not you were praying, too.

As far as he was concerned, all of aikido was a form of *misogi*, "cleansing." At the same time he understood that if you had a couple of fourteen-year-olds in the class or you had some other guy in class who was worried about his marriage or his company going bankrupt or a thousand other worldly problems, those people would not be totally committed to prayer in the same way he was. As I said, there was no policing. In fact, there was not even any feeling that some day you would achieve O-Sensei's eminence or any of that stuff.

With O-Sensei, there was no enforced piety. Aikido is not a religion. That's what's so devilish about aikido. It deals with these primary forces but leaves pretty much all the detail work up to you. O-Sensei said, "Aikido leads religion to completion," which I always found and still find a very impenetrable statement. I can think about that, and have, for a long time and still find other ramifications to it—for example, that we are charged with healing, with the restoration of balance. But is that balance Christian? What are the morals that underpin that? Who knows? O-Sensei left that up to us to figure out. He was not a moral policeman, running around telling everybody to clean up their act. That's not at all where he was. And that's so hard for us from our culture to understand, because television evangelists and all these other people say what we ought to be doing and he never did that. He wasn't in that mode.

At some point O-Sensei said that he had this experience of enlightenment and all desire for power was taken from him. And by that I think we can infer that up until that time he was kicking ass; he was really powerful. And he had a tough time, sometimes, monetarily. He was kissing admirals' asses; he was really out there stroking and toking. If you want to get a dojo and you're hoping some admiral will give you money ... the way it works in real life is you've got to sit up listening to that asshole admiral talk all night, hoping he's going to give you a check in the morning. I mean, that's the way of the world, right? So when he says that all desire for power and influence over other people was taken from him, I think that that's what really happened, that he was delivered from worrying about that whole scene. And as far as I'm concerned, the truth of that can be seen in the fact that he didn't run around trying to get everybody to go through the same mousehole. If you wanted to go around and screw bar hostesses on Saturday morning, he wasn't going to say anything one way or the other about it. It wasn't his job to do it. And I'm sure that as he saw me do that, he saw, in the other *uchi deshi,* massive failings, massive problems. But that was what aikido was for. He would say, "Well, practice aikido. Come to practice." That was probably the most proscriptive thing he ever said. And he didn't say that that much. He'd say, "Oh, you're in practice. That's wonderful, wonderful."

So I think that it's almost a testament to him that his students are not pious. It may be different now, but when I was in Japan, virtually every teacher that I knew smoked like a chimney, drank like a fish and chased pussy when they had the slightest opportunity. And that inevitably amused or outraged most Americans who were studying there and who had this conception of the noble ascetic. And then one began to find that behind all this smoking and drinking and wenching, there was some noble asceticism going on.

You see, nobody, except those people who were part of inventing another cliché, ever said that the warrior is noble and pure, you know, spends his Sundays with boy scouts. All that affective stuff didn't need to be laid on it, and the more that you subscribed to it, the deeper trouble you got into because for the most part you hadn't conquered those demons, either.

Anyway, I was an *uchi deshi* until O-Sensei died. I still have a lot of guilt about that period right around O-Sensei's death. Like everybody else, I had to teach English to support myself. Well, I hate teaching English, I hate it. I mean, I really got to hate the students. I hated them not with a general but a very personal hatred; it was just the wrong thing for me to be doing. I thought if I had to ask one more time, "Mr. Suzuki, what is your hobby?" and heard Mr. Suzuki say, "Me hoebbee is leading a book," I would just explode. I just lived in a state of permanent rage. I knew I couldn't go out and teach aikido in companies like the other *uchi deshi*—one, because I wasn't that good, and two, because the Japanese would not stomach a foreigner teaching a Japanese martial art. It took a guy with skin as thick as Steve Seagal's to pull that one off; I could never do that. So I figured the way to get around that shit was to quit teaching English and go use my head and scam something together because Japan was really getting hot and they really wanted American things and they were starting to get disposable income.

So that's what I did. I did a nine-to-five in a publishing house and I brought Beatles posters over and tried a bunch of different things so I could make a fortune in a hurry and kick back and really study with O-Sensei, because after all, he was going to live forever. That sounds so stupid as to be unbelievable but I really sold myself on that. So toward the end, there were a lot of times that I missed class and didn't see O-Sensei because I was too damned busy running around and being a hotshot, taking meetings or whatever. So there's a lot of guilt that I have about that that I've pretty much dealt with but it's very painful. That's why it's painful for me to watch videotapes with me taking *ukemi* for O-Sensei. I saw one the other day. It showed the last demonstration he ever gave, and I don't know whether I was there or not. How much I would give to run that reel back. There's so much pain in me connected with the fact that somewhere inside me I knew I was doing it. I knew I should have said, "Fuck this meeting. Who cares if the Japanese get another poster? The real feast of your life is over in Shinjuku at the place called the Aikido Hombu Dojo. Get the fuck over there and study."

After O-Sensei died in 1969, I left Japan. I couldn't stay there anymore. My teacher was dead and besides I was having a lot of personal problems. I was totally going the wrong way. After I got back I ended up in New York. I didn't know anybody so I started going to the dojo on 18th Street, which Yamada had taken over by then. I had been to the dojo before when Tohei was running New York. I was in New York at that point for an operation. I was Tohei Sensei's *uke* at the time, and when he left I took over classes. So there were people there who remembered me from that visit. Through them I met Ken Nissen. Ken was really kind to me and helped me to get on my feet, and to get acclimatized to American life. Most people have tremendous trouble readjusting and I did. It was through the kindness of people at the dojo that I was able to get some semi-normal stance. Maybe two or three years later he and I opened the Bond Street dojo, in about 1974.

Unfortunately, I soon began to have difficulty with the Japanese teachers in this country who had been *uchi deshi* with me. I've operated pretty much without any contact with them for a number of years now. I suppose it was sort of unavoidable. I'm not Japanese. I'm definitely not Japanese. I had tried to be. If I thought having an operation to have my eyes changed around would do it, as other people did, I would have done it. But it only made you look stupid. There is nothing I wouldn't have done to "pass," but I couldn't do it. And even if I could have, there were just light-years of difference between us. I wasn't about to adopt their social system and I've got too big a mouth to shut up in the presence of my superiors. I've always been rebellious and it just wouldn't have worked.

For their part, I'm neither fish nor fowl. If I was pure American, just another American dude, that'd be one thing. They'd deal with me or not as personality indicated. The fact is I do speak their language and I do know some of their customs and I was there back when. And I do know that their feet are of clay. I'm not impressed with the fact that they studied with O-Sensei, as a person of less experience would be. So what? So what have you done lately? And what have you done for O-Sensei lately? I don't mean to say that my view of them is correct. I wouldn't know how to deal with me either, if I was them. But I do know that I started out really wanting to be on the team, trying to be a team player. But I finally realized that they were never going to let me in the game. They just wanted me to go away, shut up and die; that's about the best thing I could do for them. It's hurt me a lot; it really has. I really wanted so badly to be a part of the team. Your father dies in your family and maybe you become closer to your brothers. But their feeling was "Hey man, it's every man for himself. Anyway, you aren't one of us so why don't you go away?" Initially I was trying to be accommodating in any way I could think of. After a while I stopped trying to be accommodating. I became a pain in the ass.

And I still am. I mean, my great-great-great-grandfather was with Ethan Allen at the attack on Fort Ticonderoga, the first anti-British military maneuver, the one that really saved the revolution. So that's deeply ingrained and I'm proud of that. I'm proud of that rebelliousness. Somebody's got to be a pain in the ass. It might as well be me. I was not always in that position. But they helped confirm me in it. I would have rolled over and begged like a dog if they had scratched my belly, but they didn't want to do it or didn't know how.

But let me tell you something. Me and Yamada don't get along, on any level that I can think of. I mean it's like night and day. And Yamada's been pretty excessive over the years in one area or another. He did a couple of things to me and I took them pretty hard. So if somebody asked my opinion, I'd give it, loud and full-bore. Didn't bother me at all to bad-rap Yamada. Since he was doing it to me, I figured the least I could say was my honest opinion. Well, I had a student who had studied with him. In her hearing, I gave my opinion of Yamada. And she said very simply and very calmly, in a way that totally changed my head, "Well, I don't know about your experience of him, but all I can say is he was there for me at a time in my life when I really needed some help, really needed someone to point the way for me. He did that for me and I'll never, ever forget, and I'll always honor and revere him for his help to me." The simplicity and the purity of heart with which she said it made me understand that just because I didn't like the guy didn't mean that he wasn't helpful or important or useful to other people. Seems like a pretty stupid realization, but I really got that. Since then, I've tried not to say too much bad about him, or when I do say things, I remember her and the way she said that, always.

Anyway, I was teaching in the Bond Street dojo. To support myself I had to have other work too, of course. For a while, like a lot of other martial artists, I worked as a bouncer. I put a lot of my aikido training into practice there. You know, how to spot trouble before it starts, how to keep it from starting and how to deal with it if it does start. I got into a few fights in that job, but there was one fight in particular I remember that I'd like to tell you about. One night I got into an argument with this drunk giant about going to the men's room. This guy was a good 6 ft. 6 in., maybe 6 ft. 8 in., 300 pounds. Not only was I urging him to go to the men's room, but I was saying I would stand outside and make sure that no one else would enter the men's room so he could have complete use of the facilities. And when I would say that, he would say "You mean to stand there and tell me I can come here and spend my money and I cannot go into the bathroom and piss it out?" And I'd say, "No, no, you don't understand. By all means feel welcome to use the facilities and consider me your servant in making sure that nobody else should interrupt you." And he'd say "How dare you? How dare you?" And I'm standing there and thinking: "This is aikido, man; we're going to be into non-fighting around here," trying to be ever more fulsome in my willingness to help him but he ain't taking fucking word one of it, because he wants to hammer the shit out of me though he hasn't become aware of it yet. He's drunk and I'm sober and he's trying to work his courage up.

He starts to take his leather jacket off, and I know exactly what's coming. He's gonna flare that thing over my head and his hand's going back either for a punch or for a knife or for a gun or whatever the fuck he's got back on his hip. Anyway, when that hand comes out, it's going to be coming fast. One of the good things about aikido: you get used to fast movement, close in. It doesn't bother you at all. I went right to the absolute last tenth, hundredth, thousandth of a second. And I got right up to D-Day, T-Time and I had to move. If I'd waited a split instant longer, it would have been all over. It would have been his move and I would have been behind. As it was, I took him and we went into the bathroom, I took him right like that. He was standing in the men's room door; the door was open. The whole bar was watching us and they were playing "Street Fighting Man" on the jukebox. Talk about cliché!

39

Anyway, when we went in the men's room, I got him by the throat, and his head went back. He bounced off the back wall and I didn't give him a chance. I went right in and dug my fingers right behind his eyes. And I went, as I had with the timing, right to the last possible place before injury. He was so terrified, as well he should have been, that he peed. The force of his piss coming through his underwear and his trousers turned into the most beautiful nimbus. It was a golden mist. I remember the observer part thinking, gasp of awe— "it's pink, pink." The men's room consisted of a toilet and a sort of pissoir; it was just your basic sawdust bar men's room. There was shit and piss and beer and sawdust and pink walls with graffiti and swastikas and "death to faggots" scrawled on the wall . . . and all of a sudden it was like a grotto at Lourde's. In the midst of hammering this motherfucker, in this midst of all this shit and piss and ugliness, there was a moment of pure beauty and light. When he let his bladder go, I took my hand out of his eyes and I hit him with the back of my fist three times as hard as I could hit him right smack in the nose. Retrospectively, I can see that this was the perfect plan for that distance and that time, I mean it was absolutely the perfect surface to hit him with. The first two times I hit him as hard as I could, but I didn't have quite the right range; the third time I hit him, I had the range. He dropped down and grabbed ahold of the toilet and cried "Mommymommymommymommy!"

So I get down on the floor, covered now as always with piss, and try to get this motherfucker's hands off from around the toilet, stroking his head, trying to restore a little balance, you know? I'm stroking his head and I'm telling him, "Look, I'm a professional. This is my life. I'm paid to do it." I stroked him and I told him that there was no indignity to being hammered by me, because that's my job, that's my life, that's who I am and that it's only natural that I should be doing this and that I thought he was a very fine person. Together we were going to get up and we were going to comb our hair and we were going to look in that mirror and straighten each other up the best that we could and we were going to go out there and meet those other assholes and show them that we were buddies. We stood up and looked in the mirror and he got out his comb. "How do I look?" "You look good, yeah. Oh, you missed something over here." "Oh, okay."

Then I opened the door and the jukebox is out there playing loud music and all these fucking idiots are standing around, waiting to see who'll come out first. They see me first and they roar. I felt like hosing every single one of them. Right then I really hated those people. I had a lot of love for this guy and none for those fuckers. But he didn't come out. Then one of these guys who always hang around bouncers, you know the kind. "Hey, man, when you need me, I'll be there." Yeah, right. While I was dealing with this guy, they had all been delayed by urgent business with their brokers. Anyway this guy says, "Hey, Terry, did you frisk that guy?" I said, "Holy fuck, I never did." I remembered his hand going back. What did he have back there? Maybe he had a derringer or a bootpiece. The terror grabbed me again. I yanked open the door and dived in, expecting to meet the Third Marine Division. He's still sprucing up. He sees me coming and he dives back to the toilet again. "Mommymom-mymommymommy." We've got to do the whole thing over again.

By this time I know his name. His name is Doug. I say "Doug, hey be cool, man. Get it together. Come on out." He says, "Allright." So then he comes out, leans up against the door and says, "Where is he?" I said, "Who?" He says "The guy who did this to me." I said "What?" He says "Where is the guy who did this to me?" I could tell he was trying to work himself up to the point where he was going to do it all over again. So I said, "I'll give you 'til three, Doug. On the count of three if you're not out of here, I'm coming after you. One. Two." By the time I hit three he was on the street.

So now he's gone. It's over. We had broken the toilet. It's bubbling and cracked. I'm lord and master of shit and piss, other people's. I really had a communion with O-Sensei at that time. I wondered if what I was doing was what he meant for me to do, that it was necessary for me to go into the dark to that extent, go down into the shit and piss of things and if that was where the basic lesson was. I was thinking about that. And I didn't know how the fuck

I was going to stop the toilet from running all over the floor. I was trying to figure this all out when I heard this boom—boom—boom—boom boom, this loud noise. It sounded exactly like two bodies rolling down the stairs. This place, this sawdust bar was on the first floor and there was a fern bar on the second for the yuppies. He'd gone up there and he'd run into the owner, a guy named Billy. Billy was coming downstairs. Doug grabbed a hold of him and tried to throw him downstairs. Billy fought back and the two of them rolled down the stairs and landed on the street outside.

I ran over to them, grabbed hold of Doug by the seat of the pants and the nape of the neck. Billy pushed at exactly the same instant and this three hundred pound guy wafted as lightly as a ball of cotton over the concrete and I stuffed him as hard as I could, with real malice, right down into the concrete. He rolled over and I grabbed his arm and tried to do *sankyo*. I couldn't have done *sankyo* with a fucking pipewrench on that guy. I mean, his arms were that big. So finally I said "fuck it" and I put my knee right in his windpipe, joinced him a couple of times to get his attention and then I just slid up a little and put my shinbone right across his throat. He said, "I'm suffocating. I can't breath." And I said, "I am thrilled to hear it. Use up more of your air. Talk to me a lot. Tell me things I need to know." I was really pissed. All of a sudden, just like in the movies, I see a pair of shoes and trousers and it's the cops. They had called the cops and the cops had just arrived. One of the cops looks at me and says, "All right, Mister Bouncerman, Mister Badass Bouncerman. Let him up." I say, "Sure." He got up and it took five guys to get him into the squad car.

Anyway, he's gone in the car and I go back and Billy comes through. He says, "You assholes broke my fucking toilet." And I said, "Billy, I quit. This is the end of my bouncing career." Old Doug, they put him in jail. I don't know how long he did, maybe six months. Once he was out, he came back and shot two people, two bouncers, shot them right in the ass, both of them. They turned away from him. Otherwise he'd have shot them in the gut. It seems to me that I've spent a lot of time down there in the shit and piss, my own and others'. Aikido's helped me deal with a lot of it, but sometimes it just hasn't been enough. I told you about restoration of balance, but what do you do with somebody like Doug? Aikido helped me protect myself but it couldn't restore Doug's balance.

In the midst of all this, teaching and working as a bouncer and stuff, I wrote that book of mine, *Giving in to Get Your Way*. You know, I'm terribly embarrassed about that book. So much so that when it comes up it feels like someone is touching a very deep wound. It was written with a student of mine, a guy named Victor Miller who had all the contacts. Whenever we had conferences about the book with the publisher, it was the editor and him against me. I found myself "giving in to get my way." They said to me, "Look. Do you want a book or not?" And each time, I said, "Yeah, I guess I do," and I'd wind up doing it their way. Now I feel that I gave away much too much. They were writing for the housewife and it was supposed to be the next self-help book. They would say things like "What the reader wants to hear . . ." If there was such a thing as a prototypical reader, then there would only be one book ever published. The fact is, nobody knows what the reader wants. And just because you've had a string of hits doesn't mean you really know, either. But they had me by the balls because I'd put a lot of effort in and I'd told my family and friends it was coming out and they were all waiting.

Then the editor walked out before the book was completed. When a book loses its editor in the process of being published, it's like leaving a sheep on the mountain. A book will die unless your editor is in there fighting for it all the time, fighting for promotion budgets, fighting for good artists for the title, fighting all these battles. But she just fucking split. So the fact that that thing ever got published is a miracle.

But partly as a result of her leaving they came out with a cover that looked just awful. I have a couple of the books around here and it still hurts to look at them. That's not what I saw. That's not the book I wanted. One of Yamada's students who at the time was the hottest experimental video guy in the country took the circle, square and triangle, put a video camera on it and feedback-looped it, did the whole series of photographs whereby the square turned into a circle and the circle resolved into a triangle and came out with a still that was fantastically beautiful for the cover. That cover was so important to me that I hand-walked the film all the way to the office and gave it to them to make sure that it got there. I didn't even trust the mail. But they fucking lost it.

So it really hurts me when I hear about *Giving in to Get Your Way*. Even so, I have had some people who said that it helped them. I had a letter from a guy at The Air Force Academy, strangely enough, and he said, "We ordered a dozen of these initially, but we have had many more requests. Could you get us some more books, because we use it in class?" I was just flabbergasted.

Anyway, I taught at Bond Street for five or six years. In the process I discovered that I wasn't really suited to being the head of a dojo. That weighed heavily on me. I knew I felt a deep responsibility to O-Sensei to spread the art, but I didn't know what that meant and what, specifically, did it mean in moral terms. I was never taught how to teach. Of course, none of us were. Nobody had ever given us a class on how to teach or the problems that we'd run into as teachers, because we didn't get that honest with each other. What do you do when some dynamite-looking woman makes goo-goo eyes at you and says, "I want to know you. I want to know everything about you. Feed me." Well, is that good or bad or what? What do I do, tell her to go to her room, to go study with somebody else? How do you respond to that? And we get no help from the Japanese because they are not skilled in emotional interaction. I mean, I used to teach English conversation for them. It took me a while, but I found out I wasn't teaching English; I was teaching conversation— they don't know conversation. They could know English like they know music, but they can't converse, because they don't have that within their society. None of the guys who are over here have ever been taught how to teach. Nobody was ever told, "Hey, you're going to get over there and they're going to idolize you." Those poor bastards, Yamada and all of them. Nobody prepared them for that. But although I can get very vituperative about them, the fact that nobody has been shot by jealous husbands, that they haven't ODed, is actually to their credit. If I had been in their position, I don't know if I would have done as well as they.

So I think this whole thing is a really hard place and we're all going through it. Is it good or bad to go to bed with your students? What are you supposed to do around that issue? How about asking for money? Are you supposed to give this stuff away or is it okay to charge money for a demonstration? I mean, we've all had to bootstrap ourselves around those issues. And it was no easier or harder for me than it is for anybody else. But I felt that I was not doing a hell of a good job at it. And I also felt, even though I couldn't articulate it, I felt I was starting to become a real bully. I was able to bully people. Initially it was good. For their own best interest I would push them past their own sticking point. But the trouble is you get confirmed in your success in doing that, and you start to apply this across the board. There were a couple of people I know I handled too roughly. Kindness and gentleness and not pushing them would have been the best way to their heart. But I didn't see it because I was too blind or I didn't understand or whatever. I felt I was trying to do the best I could. But all of sudden I realized that just because you can bully them doesn't mean you ought to.

Gary Snyder says, "If you want to change the world, don't move from where you are. Put your roots down and stand there." But being a solid, stable, long-term teacher of basic aikido like that seemed far more responsible and far more grownup than I could ever possibly be—that being rebellious and floating around was about all I was fitted for. And I was being seduced by the lure of California. People in California would say, "Oh, come out. You're perfect for out here." Well, like a jerk, I listened to those sirens and went, and it was not a good idea for me.

I remember the first time I came to the Bay Area. I was living in New York and I didn't have any money. Bob Nadeau had invited me to the San Rafael retreat. He picked me up at the airport and then he took me over and introduced me to the people and said, "Go ahead and teach." I just wanted to watch class; I hadn't thought of teaching it. This was at a time when having twelve people on the mat at Bond Street was rare. Ken Nissen and I would say to each other, "Jesus, there's twelve people out there! Twelve! Do you realize how many people, twelve! Double digits!" And one of us would say, "Don't worry, you can do it. Don't let it freak you out. Just go out there and do it." That was where I was coming from. So Nadeau says go ahead and teach, and there are at least 140 people on the mat. And there are all these black belts. I'd never seen so many black belts except in Japan. And right in the middle is this gorgeous-looking woman and she's smiling at me. I know I know her, but I can't think of her name. It's Joan Baez. And she wasn't the best-looking person in the place by any means. I mean, there were all these gorgeous-looking California people. So I taught the class and afterwards Nadeau slipped fifty bucks to me. The way he handed me that money was extremely kind. I'll never forget it. I'll always love him for it.

So of course after an experience like that, California seemed very attractive. I moved out there primarily at the blandishments of this guy who wanted to help me run seminars based on my book. I did a thing called "When Push Comes to Shove" for businessmen, how to deal with conflict. Everybody's using the word "conflict resolution," but I remember in '78 when I started using it, nobody else was using it that way. "Conflict resolution" was a study of international relations. That's what it meant, it had nothing to do with interpersonal work. I think I pioneered that term, but I'm never going to get any credit for it.

Unfortunately, the seminars didn't work out the way I hoped and I had a falling out with the guy I was running them with. In fact, that whole California gig didn't work out for me. It's that same shit that Californians do to everybody. They want everybody to move there and move up the road so they won't have to drive too far to see them. And it's all so superficial. They said, "If you move out here, you'll have forty-five students in a month." And they're absolutely right. The second month you'll have six.

One good thing did happen to me out there, though. I met Robert

Bly. In fact, I'm still involved with him and his stuff. I met him in a very straightforward way. A guy I knew said "There's this poet named Robert Bly and he does stuff with men. Are you interested in doing a gig?" I said, "What does it pay?" "The first year he won't pay. But if you want to go up there and do something for no money the first year, if they like you and they like your stuff, maybe the second year they'll give you something." So I said, "So what do I gotta do?" And he says, "It's a week up in Mendocino in the redwoods." So I said, "Well, shit. How bad could that be? Do they do food?" "Yeah, you get free food. A bunch of guys are going up. C'mon, man, it'll be fun." So I said, "What are they going to do?" "I don't know. It's about men. There'll only be men there." Well, I grew up in boarding schools, barracks and dojos and things like that, so being together with a bunch of men, that's easy for me. It's just being a kid again. "All right. Shit, I'll go."

So I went along. For some reason I had the impression that Robert was some aging looney who had a lot of money or something. I don't know, I had this fantasy going about some dotty old man running around and stuff. In fact, Robert just absolutely blew my mind. Without knowing it, I luckily stumbled into what I desperately needed. He's on the poetic end of psychology, the psychological end of poetry, or whatever. Anyway, he started telling me about fathers and sons and relationships and he did so with great éclat, with great panache, and his knowledge of poetry is encyclopedic. Stuff would just come out of him. I'm happy just to sit at his feet and listen to him.

Robert says a hundred things that I don't believe in or I don't agree with and I don't care. I don't have to agree with him. But I just find him one of the most engaging and amusing and interesting talkers I've ever heard. I've been to his gatherings not only as a teacher, but I've paid to go too, I enjoy him so much. I'm not a "Bly guy." I just enjoy him. I think that Robert is wrong in a lot of things. But it doesn't matter to me. He has great courage and great ability to stand up and be an asshole and say something that he currently believes in even if a child would know it's not true. He'll stand up and say it. He won't try to convince you of what he's saying. He'll say what he thinks. I've many times seen evidence of his courage and his honesty and his willingness to look at his own stuff. He's got his trips and stuff like all of us and I feel absolutely no need to promulgate his stuff. I don't know the last book he read or what he's now into or whatever, but I look forward the next time I see him to finding out what he has been reading and what he now thinks about things. He's a great figure of a man and has a great soul and a great heart and so I feel real good about that.

There's a great hunger for men's work. But even after all this association with Robert, or especially because of it, I'm still not exactly sure what "men's work" or "the men's movement" is. I think in truth it has something to do, as Robert would say, with the ability to grieve, to go into one's deeper feelings, to come down from being happy all the time, which is something this culture wants us to be. It has something to do with that, but I don't know what. I don't feel very much more able to do it now than I ever was. But I think he's on the general right track. He's very circumspect about it and he will not prescribe, but he has been, probably through his own agency, sort of leveraged into this guru thing, though he's pretty sincere about not coming from that place. It's just that it's inevitable that he should be pushed into it.

But you know, it's really funny, just as an aside, you see that process going on. I guess in the shrink business they call it "transference." Another way of looking at why I got out of being a teacher— a permanent, in-one-place aikido teacher—is to say that I couldn't handle transference; I didn't know how to deal with it. I might have been able to handle it with guys, but with women, I was hopeless. It just so meshed with my stuff, whatever "stuff" I have, that just any sanity was out of the question. I remember something Robert said one time, it really moved me very deeply; it really gave me some insight. It was the last day of a week-long retreat. I'm sure you know that everybody gets pretty emotional at these things. You've had a hermetic experience in the sense that you've all been confined in this one area and a lot of different stuff has taken place. And there are, especially on the part of newer people, great waves of emotion that come up toward the head person—in this case, Robert—and he goes to pretty great lengths not to let that happen. He does not encourage that. But there are some people who are so needful of that, if only for a day, if only for a week, of getting into this space they have locked off in their life and just haven't been able to look at. All of a sudden the door is open and this riot of transference comes out. And if you're up there and you erase that by some snotty bit of sarcasm or something, you really do an act of injury. It's very easy to be callous with that. "I'm not your father. I'm a human being." But maybe that is not always right to do. It's not that the opposite of that, encouraging that transference and making it personal and making it concrete, is good. But it's understandable, Robert said. And he said it very simply. "Don't we all need fathers?"

It was a very right thing to say. I've been thinking about it a lot. It seemed very right to me, that he wasn't encouraging that kind of transference, but he wasn't trying to deny it either, but just trying to look at it. Somehow from that moment, I really started seeing him in another light. And on this TV thing that he did with Bill Moyers, "A Gathering of Men," Robert said something about the importance of older men praising younger men, giving them some validation and praise when they do something that is reasonably praiseworthy. He started out by making the point that we rarely do it. I have taken that to heart, and without trying to be dumb about it, I have tried to oil, so to speak, my jaws so that if I see something in the dojo that is praiseworthy, then I'll say to the guy or the woman, "Hey, well-done there." That praise won't be rusty in coming from me.

I've developed a sort of routine about that in various workshops I've done. It kind of got to be a set-piece with Bly. I do a bunch of exercises around it, usually with novices, but it works with aikido people too, strangely enough. What the exercise consists of is this: there are groups of five people. One person stands in the center of the circle of four people, who are sort of at the cardinal points. And initially, I've taught them how to stand, how to do *corret hanmi* [stance], how to keep their weight below belt-buckle—basically

Tohei stuff. Then I tell them that the person in the center has to look at the person right in front of him, and that guy or woman is required to say something of an unpleasant or negative cast: "Well, I don't like your shirt," or "why do you have that silly hair-do?" People usually pick external things, shirts, hair-dos, things that are easily seen on the outside, with which they may or may not agree, but for want of anything else negative to say, they choose something.

The person in the center acknowledges that some part of whatever was said contains truth. You may choose to analyze that or not in the moment, but in any case you take it down through your *hara* [center, belly] and down through your legs and you ground that into the earth and you bring back a "thank you." You then turn to the next person and they do the same thing, and you go around the circle. And because it's external, particularly because it's external, it's pretty easy for people to take that. The first part of this exercise is always hard for the people on the outside: to take someone who is a perfect stranger and come up with something negative requires some degree of courage, some degree of discomfort for the people on the outside. For the person on the inside, it's pretty easy because people have been calling him a jerk all his life, in one form or another. We're used to slings and arrows, so we can deal with that shit.

Everybody takes turns being in the circle and then the whole thing is repeated, except this time the people on the outside have to say something of a positive cast. And strangely enough, people immediately go for quality; they go right to the heart of the matter. "You look like a kind person," or whatever. The person in the center still has the same role as before—to acknowledge that whatever they say, some part of it is true. If they say that you seem like a kind person, you acknowledge that and still ground it down and come back with a thank you. "Yeah, in fact I am. I'm a kind person." The strange thing is, it's much harder to be praised. People feel disempowered in some very perverse way. "You just said that I look like a kind person. What that means is that that made me feel good. When you said I was a kind person, I felt a warm flush of agreement. I've always wanted to be liked," or whatever, right? All that stuff comes up and you feel much more off balance and much more at sea in a sense than if someone says, "Hey, you know, man, you're an asshole." A million times of being called an asshole compare to the few times that you have been genuinely noted for some valuable thing. Kindness—you have no experience with that. And you fear it because you want it so much, because if they only knew how easy it was to manipulate you by just telling you things that you know are true. So they now have one key to your being.

I think that aikido has got to go this way. It has to start dealing with this stuff and be more than just knocking folks around or getting bashed or whatever. I think it has to be valid in our daily life, because if it isn't, it's just stupid. There's no point in doing it then. It would be on the order of playing tiddlywinks.

Another thing that Robert got me thinking about is darkness. I think that it is necessary for a man to reclaim his darkness. I don't mean to even come close to suggesting that I've done it more than other people, that I have reclaimed mine. But I do think that Robert is right, that things are essentially out of kilter because we have no initiatory process. We need as men all over the world to be initiated into manhood, and since we have no initiatory process anymore, we're really stymied. And one of the things we need to do is to recognize that we are both light and dark, and we need to reclaim some darkness that has been denied us or taken away from us. We have to somehow learn that being dark is not evil, not necessarily. I mean, there's evil that's dark, but there's also dark that's not evil. And it's very important to understand. That's why we have to go into it, because it's only from that experience that you can discover that there is a very valid deep darkness that men somehow are able to contain. That's not saying women can't and don't, but that seems to be one of our gifts or responsibilities as men: we're able to deal with this energy and we're able to contain it. And it's one of the things the older men are able to instruct the younger men in. From what we know of primitive cultures, I think it's fair to say that that's one of the things that older men do for the younger men: show them that there is this dark thing that is of benefit to the tribe in some way and that it is different from evil. And if you think about it, yeah, sure, there are older people in the dojo; but there aren't many old people in our dojos that started when they were young men, because it ain't been around that long. But you wait. Fifty years from now we'll have two or three generations who have had aikido training and are conversant and familiar with it. What it'll be then, I don't know, and I spend some time thinking about it. But you have to reclaim your power, and part of your power is your dark side. But nobody knows much about it. There are no experts on it. Nadeau, though, he's been in the dark. He knows about the dark.

I'm just paraphrasing Robert when I say this: we need less polite-ness—more kindness, but less politeness. We've got plenty of cookie-pushers, plenty of guys with creased pants—"Dare I eat a peach? Shall I wear my trousers rolled?" Got plenty of that shit. We need more hair. Robert gets into talking about wildness, and the wild man and the difference between wildness and savagery. And once you really start looking at it, you find that there is a difference, that even though we use the words interchangeably, they mean totally differ-ent things. We've got enough savagery to last us until kingdom comes. Paradoxically, wildness can reclaim us from that. Wildness is not savagery. Wildness is something that we can't even put into words because it's long before words. It's before we had the ability to talk. I know that one of the things that helps it is learning how to dance. And this is one of the things that Robert does. People bring drums to these things and they drum and dance. Personally, I don't like it. I've got a lot of things I'd rather fucking do than dance around. I'll do it to show that yeah, I can do it. I can subject myself to that and I can even get off on it occasionally. But there is something to it; I've seen a lot of people dance and I've seen people in front of me trans-formed from John Accountant into this sort of prehistoric being. And only occasionally in these retreats have I seen people mistake wildness for savagery.

So I've done a lot of work with Robert. But there was a period in there, starting when I was still in California, when I couldn't do much of anything because I got sick. Partly because of that, but also because I knew that I was going in the wrong direction and I had to consolidate or retrench or whatever. I came back to Vermont, to a place near Burlington where my family has a vacation home. I was really sick there for a while. Chronic heart failure. I couldn't, and still can't get enough air in my lungs, so my heart works overtime to pump around the little bit of oxygen I do get. Sometimes I thought I had come back here to die like some wounded animal. Riki, the woman I'm living with, was the one who saved me. She really did. But it was really touch-and-go there for a while. I didn't know if I was going to make it.

It seems to me now that those who tread a spiritual path very often tend to get sick at some point. It's a form of correction. It certainly happened to me, and I certainly have been chastened by it. If there was a spiritual OSHA [Occupational Safety and Health Administration], if there was one for the guys in the spiritual trade, there'd be a whole thing about inflation. The primary enemy of the cleric, of the religious person, is inflation. You get blown up by your own *ki.* The Romans called it *divinus aflatus,* "divine inflation." It's recognized as a pathological response to religious training, and it is one of the big evils. It really does exist and people really do get caught by it and sometimes they never get out of it. It has happened to so many people who went through the '70s, everybody who has been caught with his pants down. And those of us who haven't been caught are doomed to be. You cannot maintain a good life with the kind of attitude that you deserve to preach celibacy but get a little on the side. Little by little those discrepancies and disparities creep up on you and pretty soon, if you haven't been discovered, and you haven't been called on, you do yourself in. That's what happened to me. I mean, I was doing workshops for the peace movement. What do I know about peace? I don't know a goddamn thing about peace. So if you can't square it with yourself, somehow I think some internal process takes over and it'll square it for you if you're lucky. If you're unlucky, it'll kill you. I've seen that happen, I've heard of that happening to a lot of people. And in fact it happened to O-Sensei himself. I mean, he was a sickly person, as was Tohei Sensei. I think that probably the people most in need in our culture are those who left their country as I did and went abroad to India or wherever and came back with some spiritual knowledge, spiritual awareness or whatnot and were successful.

Eventually I got well enough that I was able to start training again. Up until about a week before I started training again, I would go and watch class. At that time the dojo here was located in the basement of a place and it was a really deep basement. It would take me probably twenty minutes to walk downstairs and maybe half an hour to walk up the stairs. I mean, there was no possibility of my getting back on the mat. Now what I do is I go and I try to get one of the students to teach and I take the class. But I don't care about the techniques. I really don't. They don't mean anything to me. But I'm very serious about aikido. I'm in a new phase, it's not the technical aspect. At some point you get bored with technique. There are a limited number of attacks and a limited number of responses. And how many ways can you do them? Okay, so you can do them fifteen million different ways. But 14,999,000 are boring and the rest apply to you, sometimes, if you're feeling good, on Tuesdays. So I'm much more interested in the community, much more interested in watching people develop. There's one guy in our dojo who has a viewpoint of himself as a real spazo. I don't know very much about his background, but I can tell that he has been helped to that view by other people. He's a very bright man, a scientist. It's just so wonderful to see him improve and to see that this spazoid is actually quite graceful and very strong and very powerful and is really coming into an appreciation of that. That's where the juice is. That's really fun. I could give a shit about how to *donikkyo*. And it's really nice to go out and have a beer afterwards or a cup of tea or whatever and to hear about who's breaking up with who and that sort of stuff. It's a family of a sort.

I'm really learning a lot about community, I'm really interested in learning about my defects and about how to repair my defects in community organizing, how to make people feel welcome. In aikido you've got so many weird people who do such wonderful things. If we ever started to draw on the community, we could draw on them forever, if we knew how to get in touch with them, how to extract the knowledge and the wisdom and the capabilities of all the people in there. I haven't the faintest idea how to do that. I don't think I'm very good at it to begin with, so for me the learning takes place in just looking at the students, just learning to look at people and say, "Oh, I see, she's very embarrassed about her feet" or "She doesn't think she's very good-looking." I'm learning to just notice what people show you instead of looking over their heads and being lost in the technique. I'm starting to look at real small details, to see that person as a person. I've got a long way to go in that.

For a while there, after I got sick, I went through a lot of hatred of aikido. "I'll never do it again. It was a period in my life. Yeah, okay. O-Sensei was a great guy and I learned a lot. But it's not my life. I'm somebody else now." But in truth, I wasn't able to get the splinter out of my system. It's still in there. Aikido saved my life. It has been both my refuge, my excuse, my living, my means of getting laid. . . . It has been a very good friend to me and a very harsh teacher at the same time. I figure that in thirty years I've learned anywhere from one to one and one-half percent of what there is to learn about aikido. There are many people who never even heard of aikido, who will die without ever hearing of aikido, who live a perfectly exemplary life or do things that are exemplary. I don't feel that aikido has any special handle on anything. But a lot of effort has gone into it and a lot of things have been discarded along the way; streamlining has happened. And it is a very effective, very systematic way to understand, on a deep level, some basic principles, and to embody those principles, to articulate them in practice rather than in simple theory. The feedback is immediate. I think it really is a genius invention.

2

ROBERT NADEAU

Powerfully built, his head covered with a thick layer of graying curls, Robert Nadeau exudes the confidence of a skilled martial artist and moves with the self-possessed grace of a cat. After working for a few years as a policeman, Nadeau traveled to Japan and trained in Hombu Dojo during the 1960s. As the editor of an English language newspaper devoted to aikido, he interviewed the Founder a number of times and would often have more informal conversations with him. Nadeau was fascinated and inspired by the universal patterns and forces which he saw in Ueshiba's teachings. In the following interview he elucidates some of those patterns and forces, particularly the pattern which goes under the name of "the Peter Principle" and the two primary forces which rule our lives: yin/yang, male/female. He also talks about one important problem inherent in the dissemination of a non-competitive art like aikido: unqualified teachers.

He first became widely known in the 1970s with the publication of George Leonard's book, The Ultimate Athlete, *in which Leonard describes Nadeau's gifted and innovative teaching style. Nadeau is the exponent par excellence of the energy side of aikido and is one of the pioneers in the San Francisco Bay Area of the kind of "energy work" for which the Esalen Institute became famous. Indeed, he taught at the Esalen Institute for a number of years. He has also long been interested in how to take aikido "off the mat" so that non-martial artists can benefit from its teachings. Although he trained in judo and karate and holds a sixth degree black belt in aikido, the highest rank awarded to any American, Nadeau prefers to view himself as more of "a spiritual scientist" than a martial artist. It is no wonder that besides George Leonard, two other Innovators were his students: Richard Heckler and Wendy Palmer.*

I was a police officer in Redwood City when I started aikido. I started aikido with Robert Tann who was teaching in South San Francisco. I'm not sure of the year. I think it was 1960, around in there.

I was in the Marine Reserve before that. Semper Fi* comes quickly to my lips. But I had to do other things. That's why I didn't end up in the Corps as a regular. The desire was there, though.

I've been doing martial arts since I was maybe fifteen. I started with judo. I've touched on a lot of things, done a little kempo karate and taught police unarmed combat. In fact, I taught unarmed combat when I was in the Marines. But I was just a kid then.

I had heard about aikido from a friend of mine who was from Asia. I'd never heard about it before and I was interested in all martial arts so I kept my eyes open. I'd bump into a little paragraph here, a one-pager there, but I couldn't quite put my finger on it. I used to go to San Francisco and check out the different schools, judo schools mainly. One day I saw an advertisement for aikido books at a judo school and I wanted to catch up on what aikido was so I went to the school, and lo and behold, there was a guy who had just come in from Hawaii, Bob Tann, and he was teaching a class there at this judo school. So I watched it. Of course he had all brand-new people, but I thought there was something there.

So I came back home and got some of my training partners. I said, "Come on up, let's go check this art out. I think there's something there." Then we went back for a second time, and this time Tann came over and talked to us. As soon as he said something about mind-body harmony, I was instantly interested because I'd been trying to hook in meditation and mind-body harmony in my own way

---

*Short for "Semper Fidelis," "always faithful," the Marine Corps motto.

with the other arts, knowing there was some relationship between mind things or spiritual things and physical actions. And here they're already talking about it. That grabbed me. So I started training and at the same time I kept doing the other arts I was doing. It was pretty interesting. Meanwhile I was getting tired of police work. It just wasn't my thing. I needed a change so I decided to go to Japan and train martial arts. I wanted to have a chance to train myself more. I'd been training quite a lot, meditating a lot, doing a lot of physical practice, a lot of mind/body practices, and then the aikido thing.

I was kind of born with an interest in mind/body practices. A lot of things I'd developed myself. But I wasn't stupid. I knew that a teacher could save you a lot of time, somebody who'd walk the way ahead of you. So I eventually found somebody who was capable of teaching meditation. A gentleman named Walt Baptiste, who I call an American yogi. He was one of the first Americans into that field that I'm aware of, and a lot of his stuff was also personally developed. I think his uncle was connected to Yogananda so his uncle probably gave him a start. But because he was also a natural, he probably developed a lot of what he was doing himself.

I had been doing a variety of practices on my own, all kinds of weird things. I'd stare at candles, see how long I could sit there. I'd go outside on a stormy winter night to see how long I could sit out there in my shorts. I'd just do whatever I could think of. I started to glom a few books. Again, there wasn't too much out in books then, just some strange things, like Madame Blavatsky. I popped into a couple of sessions with followers of hers. But they were all really old people: they were sixtyish and I was twenty. And I realized very quickly that philosophy, talking about things, was nice but you really had to train. So anyway I was fortunate to meet Walt Baptiste, and he used to do these six-week meditation sessions. It was a good basic meditation style. I got some good basics there; just learning to sit for an hour without fidgeting around really helped. I had been training my body daily since I was fifteen, and I began to realize there were energies in the body, and it wasn't too hard to start to train them also. I was becoming aware of the more spiritual, loving aspects, while at the same time training for martial arts—training to kill, so to speak—so I had a question about where meditation and the martial arts meet. So when I heard about aikido it caught my attention, it was a natural direction for me to go.

So anyway, I wanted out of the police force. I wanted to get out of town and just concentrate on training—physical, mental, spiritual. So I decided to go to Japan, not that I was guru hunting, because by that time I had enough meditation time in. I knew kind of where the answer was. I just wanted to get out of town so I could concentrate. The police world is kind of a strange world in that you really immerse yourself in it, and even if I quit the police force I'd still be hanging out with other cops: it's hard to shake loose of. So I had to get out of town. I decided to go to Japan and study all the arts that I'd been training—judo, karate, aikido and whatever else came up. This was 1962 and I'd been training with Tann for at least a year by then.

After I got to Japan I started with aikido and judo and karate. I trained aikido at Hombu Dojo. And I went to the Kodokan and I went to one of the universities, slips my mind which one, and trained with their judo team. And I trained karate at the Japan Karate Association. But very quickly judo didn't seem to fit anymore, even though I had already ten years-plus in. It suddenly didn't seem to fit. And after a while the karate didn't seem to fit, either. It just didn't quite click for me. So I began to de-emphasize those and emphasize the aikido until eventually all I wanted to do was the aikido.

The first time I was there I stayed about two years. I supported myself with some money I'd saved from my police job, and fortunately I had a very understanding wife who was a good secretary and she got a job there. And then I started teaching English. I went back a couple of times after that. O-Sensei was around a lot. He was teaching in the early mornings a lot, and his home and the dojo were in the same building.

Before I even met him I kind of knew he was somebody. I had a friend of mine who was an extremely good psychic and she had mentioned this man even though she didn't know anything about him. She had mentioned his powers, his very high spiritual nature, so I was kind of prepped for him. I had also heard about him a bit since I'd started to do aikido. So when I got there and watched him do his thing, I knew he was something else. It was also strange watching these people go down the way they were going down. I was kind of used to wrestling around, slugging it out; he'd wave his arm and these people would drop pretty good. So I figured he was good. I really wanted to try him, being the competitive fool I was. Finally one day, I don't know how many months went by, there was a class. All the students were sitting around and he looked at me, and he held out his arm and said, "Grab by arm." I'd been waiting for this for ages. I was probably in the best shape of my life; I'd been training every day, so I was up and at him like a shot. He was right in front of me, that arm was right in front of me, and suddenly I'm in a rubbery cloud going deeper and deeper and the rubber is like a rubber band starting to stretch out. And suddenly I'm flying out of this cloud and I catch him out of the corner of my eye—he's standing to the right of me instead of in front of me—I catch him out of the corner of my eye but I'm in the air and going down. I know I hit hard because I slapped hard and everybody started laughing, but my mouth was agape. I was just awe-struck. Now you've got to remember this wasn't the first time I had been thrown down. I'd been hit by judo champions and top-of-the-line karate boys and good *aikidoka*, you know, but always with them you'd have some sense that "this guy is tough, he's fast, he outsmarted me, he tricked me." But this was like something else. I don't know what kind of world I went into.

After I met O-Sensei, I would ask him questions now and then, and I guess he liked the questions because he would invite me to come back and talk to him. I was fortunate he took a liking to me. He used to travel the country and sometimes he would ask me to come along with him and stuff, so we had a pretty good rapport. Mainly I'd listen to what he had to say. Now and then I'd have a question: I would kind of say, "Okay, this is the way I think the universe works right now, Sensei, tada, tada, tada, tada," and he'd either confirm or deny. So then I'd know I was on the right track and I would just keep doing what I was doing. Again, I wasn't guru hunting at the time. You see, I had already established through my meditations how to make my approach. But just as a reference, and he was a very good reference, I'd say, "Tada, tada, tada," and he would say, "Yes," and I'd say, "Okay thanks," and then I could just go home and continue my meditations in my apartment around the corner from the dojo.

I was also very interested in his approach. I had thought there was a relation between meditation and functioning—other than the little magic things that might happen to a meditator—between meditation and some kind of daily-use functioning, but I wasn't sure how to bring those two together. I had seen signs of it because I'd meditate and go do judo and I knew I wasn't the same person. I knew I was reacting completely differently and doing quite well. I knew that in body building, with certain ways of using your mind and your attention, you'd get much better results. I just didn't know the extent of it and here this guy was doing this fantastic job of overlapping his awareness and daily life function. So when people ask, "What did you learn from him?" generally I say, "I learned I wasn't crazy." See, before that I wasn't sure. I thought things worked a certain way, I hoped they worked a certain way, but I wasn't sure. So to see him do his thing and then to ask him about it and have him say, "Yes" . . . it was like, "Whew! Thank god!" because I wasn't sure for a while how far off base I was, you know. Again, we're not talking about 1980 or 1970 when you had Maharishi and you had the yoga classes on every street corner and you had meditation going on. We're talking about pre-all of that stuff. There really wasn't that much reference, so I needed what I got from him. I respected him very much. I loved him very much.

So I would train the aikido and do my best at it. All the while I was training, I was also saying to myself, "This isn't really it," meaning just the techniques per se, just the training, that there was something else. But I didn't know any other doorway and if you're going to hang out with aikido folks, then you'd better do the aikido and do it damn well. So I would do it diligently, I mean, really diligently, but all the while leaving myself open. Because I saw the other teachers ... I hope this doesn't sound disrespectful. I respect them for their technical capabilities, and as people, there are some beautiful aikido teachers, beautiful people, but O-Sensei was just in a whole different world and that's what I was interested in and that's always what I've been interested in since before I ever heard of aikido. I respected the other teachers for their level of ability and all of that, but I didn't see any of them look like they had bridged the gap that O-Sensei had. Not that that's easy to do. A lot of folks aren't particularly interested in that kind of thing because there's a loss of ego at a certain level. You have to die to be reborn, that kind of thing. Maybe a lot of folks don't want to die and be reborn. Maybe crossing into other realms and functioning from there is easy, but maybe it's not that easy. It's one of those things that's a split-second away and it may take you a lifetime to find that out. I mean, everybody's potentially a very great spiritual being, but how many great spiritual beings do you see tromping around the street? Some people saw that as a problem, that the teachers at Hombu Dojo were not as spiritual as O-Sensei, but I think it's not just what's the problem at Hombu Dojo, what's the problem with people? This is an ongoing quest and an ongoing problem since day one. We've had the dreamers and the rememberers and the priests and the saints and we're always making that effort. In some ways it's not easy.

I know some people say O-Sensei was difficult to understand, but I don't think it was O-Sensei's fault, because those who were interested in spiritual things, even though they were Westerners, understood him. It doesn't mean we understood a particular Shinto word or whatever, but we understood him. He caught on early in the game that a lot of Westerners were very into what he was into. He mentioned that. Many of us there were interested in spiritual awareness development but there have also been many other people doing aikido who were not interested in spiritual awareness development, so I don't see the point of putting the blame on O-Sensei because they weren't particularly interested. No, I think they were doing their own numbers. In some ways he was secretive because he was dealing with a power, and he told me this power was fairly simple to do. Don't teach it to people with bad *kimochi*, or as we'd say in California, don't teach it to the assholes. So he would be careful. At the same time he was laying everything out. We had a few sit-downs, some real discussions, and I always had the impression he was laying as much out as he could. I didn't see him hold anything back. I'm certain if I'd had more questions he would have answered them. I think people who say O-Sensei was difficult to understand are people who for some reason or another didn't want to understand him.

I have a story I tell—now this is just my sense of it—but there was a lady training in Japan and we were having some coffee and she said, "I don't understand him." I suddenly had this extremely strong feeling like, "No! She's got a certain lifestyle. She doesn't want to understand him because she's afraid in doing what he's doing she'll have to change her lifestyle." Now that was just an intuitive hunch but it hit me like a sledgehammer over my head. I think there's a lot of folks like that, who say, "No, I don't understand this man because I may have to change my lifestyle. I don't understand this man because I'm going to have to let go of some of my old beliefs." Think of how many beliefs a person hangs on to. And to go into something bigger you have to let go of a lot of the smaller stuff, even if you don't want to. I was in a taxi with O-Sensei and I said to him, "You know, I really want to do your aikido," and he said to me, "That's very strange. Everybody else wants to do their aikido."

That doesn't mean you have to do exactly what O-Sensei did. If you're going to line up to the universe or god or whatever, you've got to do it through your own system. I don't have a white beard and I wasn't born in southern Japan in 18-whatever. You have to do your own form, so you can't follow somebody else's path that way. But you can understand the laws that they're working with and then just translate them back to yourself. See, that's why I didn't sit around every day and ask him a bunch of questions. I knew that that was futile. I would maybe learn some information, but I knew I had to do it. I didn't have that many questions. I would just get a little adjustment now and then, and of course I'd get a drift of how he was viewing it, but it's not like I had a question a day. I was putting my time in sitting and catching it for myself as best I could. It's always going to be that way. You know, you can learn from somebody, but you've got to do it.

There's a lot of confusion about that. A lot of people when you try to lay out a basic pattern will sometimes misunderstand and say, "No, that's your pattern," and oftentimes it is not; it is a basic pattern that they should be able to put themselves into. There are many approaches. Somebody could practice with breathing or somebody could practice with chanting or somebody could practice with centering or somebody could practice with a quality like love or balance or harmony or a texture like bright or golden or pure. They're all valid. They're in the same place. Space that has a certain degree of purity, has a sound. That same place has a center, that same space will dialogue itself through imagery. It's the same space. You don't tell somebody, "Don't chant; do this," unless you maybe are intuitive and you see, "Ah, this guy's a chanter." Then you might say to him, "Hey man, I think it's cool if you chant." But I think properly done, you're not doing a number on him. Either you have a sense of the person or you don't. If you don't, then you just let him work it out as best he can. If you do and you think he's going to be receptive, you may throw something out. But it's their thing for them to do something with. So O-Sensei threw out patterns. He was laying out patterns all the time. He always talked about center, always talked about fire/water, form/circle, circle/square/triangle—Izanagi/Izanami. He was laying it out all the time, all the time. Now it was up to them, if they were interested, to find out what that meant within their own system.

As for what has happened to aikido since O-Sensei died, it's like anything else. Somebody can lay something out and people are just going to do with it what they do with it. We've been through this before. There was Christ, then there was Christianity. There was Buddha, then there was Buddhism. We do some strange things after the great ones leave, some of it good, some of it maybe not so good.

We have to take everything with that feeling that it has helped a lot of folks and it will continue to help a lot of folks. And in there there are some turkeys, a lot of people take advantage of the art, or whatever. I don't know what to do about that. You can't be a policeman. You do the best by laying out what you can. I've been trying different things but they don't seem to work. Pleading doesn't work and threats don't work. So let them do what they want to do.

The last time I came back from Japan was right before O-Sensei died, '67 or so. I had a trip planned around '69, but he died and I haven't been back since. I came back broke. I went to work just to make some eating money and started teaching. It was kind of hard because the aikido still wasn't really known. You'd start with two or three students. You'd go to class some days, you'd be the only one there.

I started in Menlo Park and then later Mountain View and San Jose, and I also taught in San Francisco fairly early in the game. Charlie Tart, who's out of U.C. Davis and who has written some books on meditation, used to do aikido and at that time we also started doing some classes just in centering and energy stuff, separate from the aikido. Charlie thought they were great and mentioned my name to Esalen, which at that time had a San Francisco section plus the Big Sur section. He mentioned it to them and they invited me to a class. Apparently they liked it. We started an ongoing group of which George Leonard was one, Michael Murphy, founder of Esalen, another. So that was the beginning of the San Francisco class. Later on I was invited down to Big Sur and I did some classes for them. They thought it was good, so they asked me to do workshops for the general public. I workshopped Esalen regularly for about ten years. Then I thought I'd take a break. It's been a long break now.

I like doing those kinds of workshops. I did a variety of workshops. Very few aikido workshops, though—mainly centering, meditation, sensitivity, psychic workshops, movement workshops. I had a lot of students who were psychologists. The workshops were very effective, I think. I get feedback even now: people tell me that a week-long workshop just turned around their whole life. I knew they were good because I was top-draw for a lot of years in Big Sur. There were a lot of big names. I was there regularly month after month and I'd draw constantly well. A lot of that is word of mouth if you draw for ten years: all those people are telling other people. Some of the people might have gone on to practice aikido. But more importantly, a lot of them were writers, teachers, university professors, doctors, and I think they carried it out in their own work.

When we first started doing workshops, I started them with Robert Frager, and we did them separate from the aikido. We had picked up a lot and had a lot of diverse training in mind/body harmony, energy things, through aikido and other things, and my feeling was that we could get a lot of these experiences across to people without them having to do the aikido. Some people just don't have three nights a week, year after year, to do aikido, but I thought there were a lot of things that they could assimilate in a day-long workshop, so we started doing that. I thought we got real good results. The things we're talking about are inherent in a system. Everybody's potentially an energy being. It's just a matter of them becoming aware of another dimension of themselves. Everybody has a center, so we would create practices, some from aikido and some from other areas and some we made up ourselves. I just thought those were great workshops. They affected people. They caught on. It doesn't mean people could deal with a *yokomen* [strike to the head], but we didn't present it as how to deal with a *yokomen,* we presented it as how to deal with any pressures, pressures in their life and business, how to be sensitive. So instead of swooping in before the *yokomen* starts, we would maybe have a therapist swooping in on the patient before they got too sick. Of course, some people really want to learn physical aikido. They want to learn the techniques and all of that. But somebody else could just maybe want to be a little more centered in their job, and all they need is a little hint, a little clue, a little assist—whether it's a day-long or week-long workshop or whatever—and from that point on they'll play with that and develop it and then continue to function better in their career.

I'm not one for thinking that everybody in the world should do aikido. As you can see, I am a strong advocate of getting some of the principles across to people without necessarily teaching them aikido techniques directly. I think that's important and so I'm pleased when I see people using that stuff in other fields. But I think we have to be a little bit careful. People who learn that way have to be careful not to confuse that with aikido in its bigger sense. If you teach people to be more centered and they're doing quite well at it, that's good, but I'm not sure if that deserves an aikido rank. I think there may be a little misunderstanding here. A student might say, "But I've gotten so much out of it and I'm giving so much to people." Yeah, but let's not confuse that with aikido. If you've got a big draw and you're making a dollar or you're getting famous or you're doing good work, great, be happy with that. But let's be careful of crossing the line and saying, "this proves I'm a great *aikidoka*," because aikido is also your power, your techniques, and a lot of these other things. I wish people would get a little clearer on that.

Of course, if you're practicing the physical art, you don't have to separate out the principles: they exist in the very techniques. They're really in there. I realized that when I talked to some American servicemen who were training in aikido and I knew their teacher didn't speak English, definitely not enough to get any of that type of philosophy across to them. And lo and behold, they were talking about very similar things that had dawned on them while they were training that were right on.

It's not an American innovation, by the way, this attempt to explain principles from the beginning or even to try to get at the principles directly. No, I think Koichi Tohei did a good job with that, too. All the teachers are good. But I think he was one of the first to present aikido principles that way. I think there may have been others, but he's the one that I'm aware of. He was talking about principles and creating new practices to give people a sense of things, again without necessarily requiring them to be that good at aikido or even to do aikido. I'm sure he did things with non-aikidoists using the aikido principles. I know he did. So I can't say I was the first.

Anyway, while I was doing this stuff at Esalen, I had quite a few dojos. Someplace in there I had San Jose, Mountain View and San Francisco. I was probably at it seven days a week, hours and hours a day. I don't give quite that much anymore. I mean, it's not like I'm a twice-a-weeker; I still do at least five days a week but I used to do it seven plus. It's still my primary source of income, unfortunately. It's so limited as a source of income. It's really a joking phrase. There's not very much.

One thing that's a little different about us here in Northern California is that I made an effort not to have Japanese teachers in this area, because I was into the personal awareness aspect. I didn't want there to be too much confusion about saying, "Oh, I can't become aware of myself because I don't speak Japanese or because I'm not a fifth *dan* or an eighth *dan* or whatever." That's one reason I don't over-Japanese things. Not that I don't like the Japanese, but just that a lot of people will do that. They'll say, "Oh they can do it," whatever they are, whether they're the Chinese or the Indians or the Japanese or the whoever. I felt that was a problem in the earlier years of teaching. So I made an effort to break that down, and one effort I made was to make sure we had no Japanese teachers in this area. That's not an anti-Japanese statement, it's just that I thought we could hack it on our own, that we didn't need the input. And I think I was proven right through the years. Aikido has grown: a lot of folks are doing it in a lot of different places. And taking for granted that people are people, and they do what they do, I guess it's going okay. You know, if we got real picky we wouldn't be satisfied, but taking all things into consideration, it's either limping or jogging along as best as it can. Now we're reaching a point where maybe we have to wonder is bigger better and stuff like that. Now we may begin to wonder about quality control, which is a moot point because you can't control anybody anyway. But I will throw it out there now, about quality control.

Growth for growth's sake is not necessarily a good thing. Look at dog breeding. Soon as a dog becomes top ten, there is some bad breeding going on, bad breeding. Sometimes it may not be good to be in the top ten. So if a student who should be training instead of teaching says, "Yeah, yeah, but I'm spreading it in my neighborhood," that doesn't necessarily make me happy. Spreading what in your neighborhood? And why are you doing this when you should be training? Not that I think there's much concrete we can do about it; you can't control folks and I don't feel like being a policeman again. But it would be nice if they would control themselves.

Know yourself. That's the problem. But some people don't trust their peers, they don't trust their teachers. But see, if people are to lie to themselves, they're going to lie to themselves. If they're going to bullshit themselves, there ain't no rules we can make that will take care of this problem. None. They'll finagle around it. Bullshit is bullshit. They'll just finagle all around it so why make rules? They have to work harder at it and I'll have to work harder trying to be a cop. I don't want to be a cop. If I want to be a cop, I'll go back to the force. They pay better. They give you retirement, shit like that. It's a problem of people. I don't know any answer. Some of the folks have been saying something cute. They've been saying, "One weakness of aikido is we don't compete." If we were a competitive art a lot of things we have we wouldn't have. You get too cocky in karate and they knock you out. That takes care of it there. Judo, they put you down, they don't let you get up. They choke you out. A few of those, and you know you're not ready to go through. What are we going to do in aikido? You hand me a wrist, I'm going to bend it harder? I hand you my wrist and you bend it? So there is a certain problem that doesn't exist in some of the other arts. Not that I think there should be competition. I guess we'll just have to live with bullshit. It's just too bad. It just makes me feel sad. Because it creates a lot of problems and pressures among folks and it creates a lot of animosity.

But we shouldn't let the bullshit keep us from seeing that aikido is good for helping people grow and change. I think the basic components of the art contribute to that. O-Sensei did a hell of a good job. One, you've got an identity that can change and, should we say, spread. We have forms that are given room to grow. We've got energy

70

which is the life blood of forms, which is given room to flow, which creates a whole new level of consciousness, a whole new being. I think everything in the world is the same; everything in the world follows the same pattern. A company is not a *shiho nage,* but I think it does exactly the same thing. It will, if you give it room, show you how it wants to grow. I think a *shiho nage,* given room, will develop itself. A company will develop itself, a situation will develop itself, so I think all the basics are laid out. I think he did a hell of a job.

Change is not easy, though. Once you start to change, once you realize that you're starting to enter a different dimension or state or level of consciousness—choose your phrase; you can't retain your original level of consciousness. It doesn't fit there anymore. In body building, a pip-squeak who gets sand kicked in his face because he's 102 pounds may go to Gold's and develop into a 200-pounder. But his mind has to change or he's still a pip-squeak inside. So there has to be a change. Otherwise the muscles are kind of a joke. You can break through them and still touch the pip-squeak inside. There has to be a change of consciousness. And there are critical points where you should know when you're crossing a border and be prepared for a change of consciousness.

This is not something peculiar to aikido. It's a universal pattern, though I don't know if we bring it out that clearly in aikido. In one sense that may be what ranks are about, that at a certain level there are certain things that you see. Not only in aikido—I can hang around with other martial artists, which I do, and we all agree on things. For example, if a good martial artist were to go watch a test at another art, he would spot instantly who the good folks are. There would be no question. I can talk to a jujutsuist, Chinese fighters or whatever, and we always agree. You start talking the philosophy, and students, teachers, whatever, and we're in total agreement. It doesn't matter what art you're from; there are certain things that are of the martial arts world.

So ranks and certain duties you might give a student offer a possibility of a shift in consciousness. If you say to a student, "Hey, I want you to become a minor assistant teacher," it means you're starting to potentially see something in him that you want to bring out a bit more. And he should know there's been a bit of a change, too. If you say to somebody, "I'm priming you to be a teacher," then he should know there has been a change. The change will manifest itself in different ways. I think when a person is going through their own process, one thing you will see is more power. It may not just be physical power, but there is a power there, there's more energy there than the norm or more than that person had a year previously. So if they go through their process you will see that change. Another way to look at it is to say that if a person develops, goes through their own process, they get larger, to use a loose word. And you see this "larger" in relation to their training partner. We're not asking them to dominate, but if they're larger, they deal with their partner differently. They'll accept them more, they'll blend with them longer, they'll blend with them deeper, they'll be so in tune with their flow maybe they'll throw them further, you see. Which is not to be misunderstood as just overpowering them, but it'll have all the signs of somebody who is starting to develop themselves.

However, I think it's a problem if you say, "Look. If you've developed yourself then you'll handle this situation better." Immediately a lot of folks will want to go try to handle the situation better, which starts becoming tricky or dominating or whatever. But that's just a misunderstanding of the process. We have to, it seems to me, keep repeating: "Keep changing yourself, keep doing your process, and if you're doing it we'll see the results." But again, over and over, people shift their focus to the results. So we've got to keep shifting their attention away from the results and back to the process. Sometimes because they're stronger, because the results are better, they'll think there has been a change when there has been absolutely no change. They're thicker in the shoulders or whatever, but they really haven't learned anything. They've learned how to place their arms in a certain manner, but if you see absolutely no change that's when I get sad. Sometimes I see somebody training and I'll see no change in them though their techniques are getting better because they're doing them a thousand times a day or whatever. Of course, if they do that, certain moves are going to get stronger, but if you see no change in the person, to me it's sad. I like to see change in the person, knowing it won't be long before I'll see a change in the technique: that's naturally going to follow. I suspect that's again a world-wide thing. You know, if you are in harmony with the universe, you may be happier and wealthier. So people might lie and cheat to be wealthier to show that they are in line with the universe. I think it's a misunderstanding. It's across the board, not just in aikido.

One of the things I've discovered in my own process is that there isn't a good and an evil. I think there are two forces. And when you're comfortable with one force to some degree and you start to become aware of the other force, potentially it can look really strange because it's coming at you and you are not versed with it, you have no relationship with it, even though it's you. So immediately you start calling it something evil. For example, when people start to ground and settle, it's quite likely a lot of them will run into a type of power that makes them potentially angrier. Any time you grow wider you're going to be more open for your counterpart to start to make itself known. But because you don't have a relation with your counterpart you're going to have some misunderstandings there.

What might help would be for people to realize there is this other force which is equally as beautiful as anything else, but it is at first very different. We might talk about it in terms of male/female. A male in expanding his maleness eventually is going to run into his femaleness, and it could appear very strange at first. At first it could appear weakening. But it's not. The other force doing a full run is definitely not weak but when you first see it, it might appear so. In workshops I got people to recognize the presence of that other source or direction or their other half so that they started to learn a bit of how it beats. In my classes, I try to lay out what I think are universal principles of things that students will bump into eventually, if not this year or this lifetime, then eventually, because it's an ongoing law. There are two forces, period. It's not that there are two forces this year, and next year it's going to be something else. There have always been two forces: *izanagi/izanami, yin/yang,* he/she, up/down, fire/water, call it anything you want, it's still two forces.

And often what surprises is what happens when you've been opening wide. Let's say for a typical male when he opens to God the Father, it's an upward drift. Eventually one day he's going to be aware of this dark, murky stuff underneath him. After all this brightness and all the hallelujahs and all the angelic beings, it's going to look bad. It's not bad. It's time for the other force to show itself. But at first it doesn't look neat. I remember my first go-arounds. It was awful. Talk about crocodiles under the bed. I'd been meditating heavily for ten years or more, doing well, sort of working my way up the ladder, so to speak, striking out in all the astral planes, whatever language you want to use. And judging by the space I was in, I felt I was doing quite well; judging by the texture of the energy, the beams I was bumping into, all that kind of thing, I was doing quite well. One time I reached what looked like a roof of the universe and I thought, "Oh, finally." It was like a vast space and there was a sense of wide and empty and nothing and vast. I thought, "Hmmm" and I thought, "I bet a lot of people when they hit this think that's it, that there isn't anything more." But I had this feeling in my gut that I was missing something. I mean, I was happy with the height, and we're talking years and years getting there, a lot of hard work and a lot of devotion. But I had this feeling I was missing something. So I went back at it again and again. Finally I heard, "Go down." I said, "What? Go down? Go down, what do you mean 'go down'?" I hit it again, and it said the same thing, "Go down." I started to feel this downward sense. Now all the time I'd been meditating I'd always been physically grounded. I train every day of my life. I was always grounded in a certain sense. I knew it was kind of important, but I didn't understand "Go down."

So I think for the next ten years I started studying this other direction of things, which appeared at first very dark, very savage. One of my first visuals on it was a snake pit. Here I am in a meditation where I'm used to angelic beings and hallelujah choirs and all that kind of stuff and here's a snake pit. What the hell is this?

What's this doing in my meditation space? And these things were spiraling up, biting. I could almost actually feel them. I thought, "Hmm.... Well, I'll hang out here because I'm in my meditation space. I'll let them bite me. Maybe it's a death trip practice. I'm used to practicing dying, so okay. It's a weird form, but I'll try it." So I let the snakes bite me. I've got no great love for snakes so even though it's just a sitting, I'm feeling these snakes bite me. Ugh. But I hang out there and I suffer through it. After a little bit the snakes start to smile. I say, "Aha! We have us a joke here. Okay, I'm used to this. We'll see." I hang out longer and go deeper. They're not snakes, they're spirals of energy. "Oh, now we're getting some place, because I know energy is important."

I hang out longer, go down deeper and there's this beautiful lady down there and she's flipping her arms. Every time she flips her arms these spirals go up and she's the giver of energy of the universe or something. But I could see when those energies got high, if you didn't know what they were, they would start to look like biting snakes bitching at you, and you only realized what they really were when you allowed yourself to go into this other realm. And then I started to study that other realm for, god, over ten years now, I've been majoring in that.

It's probably a strange place to hang out in, so I'm sure it must have affected how people have viewed me. It has affected my techniques. I do a lot of down under stuff now. When people attack me, I just sense "deep" and they fall down sometimes. So I spent a long time going down into it. It affected a lot of people around me, but I'm basically a researcher. That's my real job. I'm a universal researcher. If you say, "Are you an aikido teacher or are you a this or a that," I'll say, "No, I'm a spiritual researcher." If I slept with my *bokken* [wooden sword] every night and got up at 6:00 AM and shadow-boxed my techniques, then I might say, "I'm a martial artist or *aikidoka*," but I don't. I don't sleep with my *bokken*. But when it comes to checking out the universe and following out patterns and stuff, yeah, yeah, that's my thing. So by majoring in what at that time, maybe, seemed to be an obscure thing, the "deep, dark" and the "deep, strange," I know that it affected some folks. I know a lot of folks that I hung out with suddenly weren't hanging out with me, but I had to do this thing. I was there, you see. I'm a good scientist and when something happens I have to let the experiment run and give of myself.

Now and then I've thought about writing about all this, but I want to wait until I feel like I have more of a total package. You know, I could have started writing about centering and things like that back in the late '60s and energy flow in the early '70s when it was just starting to become a talked-about thing, right before all of the hatha yoga and t'ai chi and energy healings and all those things. We didn't have that much faith before that, so it would have been a good time. But I also thought, "No, I don't have that much to say yet." Certainly I'm not satisfied with the package as I see it, I'm not satisfied how I see things work. I want a bigger grasp of it, so when I'm satisfied with my grasp of things maybe I'll write.

Anyway, I like to really remind folks that as they grow there's an expansion, and when you expand you're going to bump into other directions of force, energy, and they're going to scare you, potentially. Try not to be afraid, try to hang out with them. It's the other half of you. Just do the best you can to catch that. Let's say if you're male, just know that your starting viewpoint doesn't quite understand the language of your own female. And vice versa, if you're female you don't understand your own maleness. And if you're male, it doesn't mean you've got the male domain of the universe down pat. And just because you're female and it's a female age you don't sit back and say, "I've got it made, I'm a female and I know it's a female age coming up now." It's like, "Hey lady, I'm sorry, but you've got work to do, too. You can't sit on your laurels."

Because of this whole process, you'll see stages in people's training. After the first month a lot of folks might quit. The same after the third month, the sixth month, the first year. There's a cycle. And then after that there's testing time. Sometimes when students start to check themselves out for a test or something they'll fall apart. That's a typical example of somebody saying, "Okay, I think I want to be a certain level," at which time the support energies start to come into play. Now if you don't know there are support energies you're suddenly wondering why you're getting shaky when you weren't the week before. Suddenly there are holes in your technique and you're falling apart and you're forgetting and you're getting dizzy and all of that. Well, that's all the support energy, you see, and a lot of folks don't catch the connection between a statement of desire and what happens in their system after that. There's a science right there. The corresponding energies will respond to your idea, dreams, statement, and it would be good if you would understand how that works so they don't frighten you to death and confuse you. I've seen countless times where someone says, "I want to take a test and be a whatever," and they fall apart. They're doing the same techniques they've been doing for the last months before that, but suddenly they look nervous. That's the energy.

It's the Peter Principle. The Peter Principle is about comfortableness with energy. Somebody says, "I want to work here." Okay, as a worker he can eat that much energy, so fine, he's comfortable and he gets a job. Then he says, "This is pretty easy. I'd like to be something more." Then they notice him and they say, "Hey, would you like to be night foreman?" He says "Okay" and he tries it out and he gets night foreman's energies, which are more than worker energies. Lo and behold he's comfortable with that. He looks pretty good. So the folks say to him, "Hey, you're looking pretty good. We're going to make you superintendent." Dum—da da da [Dragnet theme] If he's not comfortable with superintendent energy, from that moment on he's always on edge. He can't step down because unfortunately it's not socially acceptable to step down at this point. But now, because he's under so much pressure, he's making a lot of dumb mistakes. That's the Peter Principle: He's worked his way into a place where he doesn't function very well, and he can't get out of it unless he screws up so bad they bring him down or fire him. Our system doesn't have enough testing periods: "Hey, try this for a bit, see how you feel." And it's no demeaning thing to step down. But in society it is.

A lot of what I do is to try to teach things like this and call them loosely "tricks of the trade." It's "tricks of the trade of living," because I hate to see people hurt and confused when it's all very natural. I'm interested in seeing people open up more, not just to let a *shiho nage* through but open up more so we can see better what their real job is. I'm very interested in the fact that when people open up you can get to see their real potential. It's almost like a movie, it gets that visual sometimes. You can see what they should be doing. There are certain universal jobs that are good for us to do, and if you look you kind of see them. So I may not be interested in your *shiho nage* but if you have to open to let a better *shiho nage* come through, by the very nature of your opening, you're opening to the "more" that exists within the system that's related to you. Yet in letting a larger *shiho nage* form come through, you must have learned some tricks and you also have to let the energy in relationship to that come through. If you learn a few tricks for that then you can transfer exactly that same pattern to a job increase or job change. The patterns will be the same. That fascinates me.

I think it's too bad when people don't see that it's a process. If you said to me, "Stop aikido right now and go do something else," I wouldn't have a heart attack over it. Oh, I'd have some tremors because there would be new energies coming in, but it wouldn't be a great shock, even though I've got a lot of years in. I think that would be nice if people had a little bit more of a sense of aikido as a process and not hang onto it in a small way. By tightening in on it, they miss the message or potentially maybe even bastardize this beautiful pattern net that we have.

When you open up bigger to deal with being a bigger *aikidoka*, you're opening up to all the other facets, too. So if there have been little secret hidden things in there, they may show. And if you don't recognize them and don't want to deal with them, then you could be opening a can of worms. To some people who say, "I'm really happy, I like life just the way it is, don't bug me," you might say, "Fine." You might not say to them, "No, no, you should meditate; no, no you should open up." They're not ready to deal with the amount of stuff going on when they open that door to the next level of consciousness. So I really wouldn't tell everybody to meditate, everybody to open up, I really don't want to do that. Some people are hanging on by a thread and in opening up they may not know how to deal with it. They may not have the ability to learn the tricks or rather to remember the tricks, because we all inherently know the tricks: we've been the route before but we've forgotten so badly that for some folks, it's like starting on day one. They don't have a memory of who they really are. They really think they're just "a human being" period and there is nothing else.

We're so encased. Since the dawn of time we're so locked in and merged that we don't even remember who the hell we are. Guys like O-Sensei come along and say, "Hey, look. When I line up with the whole universe, the whole universe is going on through me." He's trying to tell us, "This is your real state and anybody can do it because this is your heritage, this is your right, this is who you really are." But if everybody hangs on to their small, tiny self and says, "Oh no man, I'm not going to let go of this. . . ."

When you begin to let go, you first don't know what you're letting go to. If you're going to open up, if you're going to let go, you can work out the things that show. You may bump into potential quirks and things, but it can be worked out. Just know that they're there. See, in meditation we kind of know that, so we're always kind of watching for it. In aikido we may not know that, so we're not watching for it. So somebody could look at somebody doing a strong technique and say, "Ah, he's coming along good," and I could see that same guy and say, "Oh shit! What have we wrought?" because I'm maybe seeing something ugly coming through. It can be worked on but they're not looking at that. They're looking at his wrist getting bigger. Who gives a shit?! The shadow self thing may come up more because a lot of people have been training for a long time now. There comes a time where they're going to have to bump into a major "other." That may be starting to happen more and more, so if you find higher-ranked people quitting, higher-ranked students quitting, it might be a clue. They're starting to bump into something they don't know if they can deal with.

Now what would be a shame is if they pointed the finger away from themselves at something else, at aikido, at their teachers, at the system or whatever, when really it's a result of their bumping into a major portion of themselves that they didn't know was there. Instead of feeling and at least facing it, they're afraid of it. "Oh, it's that, but I don't feel like dealing with it." That's fine, but they may say aikido's too harsh or something like that and confuse the issue. I don't feel that aikido is any harsher now than before, but if you're bumping into more power that scares you, you may see everything in terms of power or how hard the hit is. For example, you may have never noticed a teacher growls when he throws. They've been doing it for years, but if you're going to be opening up, you'll suddenly bump into power and in its first onslaught it'll maybe growl as it comes through. Suddenly you're seeing the growl and you'll see that you never noticed it started here [inside] first. You were seeing it out there. You may think, "Gee, growling is not good," but if you really move away from your growler, that's not good. The son of a bitch has always growled. He's just trying to show you he's got one too or whatever.

Aikido is a great art but there are some developments or trends I'm not too fond of. For one thing, I don't want people to get too religious in a dojo because a lot of people that are going to be teaching in a dojo have no religion. That's why I don't like the Shinto clap at the beginning and end of class. As I said, my real job is I'm a scientist. I know how the universe works and I'm a damned good meditation awareness teacher. That's my thing. And even I don't like too much of that. That's why I'm casual on the mat. That's why I say "Fuck you" a lot and stuff like that just to keep it down a little bit. Just a little bit, though; if you get too disrespectful then at a certain point that becomes bullshit too, so I'll say, "Hey, don't overdo it, man." But just because you've learned to do a *nikkyo* strongly, you shouldn't be approached as if you're some kind of spiritual master. So I don't like things like long bows. It's a small thing but I don't like it. I don't like it when Joe Schmoe's out there and he bows in and all the students bow, and they stay bowed and he turns around and then he bows and they're still down. I don't like it, it's too much. It's a small thing but it's too much. Hey guys, it's just an aikido dojo. Yes, we bow in aikido, but not to Joe Schmoe up there because his *nikkyo's* a little stronger than somebody else's.

A teacher, particularly a new teacher, may be in a position where he is receiving a lot of stuff that may not be his to accept. There are a few of us in the aikido world who are very keen on spiritual aspects and spend a lot of time in different parts of it. So if someone approaches me on a spiritual note, I accept it because after a certain amount of years I've accepted that that's what I do. I've been very careful: for a long time when people said, "Please teach me to meditate," and stuff like that, I'd say, "Oh no, not me, man. I'm just a student." But if a new teacher answers a question like that with, "Yeah, sure," I say why? Because they're a fucking *nidan* [second degree black belt]? That's bullshit. Unless they've got something else going for them they are potentially putting themselves in a dangerous place. They'll start to think highly of themselves, not because they have it, but because they're in a situation where people bow to them in some form or other and say, "Sensei, sensei." They'll start to believe they deserve all those bows and not do anything inside themselves. So there's a problem with jumping the gun on teaching. They don't have that trouble too much in Japan. You've got to go through a long, long process. And even then you're going to have some turkeys up there but at least they've gone through the process, you've done the best you can. You've washed the work pants thirty-three times; the stain doesn't come out but at least you've washed them thirty-three times. We don't wash 'em thirty-three times here. Sometimes they don't even want you to sprinkle them.

Some people, teachers, whatever, complain about the "costs" of doing aikido—injuries, poor pay, broken marriages. Well, years ago somebody asked me if aikido should help a marriage and I'm not sure what difference it makes. If the marriage is over, it's over: it's just a growth pain, unless you're going to make a marriage that lasts forever as some kind of great spiritual symbol. I'm not sure how valid that that is. I was married to a very nice lady and reached a point where I had to leave, but not because there was a problem. There was not a fight, there was no problem. Nobody could believe we were getting divorced, but the thing was I had to go and do this weird spiritual thing and really major in it. Although she had been very supportive for the degree that I was going to major in it, I didn't think she'd be comfortable with it. And in retrospect she said to me, "You were right." She hadn't realized she was starting to be under pressure until after we broke up. It was only afterwards that she realized she really couldn't see herself as a spiritual scientist's wife. So in retrospect it worked out well and we're very close, very friendly and all that stuff.

Sure there have been costs. Sometimes I can bitch that the financial remuneration is very poor, for example. But nobody forced me to do aikido: it was my choice. I could have quit any moment I wanted to. I do it because it's in me to do it, and if I stop doing it or stop doing it as much it will be because I want to and it feels right. I kind of made a deal with myself. I said, "I'll do aikido until I get word otherwise" and I never got word. And then I got hurt a few years ago and pretty badly, the first serious injury in my whole life. I went to a doctor who's a specialist in his field, and when he said, "You'll never do aikido again," I broke out laughing because I was beginning to get the word and I knew it didn't mean I wouldn't do aikido. In fact I did aikido the next week [laughs], mainly with one arm but most people didn't know. But I knew that I should start keeping my eyes open, that other things were going to start to show for me. So I didn't take it to mean quit totally, get out, just start to keep your eyes open. That's when some other things started for me: the art world and other business opportunities started to show. Far as I know, I'll keep my hand in the aikido unless I get word otherwise. I just hope the next one's not a real physical-breakdown form.

3

ROBERT FRAGER

Robert Frager possesses an interesting combination of talents and accomplishments.

Of slightly less than medium height with short, thick white hair, he has the compact build and self-confident gait of an athlete, possessing a sixth-degree black belt in aikido. He is also an academic, heading and teaching at the school he founded, The Institute for Transpersonal Psychology. He expresses his fascinating ideas about aikido in complete, well-formed sentences and talks with the authority natural in a professor and administrator. But the self-assurance and calm authority he radiates also bespeak his role as the spiritual leader of a local Sufi group.

Robert Frager is one of the three people in our book who spent the most time studying with Ueshiba. Frager was preparing for a year in Japan when he began practicing aikido in Hawaii. When he went to Japan, he carried a letter of introduction from his teacher in Hawaii which enabled him to meet the Founder on his arrival at Hombu Dojo. In his first class he met Robert Nadeau with whom he became good friends. Later, after Frager was awarded his black belt, he began to accompany Ueshiba on trips and had the privilege of taking ukemi *from the Founder. Meeting the Founder changed Frager's life. It altered his view of what was possible for human beings and thus changed his orientation in his chosen field of study, psychology, away from research and toward the kind of exploration Abraham Maslow was doing with human potential. It also had a profound affect on his spiritual devel-*

opment: through his exposure to the Founder he became aware of the reality of spirituality.

Although we have included him in the group we call The Disciples, Frager could just as easily be considered one of the Innovators, since he has devoted much energy to considering how aikido can be taken "off the mat." He was the first one, along with Bob Nadeau, to present aikido at the Esalen Institute. Aikido is also an important part of the curriculum at the Institute for Transpersonal Psychology, even though most people who take it there will never pursue it as a martial art. Frager's ideas about aikido are also innovative. He feels aikido unites aspects of three important human archetypes: the Warrior, the Healer and the Magician, as he explains in this interview.

My first introduction to aikido was in '63, I think. I was a graduate student at Harvard at the time and had received a fellowship to attend the University of Hawaii to study Japanese language and then go to Japan. I had done a number of years of judo and karate, and I brought my *gi* with me to Hawaii and decided I was going to do some martial arts in Japan. While I was in Hawaii someone handed me probably the first book published in English about aikido, Koichi Tohei's book, *The Art of Aikido*. In it there were several quotes from O-Sensei. I remember reading something about "aikido is love," and having studied enough of the other martial arts, I knew they said that and didn't mean it and I somehow felt that O-Sensei said it and meant it. There was something in the idea of martial arts and love that was very profound and that I really wanted to learn. I had in one sense almost a satori experience after reading the book. I went outside and the grass was greener, the sky was bluer, the trees more alive; everything was just heightened and I knew at that time that I had to study aikido. So I opened up the phone book and found out where the nearest aikido dojo was, which just happened to be the aikido headquarters for Hawaii. It was about a five- or ten-minute drive from campus. Then I started training maybe two days a week because I was really busy with my studies at the time.

The head of the Hawaiian dojo was Yamamoto Sensei. After a

couple of months I was done with my Japanese language study and was going to go from Hawaii to Japan. So I went and told my instructors. Yamamoto Sensei took me into this little office they had in the back area and he said, "So you're going to Japan? Wonderful." And he took out this big roll of rice paper and an inkstone, watered the inkstone, made ink, took his brush out and made a beautiful calligraphic letter of introduction to O-Sensei. He said, "You know, you will be representing us. You're of good moral character and honorable and will represent us well," and gave me the letter. I realized that I was going the way one should go.

So I went to Japan and took the first opportunity to find my way to Hombu Dojo, and with my schoolboy Japanese—I had had nine months of Japanese full time but it was still awfully rough—I kind of mumbled that I had come to study aikido and that I had this letter for O-Sensei. The man behind the window said, "Just a moment." He went into the office in back of his and then he came out, ushered me in, and there was O-Sensei and Doshu. It was about one or two in the afternoon. When I met O-Sensei, I had this flash: I remembered reading all of those articles in *Readers' Digest* about "The Most Remarkable Person I Have Met," I remembered reading those and thinking I would never be able to write an article like that, but it flashed into my mind: "Oh, now I'm meeting one of those people." I kind of stammered how honored I was to meet him, that I was here to do aikido, and he smiled. We chatted and had tea and then Doshu said, "Well, it's time for the three o'clock class," and ushered me out on the mat and paired me with the one foreigner who was there, who was Bob Nadeau. I knew just enough aikido to be in trouble: I didn't know enough to really do anything but I knew enough so I couldn't be taken for a rank beginner, so people could throw me around. I got to know Nadeau very well, we became very close. And I got to know a lot of the other foreigners. There weren't very many back then, this was now the summer of '64. I started by training three or four times a week and then five or six and by the end of the year I was training seven days a week. It got so it felt strange to have a day go by without doing aikido.

Nadeau spent a lot of time with O-Sensei. He really encouraged me to go with him sometimes when he interviewed O-Sensei for a little English-language newspaper that he was the editor of. We ended up going a number of times with O-Sensei to the local Omoto-Kyo temple in Tokyo when he would put on demonstrations. One time I asked him would he use me as *uke*. He didn't say anything and I thought, "A little faux pas there, Bob." He never said a word. But the moment I made *shodan,* the moment I put a *hakama* on, he would sometimes use me as *uke*. So I had the wonderful experience of taking falls for him.

The best way I can describe what it was like to be thrown by him is this: It looked like I would focus on him and as I thought about attacking, my felt experience was that I would deliberately or some-how swerve to the side, miss him and take a roll, you know, just like an obvious tank dive. I would get up and go, "No, I don't care if he's a wonderful little old man with a beard, I'm going to go right at him," and would have that intention and I would feel myself swerve to the side and fall to the ground. And I would get up and go "What the hell happened?" I noticed other people would get up with the same kind of bewildered expression, except for his common *ukes,* who were really used to it, I suppose.

Then at one point he must have seen how I didn't know what was going on. We were sitting in *seiza,* as if we were going to do *kokyu dosa,* and he put his hands over mine. He kind of put my two hands together and put one hand over my wrists and he said, "Push." Now his hand over my wrist felt like a feather, just very light, soft. I pushed and I didn't move nothing, I didn't move nowhere, but the feather didn't get any heavier; his hand was still like a feather on my wrist. And I realized if he could absolutely stop me from mov-ing and I could barely feel him—we were just sitting there so there was a lot of time and I still couldn't feel it—he could probably do anything with me at speed and I wouldn't know what happened! So I understood that there was a level at which he could affect my mind, my consciousness, my *ki* that was so exquisite, so powerful and yet subtle, that I didn't feel anything physically.

And at the same time it felt like a blast of *ki;* it didn't feel very physical, but there was a blast of something that was palpable. With many of the instructors, there was a real blend of the physical and power. But with O-Sensei, I would just seem to go down. I don't know why I went down, but I went down again. He'd also never tell you how to attack him. I can remember later with him, after I was a *shodan,* we would go together to Omoto-Kyo; I'd be in a suit and he'd be in a formal *hakama* and wide, formal kimono with long sleeves. We wouldn't change clothes beforehand because they would ask him to talk. He'd get up and begin to talk and then motion to me to begin demonstrating. I'd whip my jacket off, whip off my watch, throw my tie into my shirt and attack him, always scared to death I was going to catch in his long sleeves. But he would also never say how to attack and I knew he had something he was going to demonstrate no matter how I attacked him. There was a way to attack that would probably be much easier on my body, you know, that was probably the way he wanted me, but he wasn't going to change a hell of a lot if I didn't do what he wanted. So my mind would always become a blank and I would pray that I was doing the right thing.

What most of the accounts of O-Sensei don't give you, unfortunately, most are simply about what happened or how tough he was— is this: there was an extraordinary twinkle in his eye, there was a wonderful, loving, compassionate aura around him. I literally felt that he lightened the dojo. Most of the accounts of O-Sensei it seems to me draw on people who knew him when he was younger and were scared to death of him. Even when he was older, they kind of carried that "Oh god, the old monster, the old terror is around," and he just wasn't that. He did smile and he did indicate that he had softened up a lot. He once said to me, "You know, I didn't really master aikido until I was in my seventies, when I didn't have my physical strength to fall back on."

I'll tell you something I experienced over and over again; it's real strange, but it's an interesting experience. O-Sensei would frequently go on trips and I would have this funny feeling that when he would leave, just little by little the dojo would kind of get dimmer. Hombu Dojo would kind of lose a certain sparkle. And one day I'd come a couple of weeks later and the dojo is all sparkly again and I'd say, "O-Sensei's back." And I was always right. This happened I don't know how many times. Just over and over again, I would know it when he was back in town. The only way I can describe it is to say the dojo would seem to get dimmer and less sparkly and then all of a sudden it was sparkly again. There was no question in my mind there was only one way that could have happened.

He had a wonderful sense of humor; he also had a temper at times. But he really was wonderful to be around; it always lifted me up to be around him, except on the two occasions he was angry at someone, never at me, thank God. His anger was like thunder and lightning, this blast of incredible energy and power. I'll tell you one of the stories. I was with a Japanese friend, a man named Tomita who opened up aikido in Sweden. He was one of Saito Sensei's students.

We were very close and he invited me up to train with his old college aikido group. A week or two before that, someone had been killed doing aikido in Japan. It was someone in Osaka, I think. O-Sensei was nowhere near the dojo. I don't even know if the teacher was someone who had studied very much directly with O-Sensei, but it was a great lesson because O-Sensei felt personally responsible. "Pardon me, how could you feel personally responsible for everybody on every aikido mat?" But he did, and it was a great lesson. He felt that quality of responsibility for everything he did. He lectured us about it that day. "Look, this happened because these people don't understand aikido, what aikido is about. They're treating it only as fighting, only as a physical art. If they understood it spiritually, people would never get killed."

We were in Iwama at the time. Iwama was of course the dojo that O-Sensei built. He built the Aikido Shrine there; it was his personal dojo. And Japanese etiquette has it that if you're bringing in a group to teach in someone else's dojo, you go to the *dojo cho* [head of the school] and you say, "May I please teach for you this class," because in someone's dojo, the *dojo cho* is the head of the dojo in every class. So even if you're scheduled to teach, the form is to say, "May I teach for you?" Now, it's not only O-Sensei's dojo, but it's his art, so there are two very good reasons why one should ask. So Tomita did that.

We trained early in the morning, we did exercises all morning long, we had a long break for lunch, and we did some farming on O-Sensei's farm. And the time came, after we had digested, for the afternoon practice and O-Sensei was still taking his nap. So Tomita decided not to wake him up and ask if he could teach. He felt it wouldn't have been right to wake him up for that. So we started practice. Well, after the first or second person hit the mat, I think it was like hearing a starting bugle for an old race horse. O-Sensei woke up and he came in with his eyes just flashing. Now, I was good, I was just training, I hadn't done anything. Well, I'll tell you, I really had the feeling I did not want to be across the room from him when he was that upset. What I felt was I wanted to flip a tatami and go under it, just go right into the crawl space. He was incredibly angry and he went on and on with this lecture about how this was an example of the kind of discourtesy he had spoken of and this was an example of what was wrong with aikido and this was why someone had been killed. Poor Tomita was sitting there, shriveling up. And then, O-Sensei only knew two people who were training in that class, Tomita and me, so guess who he chose after he finished this talk to demonstrate what aikido was all about? He motioned to me and I got up scared to death. What flashed through my mind was it was like the time I had been in a bull ring: make any mistakes and it's all over. So I walked up and I feared that if any of that anger, any of that came out, my body was gone. But when O-Sensei threw me, it felt lighter and more controlled and softer than he'd ever done before. He kind of smiled at me and the message I got was "I'm the master of aikido. I'm also the master of myself, you don't have to worry." There's a level at which he smiled and kind of twinkled at me. It was just wonderful. He was very humble.

I consider myself his student though in a sense I didn't learn anything from him. I learned all the techniques from all the teachers with whom I trained. But there's a wonderful old Hassidic story about a man whose teacher lived miles and miles away. Every week he would walk miles to go see him. And his friend asked him, "Why do you go see him? You walk miles through the snow, miles through the rain. What is so amazing about him? Is he a great lecturer? Why do you go see him?" "I don't go to see him for his lectures. I just go to watch him tie his shoes." I learned what aikido was all about just from who O-Sensei was, not from what he did. I also had the feeling that you could take O-Sensei's aikido away from him, you could take his skill at the techniques of aikido, and he would still be O-Sensei, because what O-Sensei was for me was what he had become inside, the inner self. There was something inside him that was different. I had met men who were strong and fast and who were brilliant, men and women at Harvard, but you know, they were men and women who might have too much to drink for lunch or be mean to their kids. Outside of the brilliance, there wasn't a special person there. What I felt about O-Sensei was outside of the brilliance of his aikido.

There was a trick he pulled all the time as an old man. I saw him do it over and over again. For example, in the winter, he would suffer from arthritis, he was in his eighties. So he would get one of the young men, one of the *uchi deshi* to kind of help him onto the mat. He'd kind of lean on him and the *uchi deshi* would help him sit *seiza* and he'd go several paces in back of him and sit. And then O-Sensei would bow and clap his hands. Then he would get up, turn around and wipe the mat with this guy, absolutely clean up on him and he looked like he'd never even heard of arthritis. And then he would bow, finish up and motion to be helped off the mat. He did have arthritis and he did say to me at one point, "Whenever I talk about or practice aikido, arthritis and my age, none of that is relevant to me."

When I first met O-Sensei, I was twenty-three years old. I was a young, ambitious graduate student in psychology, somewhat committed to doing what would make me successful in psychology, which was mostly doing research, and eventually becoming a psychology professor. Meeting O-Sensei changed my whole focus in psychology. It really opened me to the possibility that human beings could be more than I thought human beings could be. I mean, here was a little old guy who could go out every morning and do miracles whenever he felt like it. That tended to open my view of what human nature could be, to put it real simply. I mean, he would pull off something that was impossible whenever he felt like it.

The question I began to ask was how could I as a psychologist begin to explain O-Sensei, i.e., how could someone be that extraordinary? Most psychologists didn't even ask the question. But it struck me that Abraham Maslow was at least asking the right question. I had met Maslow at Harvard probably in '62 before I went to Japan. I kind of dismissed him as this wonderful fatherly, avuncular armchair theorist, kind of like a nice old Jewish uncle. But I couldn't afford to be interested in that, because that's the kind of psychology you do when you retire, not what bright, young, ambitious psychologists do. So I kind of dismissed him. But with no new evidence about his thinking, just from having met O-Sensei, it flashed through my mind that what he had to say about human nature was very profound and correct. Or the way I put it, "At least he's the only one asking the right question." Nobody else even asks the right questions or has a theory that would allow you to ask the right question. I mean, there is nothing in Freudian psychology that would allow you to ask how someone becomes like O-Sensei."

It was the beginning of a whole shift for me in what I was interested in professionally. And it was also the beginning of a lot of spiritual change for me because again through my friends in aikido, I was exposed to various spiritual teachers and traditions and I began to understand the reality of spirituality. I began practicing meditation and that began many years of a spiritual quest. O-Sensei said all of these crazy things about standing on a floating bridge between heaven and earth, all these wonderful, mystical things, and I had to take him a little bit seriously because he was capable of doing things that indicated that he wasn't simply talking through his hat. When I first started working with meditation, I did a lot of "yogic" meditation; I studied the system of Paramahansa Yogananda. That's a very wonderful, powerful devotional meditation system. What I found was I was getting very inward, very "yin," very sensitive and introspective and it was very hard to be out in the world. Someone could just say "boo" to me and it would pain me because I was becoming so sensitive, and aikido was the perfect balance for me. Aikido was a way of being more "yang," of putting my energy out, but in a way that matched and supported my spiritual work rather than being jarring and antithetical to it.

I became very much committed to doing my own spiritual work starting about 1965 or '66. For roughly ten or twelve years, from 1965 to '76 or '77, I was deeply involved and committed to daily meditative practice, often an hour or more a day, and aikido was a very important balance to that in terms of my spiritual practice, with my eyes open, in the world. I saw it as a very profound system of karma yoga. Karma yoga is usually talked about as work only. "Oh, let's do karma yoga," which means "weed" or "do the dishes," but really it's much more profound than that. It really is a full discipline of yoga as profound as any other discipline based on the notion that action forms who you are. I think in that sense that aikido is a very profound way of acting. It's not at all trivial how you act, and aikido is a way of acting in accord with one's entire self, with body, mind and spirit as it should be, in the center. In that sense it's a very profound kind of karma yoga without a lot of the metaphysics and the naming of what it is as a spiritual system.

Now I do think the naming is important. If you don't know it's a spiritual system, you may not do it well. But I remember many years ago, Phil Kapleau wrote something to the effect that aikido is only a physical art and it can't lead you to enlightenment, and I think that's absolutely wrong, that aikido can lead you to enlightenment. He may be correct in that the aikido that he saw, given the consciousness of the teachers and the people he saw, may not get you there. But a roshi who is a very good friend of mine who has seen aikido said that understanding the flow that aikido practices and works with—the kind of flow of the river that never stops but that never shows the same water twice, that constant change of life—

understanding that deeper flow can lead to enlightenment.

O-Sensei's technique was an expression of a very profound understanding of human nature. Aikido is a vessel which contains a tremendous amount of truth. There are a lot of forms out there but most of them don't contain a hell of a lot. Most of them are really like vessels that have had holes punctured in them, they're not really big containers. I studied with another wonderful spiritual teacher who was magnificent as a teacher. He was much more linear, much more effective at teaching spiritual truth than O-Sensei was, but in a sense his system died with him because he was the system. He inspired us through his practices, but he was primarily the system. I think that O-Sensei did something that really is quite profound. Over and over again, I find new things in the most basic of techniques. I'm always finding new stuff teaching things to beginners. And I'm not even talking about the fancy stuff. I think there are some incredibly profound things going on.

I think that aikido developed as O-Sensei developed. So I don't think it was a question of "efforting," that he tried to do something. I really do believe that one of the keys to understanding aikido for me is the statement that there are two aims in aikido. The small aim is to purify oneself so that in a sense divine energy can flow freely and fully through one, and the larger aim is to free all creatures and make the world happy. It's not new, it's very Mahayana. But to be that clear for a martial art and to have a martial art that doesn't just pay lip service to it but that somehow has integrated it into the very warp and woof of what it's really about, is extraordinary. Of course it's possible to do aikido without understanding that, without practicing that. I don't think that there's any technique in the world that can't be misconstrued, made shallow or turned to the dark side, if you will, because I think we're really talented at screwing things up. Right now we are not capable of using aikido the way O-Sensei used aikido because we haven't developed ourselves as human beings the way O-Sensei did. I think that's really the limitation in aikido. People who have developed great and powerful technique and haven't developed themselves as human beings in a way are cripples as far as the real art of aikido is concerned. I think that there are a lot of cripples out there. I don't want to be controversial, but that's the truth!

But aikido is also an effective martial art; it's not only one thing. I'll tell you another interesting story. Once, in 1970, the head of one of the great Sufi organizations came to my psychology school and I decided to do a little aikido demonstration to entertain him. So I did very smooth, very blending aikido, I mean, he's a spiritual teacher, right? I thought I wouldn't use the martial end of aikido. Afterwards he looked at me kind of quizzically and said, "I thought that was a martial art." I said, "Yeah, well it is. It's also an art of blending." He said, "If you do a martial art, you have to be able to absolutely put down someone who would be harmful to someone else. Otherwise it's not worth doing." And recently in thinking about that again, I think that that's an incredibly important gloss on aikido, that at one level it's a martial art that should train us to be warriors.

You know, I have this interesting position. I may not be anybody in the aikido world, but I don't know anybody else who quite does what I do. I don't teach aikido in a public dojo on a regular weekly basis. I teach generally somewhere between three to six hours a week to graduate students in psychology and theology. I have priests and nuns, counselors and therapists; the average age is over forty. It's a very rich, very wonderful aikido. I miss doing more of the technical, interesting *waza* [technical] level of aikido, but it has been a very enriching experience for all of these years.

One of the ways I've been explaining aikido to people who are not eighteen years old and don't want to be black belts, don't want to sweat necessarily, is by saying that aikido for me is in some sense a way of learning three different archetypes—the archetype of the warrior, the healer and the magician—and that they're all important. The archetype of the warrior is of someone who can handle power, who is comfortable with power in and of itself and who can handle both fear and violence, to put it really simply. My Sufi master said, "A real warrior is someone who has the power and capacity to take life but who won't even pluck a flower if it's not necessary.

He's someone who reveres life but not out of fear." That's the warrior. Some people think that's all aikido is about. But I think those other two archetypes are both very important.

The archetype of the healer is this: a healer is someone who works with energy to heal inner fears, to heal oneself. It's connected with the notion I learned years ago that you work with a partner, not against an opponent. If you can do aikido as a martial art, you start to think you're working against an opponent. O-Sensei said years ago that you shouldn't train in aikido that way, because you don't learn a quality of blending and sensitivity and empathy if you're training as if you're always in a fight. It took me about ten or twelve years to learn that I was only doing good aikido if my partner bowed to me at the end of class and really wanted to train with me again because they had a wonderful time. I was not doing aikido if I taught them a bunch of things and they ended up having learned things and feeling bad. I wasn't necessarily doing good aikido if I bounced people on their heads or any of that. What made good aikido was a sense of a loving relationship.

As a matter of fact, on one of those trips to the Omoto-Kyo temple in Tokyo, I was sitting in the back seat with O-Sensei and I said to myself, "I ought to ask him a question. I mean, here I am with someone who knows. I should ask him something. But I should ask him something significant, I shouldn't ask him something stupid. It'd be a waste of time." So I thought and I thought and I said, "Sensei, what's the right attitude toward your partner?" He smiled and I thought, "Thank god! It wasn't such a bad question." He smiled and indicated it was a good question and said, "Your attitude toward your partner should be that of a parent to a child." I've thought about that for years since. There's a lot in there. I think part of it is unconditional love, nurturing and caring, but also part of it is that there's a kind of expecting the child to follow. You don't say, "Would you like to have dinner now?" There's authority and power but also unconditional love. Anyway, it was a very profound answer and you don't find that in the archetype of the warrior. Seems to me that's an aspect of the healer, the notion that aikido really is about healing oneself.

I really wish that in more of aikido there was a built-in healing component. Other arts do that. It would be nice to say that "So-and-so is *sandan* not because he can smack you into the ground, but because he can heal a broken shoulder" or bruises or whatever. I know Tohei Sensei teaches something he calls *kiatsu*. I have no comment about it. I will only say again that I wish more schools of aikido had real healing as a part of it.

The third archetype, the archetype of the magician, concerns the transformation of energy. I think that's O-Sensei's notion. He used to say that the character for *bu* in bushido, which is the same character for samurai, has two parts: one is *kameru*, "to stop," the other is *hoka*, which is old Chinese for "halbard." So it really means "to stop the weapon." It does not mean "to use your weapon faster." It seems to me that part of what aikido is about is that by doing the work of the warrior, which is dealing with fear, being comfortable with violence and aggression in oneself and someone else, you can then take the compassion of the healer and transform that energy so that you move with the person in a way that the attack becomes something else, and there is not an attack-counter-attack, but it turns into some sort of blending and someone ends up on the ground without there being a clash at any level, be it physical, emotional or spiritual. And that intention, that whole notion that aikido is not merely about fighting but about transforming energy, is critical to the notion that aikido is about stopping the use of weapons. Frankly I'm kind of sick and tired of pictures of aikidoists with macho poses, waving swords and spears, looking like the old archetype of the warrior. I think O-Sensei said very clearly that that has been out of date since the atomic bomb was dropped. We can't afford to play warrior in the old way anymore. Unfortunately, it's still being played. There's another problem, which exists in some dojos in California and elsewhere: aikido practice can become like aikido-dance so that there's no honesty about attacks or throws. I don't think you learn to transform energy if there hasn't been any real energy going out on either part. So I really honor and love the warrior piece, but I really think that it needs to be balanced with other dimensions, like that of healing.

I went to Japan in the summer of '64. I stayed there for about two years. I left in the summer of '66 to return to the States for my doctoral dissertation. I spent about nine months in the States, finished my dissertation, got a post-doctoral fellowship and went back to Japan. It was wonderful to see O-Sensei again. I was gone just long enough to develop an even more profound appreciation for him and for aikido. I stayed in Japan for approximately six months, until December of '67 or January of '68 when I returned to the states. I got my degree in June of '67.

I came back carrying my research data under my arm and spent about six months in the L.A area. I visited my family, practiced aikido at the various L.A. dojos, analyzed my data and was offered a job at U.C. Berkeley teaching psychology. I started teaching at Berkeley in the '68–'69 academic year. There were a few aikido students around but no high-ranking *aikidoka*. Stan Pranin had just come up from Los Angeles; he was a first-year graduate student in Romance languages and a *shodan* at the time. I was *nidan*. So he and I started the Berkeley Aikido Club together. Also, during the time I was at Berkeley I ended up meeting the people at Esalen and started to set up the first aikido classes there. I'd remained close to Bob Nadeau so I asked Nadeau to jointly teach with me at Esalen. So for a couple of years we taught aikido there together.

I taught a year at Berkeley. That was the year of People's Park; there was a riot each quarter. The interesting thing was that although everything else stopped—I had no interest in teaching psychology—we didn't stop our aikido classes. It was very interesting. Not only didn't we want to stop our aikido classes; the students didn't want us to. They didn't want to do anything in terms of their regular classes but we were all convinced that there was something that we were doing in aikido that was absolutely relevant.

Anyhow, the next year, '69, I started teaching at U.C. Santa Cruz. Pranin went off to the army and we turned over the aikido club to one of Nadeau's students, Allen Grow. And then I opened up the dojo in Santa Cruz, the one Linda Holiday is currently running. Almost half my Berkeley class stayed with it all the way to black belt. Linda came in somewhere in the first year. Jack Wada was with me the first year, too. I taught there for six years. We did a lot of training on the lawn, we didn't have any other place to train. And we had a wonderful time. At the end of that time, three of my students went to study aikido in Japan. I actively encouraged my students to go to Japan as not a lot of teachers do.

What happened was that one of them, Kathy Bates, had gone to Japan and had met Mary Heiny, who brought her down to Shingu in order to meet Hikitsuchi Sensei. About a year later, Jack Wada, Linda Holiday and Dick Revoir, all from Santa Cruz, decided to go to Japan. So they went to Shingu and trained with Hikitsuchi Sensei. When they came back they invited him to come here. This was 1973. It was just a local trip. He spent most of the time in Santa Cruz. Then I brought a whole group back to Shingu and we spent about half a year there.

I finished up my teaching at Santa Cruz in June of '75 and opened the Institute for Transpersonal Psychology in September of 1975. I made aikido an integral part of the curriculum from the very beginning. The dojo has always been in the biggest classroom and all students have taken aikido. The model of human growth that we started out with is this: we need to become balanced, body, mind and spirit. The model has now become more complex. There are now six areas instead of three: body, emotions, intellect, spirit, community and service, and aesthetic. We've always stressed that students should know about the body both theoretically and experientially, and that they should know something about aikido and its uses. They also learn some t'ai chi and yoga. They study acupressure and other healing forms and, of course, psychology.

Aikido has been amazingly successful. It has been there from the beginning because I insisted on it. Everyone thought I was crazy, but since I was president it was real hard to say no the first few years. But what happened is everybody realized how important a part of the curriculum aikido is. One of our students said, "You know, aikido just ties everything together. Everything I'm doing in our program somehow all comes together in aikido." We've done surveys and the psychology students rank aikido as the second most valuable course after psychotherapeutic techniques. They all know it's not going to be professionally relevant. We've only had two students go on to black belt since I've been teaching aikido. Many of my students have bad backs and can't even do a forward roll, but they stay with aikido as much as they can. It has been incredibly valuable for them. Aikido's a mirror to show them where they are and to work on where they are. And in some ways I'm more and more trying to use aikido to show them where they *can* be, to help them get into a place of being centered and full and rounded and fearless and begin to experience at least within the boundaries of the aikido mat a new way of being. That's really very exciting: to show people that there is another way of being that they may have tasted, glimpsed here and there, and that they can begin to experience for themselves.

The way aikido is presented here is different from what you might experience at a typical dojo, of course. It's something I learned years ago when I started teaching at Esalen. The Esalen experience was a great learning for me because I had so many people for a weekend, period. It's a little different from an hour a day three or four days a week, for years. I started with "How the hell can I do anything with them?" If I was going to teach any traditional technique, the weekend would be over and they would have just started on one! So what I did was to use a lot of aikido but often without the throw. In other words, how do you get out of the way of an attack? Or how do you work with energy? How do you work with centering? We did a lot with centering stuff, a lot of energy awareness stuff. And we did a lot of experimenting. It was very powerful to work with people in the context that there was no desire, no time or place to learn traditional aikido, so what else could I teach them about aikido?

I do a lot of that in teaching aikido here. It's not nearly as physically demanding as teaching in the dojo. By the end of the first year, they can do forward roll, backward roll, basic aikido techniques. But I'll often spend the whole class on one technique. I'll start them off by just doing the very beginning of the technique—how do you handle the attack correctly, how do you move the attack to a place of unbalancing your partner?—and we'll spend a lot of time there. Then finally, how do you carry that unbalancing until you effectively can take a fall? I go very slowly and I give them a lot of time and I also pay some attention to the emotional and metaphoric parts of aikido.

For example, we may look at a classic technique, say *katate tori kokyu nage.* What does that teach you? One of the things it teaches you very directly is how to extend energy and still not clash. How can you be very direct and not clash? That's a very important thing to know. It's not very important to know how to throw someone down and break their wrist; that's not a universal experience outside of the aikido mat. But it is very important to learn how I can extend energy to you and be real powerful and not clash with you so that you don't feel that I've clashed with you. Or how can I let your energy come to me very fully and somehow let it go by and blend with it, say with *shomen uchi irimi nage?* The first thing is, how can I handle all that energy coming in and still be full and not back off? And so with something like *shomen uchi* [strike to the top of the head], I spend a lot of time just with shomen. First I have them do it and then I work with them on putting energy out; that's worth half an hour to an hour. Also, what do you feel as it comes at you? And then how can you step out of their way and how do you feel? And then how can you extend energy back and step out of the way?

I find the most important part of aikido is in the first second anyway. The first thing that happens when the technique begins, that's the important part. Once you've got that right you can do anything. I notice so often that people are slightly unconscious at the beginning but spend a lot of time being powerful throwing. That's how we trained when I started out, but that's very bad martial arts. For one thing, your partner usually cooperates with a weak attack and then sort of stands there, hands you their head or their wrist, tries to be strong and if you don't lop their wrist off or lop their head off, they go "Well, your aikido's not strong." Well, in real life, nobody's ever going to do that. One of the great pitfalls of aikido is the focus on power, on one-upmanship. I think unless aikido is both partners growing, helping each other grow—if it's "I'm going to show you that I can knock you down, but you can't knock me down,"—it's not really useful. I think that any martial art has to deal with the issue of power, and unfortunately it's a trap that's easy to fall into, the trap of power, the feeling that I'm going to be better than someone else, that I'm more powerful.

As for other traps and pitfalls, I think there's one in being a *sensei*. Of course it's a position of responsibility, it's a position one should rightfully be proud of, but it needs to be tempered by the fact that we who are *sensei* don't really understand aikido that well. It's real important to remember that, that I'm working on it too and that some *sensei* somehow put out that they're done, they're finished, perfect. This is the trap of ego, a kind of "*sensei*-itis." I'll tell you something that's very personal. When I became involved with Sufism I got to know my brothers in the order who are all Turkish men and who have all been soldiers. The Turks are some of the toughest soldiers in the world, but they didn't walk around playing tough soldier. They would tickle each other and fight to serve each other, to light someone's cigarette or pour someone tea or a glass of water. I found a genuine humility and service and lovingness among them. Seeing a real community in which men were really loving and open and warm with each other in a very wonderful way, I suddenly realized that in aikido most everybody plays cock of the walk. It's like, "Well, you're lower than me, you serve me." "I'm lower than you, okay, I'll serve you." There's a hierarchical thing that I find pernicious, it's not useful. And believe me, in my Sufi order, hierarchy is very real. Hierarchy and respect for one's elders is very real, but that doesn't stop an incredible warmth. So ego is a danger in aikido.

I tell people that if you want to judge an aikido dojo, look at the teacher and how the teacher behaves toward the students, but also, how do the students behave toward each other? I've known teachers who talk a good line while subtly allowing or encouraging students to beat the hell out of each other. I believe everything going on in a dojo is a teacher's responsibility, and that by the time a student gets to be a senior student, if that teacher hasn't corrected their behavior, it means that the teacher has approved of it. There's no excuse for dojos where the teacher says aikido is love, peace and harmony, and the senior students are being brutal to everybody else. I don't think it's really excusable when there's an atmosphere of dominance, hierarchy and fear in the dojo. I think there can be a real dishonesty when people talk about the love in aikido and they're not really practicing what they're saying. I've seen it in other arts, but it's real unfortunate when the teacher says something and it's not really practiced, so that there's a set of ideals on the one hand and the reality of what goes on on the other. That sort of thing does a real disservice to the art of aikido.

But I can't really talk too much about what other people do because I've tried to tend to my own little garden for many years now. I've come out of the mainstream partly because of a real personal disappointment with other people in the aikido community and also just because I no longer have a public dojo. I'm also very much involved with my secret practice among the Sufi community here. There's a connection between my Sufi practice and aikido, though it's very hard to explain. When I work as a Sufi teacher, there's a way in which my mind gets out of the way and I allow words and advice to flow through me. People come to me with problems and issues and I will tell them things, what to do or what certain things mean in their lives. And later I don't remember what I said because it's so caught in the moment. And I find aikido has become much the same way. I guess it's a way of being fully in the present. I don't do it all the time; I wish I could, but it is more and more on tap for me. I can be totally and fully in the present with doing aikido or teaching aikido or being a Sufi teacher in a way that is timeless, and I literally don't feel I'm there with my personality. And, as I said, the strange thing is I find it very hard to say what the hell I did or what I said five minutes later. That's why it's hard to talk about; there's something very elusive about being fully present in the moment but not being reflective or even being able to reflect on what I did.

I think my Sufi practice has informed my life in many ways. When I teach aikido I talk a lot more than I used to about opening the heart and about opening the *hara,* the belly. In some Middle Eastern traditions, heart, belly and mind are the three great centers. I find it very interesting that different things happen when you open your heart and do aikido than if you just "do belly." If you concentrate only on opening the *hara,* it's just more power and it's grounded, but something else happens when you do heart as well. I think that Sufi practice has opened my heart and made me somewhat less egotistical, and I think that's reflected in my aikido, but it's very hard to judge oneself.

4

MARY HEINY

If you first meet Mary Heiny outside of an aikido class you may find it hard to believe she is the highest-ranking woman aikido instructor in North America. Though solidly built, she is bespectacled, small and unassuming, the kind of woman you might think was a librarian or a professor. But once she gets in front of a class it becomes clear why she has earned a sixth degree black belt. Though still modest she speaks and moves with confidence and effortless power. Heiny spent six years training in Japan, starting the last year of Ueshiba's life. Her decision to study aikido came after she saw Ueshiba demonstrate. Invited by her friend Bob Frager to watch an aikido demonstration while both were in Japan studying Japanese, Heiny was so affected by what she saw that she decided then and there to devote the rest of her life to studying Ueshiba's art.

It is typical of Heiny that she did not return to Japan until she had prepared herself for a lengthy stay by completing her degree in Japanese and that once there she did everything she could to "become Japanese." In the following interview it is clear how difficult that was, particularly since she was a woman studying a rigorous martial art. Many of her Japanese fellow students and teachers ignored her or did everything they could to discourage her, but her determination was so strong and her dedication to the art so deep that she vowed to learn aikido despite the obstacles thrown in her way. Her refusal to give up and her undaunted dedication to her training eventually earned her wide respect among the Japanese who knew her, but not before she had injured every part of her body and adopted a fiercely physical style of aikido. After coming back to the United States Heiny had to completely relearn aikido because, in her own words, her body was so "trashed." In the process her aikido has become more refined, subtler and deeper. Struggle has characterized Heiny's life in aikido, and much as with Terry Dobson, that struggle has made her into an inspiring teacher and example to several generations of aikido students.

I first heard of aikido from my co-student, Bob Frager. In 1964 I was in Japan as an exchange student during my sophomore year. I was a Japanese language major and I was attending Keio University in a special program for foreigners. There were five or six of us in the class, one of whom was Bob Frager. He had been doing aikido in Hawaii and was continuing his studies at Hombu Dojo in Tokyo. He used to talk to me about aikido and O-Sensei; he would lecture me about the things O-Sensei could do, and I would lecture him back about physics and mechanics and leverage and fulcrums and contact points and the total impossibility of what he was telling me. Finally after about three months of effort he talked me into going with him to view aikido after our classes were over. And it just so happened that the first aikido class I went to see, O-Sensei came out and demonstrated aikido, talked a little bit, and then went off the mat. And I had such an extraordinary experience viewing him that I decided at that moment that understanding aikido would be my life's goal.

The experience I had was a little bizarre. It sounds like it belongs in a New Age book of psychic phenomena or something. But, it was the old dojo, the wooden, Japanese-style dojo that I went to. I sat near the entrance to the dojo. The entrance opposite me went through a corridor to O-Sensei's house, and that's where he came from when he came into the dojo. I was watching class; I was thinking, "Well, this looks kind of interesting, but I don't really understand why people are falling down. I don't quite get it. Nobody seems to be really pushed down." I couldn't quite grasp what was going on. And during class, this rather small man who seemed to twinkle walked into the room, and everybody sat down.

I knew from Bob's descriptions that this had to be O-Sensei. He went out to the middle of the mat, gestured, and some young guy came up and went flying even though O-Sensei did not touch him. Now this was the crux of my argument with Bob Frager, that you simply could not throw somebody without touching them because you had no point of contact or fulcrum over which to throw them. As O-Sensei continued to do this, I had this strange sensation that I had split in two. Part of me was going, "This man knows something about power that's totally outside my realm of experience." The other part of me was saying, "He's old; Japanese respect age; perhaps they're just falling down for him in some fashion."

After a few minutes of watching him do this and perform other amazing feats that Bob had described and I had not believed in, I suddenly felt as though my brain blew up through the top of my head. It blew up like a cloud of particles, and it hung over me, just like little particles, like a cloud of sand over my head, and I just went into a state of suspension of some kind. After a while O-Sensei finished up and walked across the mat. He turned around before he left the room, and he stared. I thought he stared at me; maybe he just stared in my direction (I heard he was nearsighted). But what I experienced was that he looked at me, and when he looked at me, I felt a beam of something come from him and it entered my belly. It wasn't aggressive or intrusive. It was very gentle and I felt something open up like a flower bud in my belly. It opened up and I felt like my whole life made sense, and I understood that everything that had happened so far was to direct me to this moment in time and space, and that aikido would be my life's path.

When he left the room, my little cloud-particle brain came back down into my head, but it was settled in a different pattern. I felt that. It's hard to talk about because it does sound kind of arrogant to say he looked at me and then I knew. But to be truthful, it's just what I experienced; it's how I felt at that moment. And I decided then that aikido would be what I aimed to study. But I wanted to study it very, very seriously. And to do that, I felt that I should prepare myself to live in Japan indefinitely. Part of me wanted to just drop everything and start aikido training, but I had only a few weeks left in Japan on my visa and then I was supposed to return and resume my education in Seattle. So I decided to return. I finished my degree in Japanese and organized all of my studies so I would know as much about Japan as possible and be able to teach English as a second language. And through contacts made on my first visit I was able to get a working visa to teach English, and I went back to Japan in '68 and started training at Hombu Dojo in December.

I had earlier thought that learning some martial arts would be an interesting thing to do. I tried to study various things during my year as an exchange student, including the *koto*. I loved *kimono* so I was learning how to sew kimono. And I'd watched a number of martial arts, but it was clear to me that in karate, kendo, judo, which were the ones that I had seen, my ability to progress in the art would very much be a matter of my physical conditioning and strength. And since I'd had polio as a kid I didn't think I could go very far in my understanding of the art because of my physical limitations. But when I saw aikido, I realized it would be irrelevant, and that how far you went in your understanding of aikido depended on your determination to study, and what effort you put into it, not how good your body was. Technically, there could be a ceiling, but I don't really believe that either, because as you start to get a glimpse of how it really works, you understand that it's not a physical situation: aiki is not physical. That's why O-Sensei at the age of eighty could be tossing people around without even touching them. He was manipulating their energy in a way that didn't require him to have the body of a twenty-five-year-old jock. So I felt that although I had physical limitations, they would not obstruct my understanding of aikido. I may never be as strong as a guy who's six feet tall, but that was not really important to me. I felt that I could go as far as I put my energy into it.

I arrived in Japan in September of '68, about half a year before O-Sensei's death. Sometimes I regret waiting. I mean, during the three years I spent in the university I was terrified he would die before I got back to Japan. But I felt that to go without the preparations

I had made would mean that what I could get out of the experience would be limited. I just hoped that he would hang on . As a matter of fact, I only saw him a few more times before he died. He never threw me, and any time he walked into the room, I just felt like disappearing between the cracks in the mat, I was so overwhelmed, I was in such awe of his presence. But each time I saw him he had just a stupendous impact on me.

I was lucky enough to understand his Japanese, by which I don't mean to say that I necessarily understood what he was talking about! But I do remember a few things he said. The things I remember best were the things he had to say about women, because as the lone foreign woman training there, I really felt isolated. I remember one class where he came into the dojo. Any time he came in the room, everyone would sit down and then he would demonstrate. On this occasion he came in and scolded the men in the class for training in a manner which was merely a contest of strength. He said they were just doing *ude korabe* which means "comparing arms;" they were having a contest with each other to see who was stronger; they were just trying to one-up each other. He said you should train like the women train; the women train to learn aikido.

I think on that occasion too he said that men have to really struggle to learn aikido, but women have a kind of innate knowledge. I found that hard to take, actually, you know. That sounds a bit like "You're really special; you don't have to do a good job; you can stay home and take care of the kids, you're so special." I wasn't really sure how to take that. But he said that. He encouraged the men and women to train together. But everyone was entirely too embarrassed to pull that one off as he left the room. Everybody went back to men training with men and women training with women and me trying to train with men. He said that men have to sit in meditation a long time to become enlightened, but that if a woman has a baby, she becomes enlightened instantly through that experience. He said a few things like that. I didn't have the same point of view, but anything positive he had to say about women was like nourishment to me. I remember him talking to a woman during one morning class, saying, "Oh, you're new. Please continue to train. Don't give up. It's very important to come every day."

The most significant thing for me personally was that there was an unexpected spring snowstorm in Tokyo. At that time I was working outside of Tokyo. We were let out early to try to get back into Tokyo because it was obvious the transportation would come to a halt with this blizzard that was going on. And by slogging through the snow—it took me three hours—I got to Hombu Dojo. Unfortunately, nobody else got to the dojo, including the regular teacher of the class. But staying at the dojo was a group of women from some flower-arranging school in Kyoto. When the class started, it was myself, them, one poor startled man who, I guess, lived in the neighborhood, and Fujita, who came up from the office to teach the class. He was teaching the class and we were training when O-Sensei came in. He had a scroll with him. I think it was March or April. It was very close to his death. He thanked all the women for coming so far to train aikido, and he said that he was really grateful that they cared enough to come and train at Hombu Dojo, and that he hoped they would always continue their training throughout their lives.

He read from the scroll. It was the Kojiki story of Izanage and Izaname and the purification of Izanage after the death of Izaname, where he goes underground and comes back. What I remember best of the whole thing was that he came in and said it's important for us to train and to keep training and that he was grateful that we were training. That stuck with me for a really long time, because at that time at Hombu Dojo, there were few women training, very, very few. At certain times no other foreign women trained and it was difficult.

I also remember a change that came over him when he was in the dojo. I remember a couple times where he really couldn't get up the stairs. By this time they had rebuilt the dojo and it was that kind of concrete monstrosity it is now. The general practice room was on the third floor, so he had a lot of stairs to climb to get up there, and I remember him being assisted by a person on each side of him. He kind of struggled up the stairs, but as soon as he set foot on the mat, his presence filled the entire room; I mean his presence was so strong, his projection was so strong. He never gave the feeling of being frail when he was in the dojo, not to me, anyway.

All in all, my experience of him was rather limited. But it had such high impact on me that it has really filled my brain, I guess. I feel something that I consider his presence, and I feel it or I don't feel it. I was just thinking about this the other day. I was wondering why, when I came back from Japan in '74 and started teaching, that it didn't occur to me to go and seek one of the Japanese *shihan* as my teacher. It simply didn't occur to me. It also didn't occur to me to have my students tested, to send them off to some seminar or camp run by one of these men to be tested for me. I just never thought of it. And I think, even though I had a relationship with Hikitsuchi Sensei, where his impact was great enough that I called him my teacher, I still didn't feel that I had to train my students to please him or that he should test them or that I should go back to have him decide whether my aikido was okay or not okay or whatever. I think that it's because I didn't relate to any of these people as an ultimate teacher. I had seen O-Sensei. In the back of my brain I guess he was there as a kind of ultimate teacher though I never considered him as a personal teacher because I was new at the dojo when he was at the end of his life. I mean, Terry Dobson was an *uchi deshi* for a while but I didn't have that kind of experience. But there was some connection made in my mind that made me look to aikido as a source of information about aikido instead of going around and looking at individual teachers. I mean, they're resources and I can learn things from them, but I'm not motivated to go and become a student of one of them.

In my own training when I try to figure something out, I just look at what is, right in front of my face, then and there, and work with that. I guess I don't consider the source of aikido to be a person, even though O-Sensei, as an individual human being, brought aikido into the world. Aikido had its source, and there was a source for him of aikido, and that's what I try to connect with. Maybe it doesn't make sense verbally, but the art teaches itself to you. O-Sensei said that aikido *waza* [techniques] were *michi shirube*, "signposts along the way." It's something for you to use to direct your attention to what you're supposed to be studying.

My attitude toward Japan changed dramatically during the time I was there. For one thing I felt instantly at home in Japan. When I stepped off the plane at the airport in Tokyo in 1964, I felt like I had come home, which was bizarre since I could barely speak the language. I had had one year of Japanese at the university. I had never been there, but I did feel very at home, at first. And when I went back the second time it was even easier to be there. I also had this idea that I should "become Japanese." So I really did totally immerse myself in the culture, particularly the study of the language.

During my first year, I would sit at the table in the kitchen of the family that I stayed with, a dictionary in each hand, watching soap operas on TV, asking "What does this mean?" and "Why did she do that?" because the motivations of characters come out of the cultural experience. Sometimes people would do things for reasons I could not grasp. I would just really concentrate and repeat what the actresses said; I would repeat their body language. I would do everything I could to make myself experience myself as Japanese. What I wasn't aware of until some time later was that it didn't really matter, because Japan was a closed society and you don't get let in anyway. But I think I had an idea that if I could really be Japanese in my heart and in my behavior, that I would be accepted with open arms into the society and of course, that wasn't the case. It did, however, make my Japanese very fluent, though not right away. I mean, even on the second trip after I had graduated with a B.A. in Japanese, it took a while being there before I reached the level of fluency that I wanted. At first I found Japanese society very easy to be in. It wasn't until I had grown as an individual and matured more, until I had stopped being so introverted, as I just sort of took the blinders off my eyes and started to look around, that it started to become intolerable.

The bureaucratic mindset in particular was intolerable. The fact that you'd go to a bank and stand in line to get a piece of paper that could have been left out for you to pick up. Then you'd have to go and stand in another line, and then if you hadn't filled it out completely right, instead of correcting it, they made you go back to the first line and get another piece of paper and start over again. That type of stuff began to drive me nuts. The oppression of women in Japanese society also really got to me. It didn't bother me as long as I felt like a guest or an outsider, but what happens to most Americans if they go abroad happened to me: if you're there long enough, you begin to feel a part of things. I began to feel a part of Japan. I had Japanese friends who were women and I taught English at a school in which there were many young Japanese women who just had so little available to them if what they wanted for themselves was outside of the traditional path for women. If the traditional path was what they wanted, they could hope for and find some happiness within that. But if they had any other ideas, there were just so few options for them that I found it hard to take.

I did not have the same problems as Japanese women, because as a foreigner, I was always set in a special category. I mean, I did have problems, but not like their problems. But because I acquired what I felt were close friends among Japanese women, I heard about things that really used to drive me nuts, such as one woman being beaten up by her father because she fell in love with a co-worker in the little office she was working in and wanted to marry the man even though he wasn't the right guy according to her dad; such as the fact that birth control devices were unavailable to Japanese women and the fact that if they worked in a company, they were basically let go at the age of twenty-five so that they could get married.

In the dojo I was treated different ways by different people. There were always a certain number of men who would not train with a woman. There were a certain number of men who would train with a woman for the purpose of teaching her a lesson. There were men who would train with a woman but who were terrified that she would shatter on impact, and therefore trained with you trying to throw you and catch you at the same time. And there were men who would just train with you, and it was no big deal. I would say the impression I left Japan with was that I had simply never been taken seriously as an *aikidoka*. The Japanese were always trying to figure out why I was doing aikido. It simply never occurred to them that I might be doing aikido for the same reasons they were doing aikido, it was inconceivable. I had to have some reason, you know, like I wanted to find a boyfriend in the dojo or I wanted my beauty exercise or I wanted to become graceful or something. They just couldn't really figure out that because I had such an intense interest in aikido I was driven to train; it was beyond their comprehension.

I gave up trying to explain after a while. I would just say "*keiko* is fun," "training is fun," and I enjoyed it; and that's all I would say because I just couldn't express myself in a way that made any difference. Many years later, I ran into Nakazono Sensei's son in Stockton, California. He was teaching a class there and I went. At the end of class he said, "You know, very few people were serious about their training. We were serious. You were serious and I was serious." I was shocked to hear that because I never felt that I had been treated in any way that made me feel that I was taken seriously. I got into a mindset at Hombu where I felt that I really had to prove myself. And it may be that I was so tense over proving myself that I didn't notice that I had proved myself to some people. It was such a struggle, I experienced it as such a struggle that I may not have noticed that there were people who took me seriously.

It was not expected of me, as it was of the men, that I would come to every class and train hard. In fact, I felt that the opposite was expected. What was expected was that I would simply give up and go away. It was expected that I wouldn't be able to handle it. It was not expected that I would. I saw this as a challenge to overcome. First of all, I kind of bought the whole samurai macho ethic hook, line and sinker. You know, you train 'til you drop; you train 'til you can only crawl off the mat; if you're injured you train anyway; you train as hard as you can, as physically as you can. You never complain, you never say *maita*, which is like crying uncle or giving up. I kind of knew innately that if I showed any weakness, that would be that. I mean, men can maybe get away with it now and then, but a woman? They were waiting for me to show that I couldn't take it, so there were no options. I couldn't just have a bad day and then come back later. So at times when I just felt overwhelmingly frustrated and in tears, I would make sure nobody saw me. I was on any number of occasions up on the roof crying my eyes out.

I remember one day, I'd had a particularly hard time. I really had trouble trying to get people to train with me; I'd bow to them and they'd look away or go away, not train with me. And one particularly bad day I'd been ignored by the teacher, I'd had a hard time getting anyone to train with me during the class and the guy I had gotten was obviously just pissed that he'd wound up with me as a training partner. After class, this guy named Kato-san was working out with another guy named Sasaki, and I was really interested in these guys and their technique, they knew something that wasn't being shown and I wanted to get in on it, but Kato in particular was like, "You're kidding! Me work with a girl?" I just was so frustrated I went upstairs on the roof and I just beat my fist against the concrete wall and I said, "Okay, don't teach it to me, don't train with me, I'll learn it anyway." That's the kind of attitude I had in order to endure what I felt was the discrimination at Hombu Dojo.

Now, on the other hand I had other types of experiences. I usually trained the afternoon set of classes. There were three classes starting at 3:00 PM and I would do each class and I would train in between the classes. I remember one time when it was Kobayashi Sensei's day to teach. I'd done all three classes. Each time I bowed to a guy, he said, "I don't train with girls" and turned away, so I got stuck with a beginner who didn't know how to escape from me yet. The third time that happened, I just was left standing there; everybody had paired up and I was left. I was just fuming and fuming and I think I looked like I had steam coming out of my ears, because Kobayashi Sensei came up and said in his jovial fashion, "Oh, Mary, what's wrong?" I just said, "I want to kill every man in the world." He was so taken aback that he literally stood back and said, "Why?" So I told him what it was like not to be able to get a training partner, to have people say "I don't train with girls" all the time. And he said, "I'm really sorry that happens. Here, I'll train with you." So he trained with me for about ten minutes, and you know, the quality of his character is so wonderful and his heart is so wonderful that it calmed me down. Then I picked somebody and I trained a threesome during the class. But I used to talk with Kobayashi Sensei after class, and he would kind of listen.

But you know, it was rough. The thing is, I don't have a strong body. I don't have a well put together, athletic, strong body. So I was always injured and I was always in pain. I always had supporters over every joint of my body to train. But I was driven; I was a fanatic. I think when I first started I trained three days a week until I could get rid of the rest of my evening English classes. And then I started in; pretty soon I was doing seven days a week. And it really wore my body down. I didn't know anything about conditioning, about preparing yourself for vigorous training. It was difficult.

Ironically, part of the value of my training was the frustration of it. I really learned to be very independent in my aikido training. I realized that I had to get it; it would never be given to me. I would never be touched with the magic wand and invited to private class or invited to join with the boys who had been tapped to be the next generation of teachers, even though I had the level of seriousness and dedication to aikido that they supposedly had. I knew that this would never ever happen to me. So I had to actively go and get the thing that I wanted out of my training. I became very proactive that way; I always sought out people to train with between classes. And a lot of knowledge of aikido came outside of the regular taught class, when I could just get somebody to work with me individually.

I taught English for a living, so I'd go to the school in the morning and teach until 2:30 in the afternoon. Then I would race to Hombu Dojo and start training at three o'clock. And I just trained straight through until the last class was done at eight. Then I'd go home and crash and get up the next morning and do the same thing, a very routine existence.

I didn't train with all of the teachers there. I couldn't make Doshu's class, for instance, because it was in the morning and I lived kind of far out of town. I just couldn't get to it. But I liked Arikawa Sensei for one, or "Harry" as the foreigners took to calling him. I'm not sure of the psycho-sexual connotations of this statement, but I enjoyed his classes. I liked him as a teacher partly because he was so indifferent as to how people liked him. There was a kind of jockeying and politicking going on to be popular and he didn't participate in that at all. I felt that in his class I could just go and I could work out; as long as I worked out seriously, he was happy to have me around. He tended to show a technique and then just ignore everybody. But the thing was, if you asked him a question, he'd spend ten minutes with you. He would go all out to try and answer your question and work with you.

People were really terrified of him because his technique was brutal. It was big and it was very difficult to take *ukemi* out of. But if you relaxed, you really didn't get that hurt. So when he threw me around after I'd asked a question or something like that, it took my body out to the limit of what it could do, but it never hurt me. A lot of people did get hurt with him but I found him to be very supportive of my training. He never said to me, "Women shouldn't do x-y-z," which sometimes happened with other people. So I liked his training. I felt that Arikawa supported me the most. And when I left Hombu Dojo, he gave me a doll. It had the character *shizuka* on it, which means "quiet." And he said, "You need this. You need your quiet spirit. You need to develop a quiet spirit," because my spirit was very yang at Hombu Dojo. It was aggressive. It was push, push, push. There was no yield. I had no yield in my technique at all until after my body totally fell apart, which happened about the same time I started a dojo and I had to figure out how to teach classes and do aikido with a body that was barely mobile. But my aikido was pretty aggressive in Japan.

Saotome Sensei's classes I liked almost for the opposite reason, because they were less physically rigorous than the other classes. And he really emphasized smoothness in movement so I knew that I wouldn't get damaged in his class; he didn't put up with that. I liked Kobayashi Sensei's classes because he had such an evenness of character. His technique was very clearly defined, it was easy to see what he was doing. He was very egalitarian in his teaching, he kind of always made sure to get around to everybody. I enjoyed Tohei Akira's classes also, because he did not seem to have any airs about him. He showed his technique, he went around and tried to help people, and he gave me a lot of attention when I was first there.

I didn't care for Koichi Tohei's classes. I went for about four months to his Saturday afternoon class, but I just found what he was doing so apart from the rest of what was going on in Hombu Dojo. And I felt that the principles that he stated, you know, to be relaxed, to be centered, to extend your *ki,* were nice, but I didn't see how his exercises were related to what I was doing in the other classes. I eventually stopped going to his classes.

But the teacher who had the greatest influence on me didn't even teach at Hombu Dojo. He was Hikitsuchi Sensei, who taught at a place called Shingu. Let me tell you about how I met him. I had this friend at Hombu who was a really strange guy, but I liked him because unlike a lot of the Japanese, he was very opinionated; he just let you know what he thought, so talking to him was fun. He also had a lot of interesting ideas about martial training and *shugyo* and all this stuff. Anyway, he said he was going to take a ten-day hiking trip around the Kii Peninsula, and he was going to visit Issei, and he was going to visit the town that O-Sensei was born in, and he was going to visit Shingu because there was a teacher there whom he had seen briefly in Tokyo and been impressed with, and would I like to come? I thought, sure, that'd be a good thing to do because I didn't really like to travel by myself. So we set off on this journey and we went to Shingu and that's where I met Hikitsuchi Sensei. At that time the dojo was really booming; there were many people training. Aikido had been in the city for a long time, so in the average class the majority in it were third *dan* or higher. I was attracted and kind of scared off at the same time because training was very different from what I had been doing at Hombu. But I was very excited by it nonetheless.

I really didn't spend that much time in Shingu. I'd go to Shingu for a weekend here and a couple weeks there. The last six months I was in Japan, I went and lived at Shingu and trained. And then I went and visited again for a couple months, so the total lapsed time in Shingu was really quite small compared with the time I spent at Hombu, which was five years. But the impact on my training was disproportionately large.

After I returned to Tokyo I started visiting Shingu when I had vacations from work; I think I went down for two weeks the first time. One of the reasons why I liked training there was that unlike at Hombu, where I always felt that I was having to prove myself, in Shingu I was automatically accepted as somebody who was training seriously. I don't know why that was. Partly it was because in Shingu it was assumed that anybody who came to train was there for the most serious of reasons, and that anybody who trained seriously could become a teacher. They just had a general attitude like that. So everybody came in and was met with the highest expectations, not with the lowest expectations. I was overwhelmed, I was really overwhelmed.

Another thing that appealed to me and scared me a little as well was the kind of training, which was very dynamic. It was at a much higher pace than I was used to. At Hombu I was used to training three hours or five hours a day—three to five hours of continuous body in motion. But when I got to Shingu I was dead after the first fifteen minutes of class, because they didn't do those little, subtle, tiny pauses that we usually do in our training. The reason was that they emphasized continuous connection between yourself and your partner, so the space in between the throws was just as important to pay attention to and manage as the throw itself. There was no rest. You couldn't stop and hitch your belt or turn your back or wiggle or take your time getting up or any of the zillion little rest habits that I had gained in Tokyo.

But I think that the most important part of the training for me there was the holistic aspect of it, the fact that every class included a technical and a spiritual aspect. When he demonstrated technique, Hikitsuchi Sensei would not only talk about how to do the technique but he would talk about the meaning of aikido and the meaning of doing aikido. I came to enjoy the fact that I felt at all times that I was learning something deeper than just a physical motion. He quoted O-Sensei a lot and would often say, "O-Sensei said this," "O-Sensei said that."

It was really hard to elicit any information in Tokyo about the spiritual side of aikido or about what O-Sensei talked about. One of the reasons that I liked Arikawa Sensei was that he had done all those interviews with O-Sensei in *Aikido Magazine*, [the aikido newsletter that comes out of Hombu Dojo], the ones that are called "In Memoriam," so I could talk with him about what O-Sensei said. Of course, Arikawa Sensei would say, "I never understood anything of what O-Sensei said. I couldn't understand him at all." But people were very, very reluctant after O-Sensei died to talk about O-Sensei. I'm not sure what all the reasons were. Maybe it was just that they were really in shock, you know. For whatever reason, they were reluctant to speak of it. When I got to Shingu, nobody was reluctant to speak of it; people talked about him all the time. They talked about what he did, what he had to say, how they related to him, what he felt like.

I think that the majority of people just wanted to look at the part of O-Sensei that they could understand. I think many of the Japanese teachers experienced O-Sensei as unique, set apart, unrepeatable, and a person who they had a great deal of respect and awe for, but they felt it was simply an impossibility—and it would even be disrespectful—to try and examine what he had to say or anything. They would just preserve his technique; they would preserve what knowledge they had, which was primarily a technical knowledge, try to share that or spread that.

I was also drawn to Shingu because, strange as it sounds, Shingu is a kind of power spot. It had a lot of energy there; it's an intense place. I remember sitting in *seiza* in Shingu. Now I played the *koto* and I took aikido and I lived in a Japanese-style apartment and I sat *seiza* a lot; I kind of prided myself on how much *seiza* I could take. But in Shingu in the very first class I attended, I noticed that my legs went totally to sleep after I had been sitting for only about ten minutes. I could not get up out of *seiza* and when I did get up out of *seiza* I had left blue streaks on the white canvas of the mat from my *hakama*.

That was just one of a whole series of psychically bizarre things that happened to me in Shingu. O-Sensei's beard is in the shrine in Shingu, and there was a ceremony every morning at that time. There was just this level of energy that I felt that I responded to. It was in the atmosphere of the dojo and the place. I loved visiting the shrine; I loved the energy around the shrine. I liked being out there among the trees and the rocks and the ancient buildings. I just felt that the whole place was kind of imbued with the spirits. I was drawn to certain aspects of Shinto; I was drawn to the feeling that nature was special and had a dimension beyond what we saw. I liked the ritual; I liked Shinto ritual better than I did Buddhist ritual. Buddhist ritual reminded me too much of my Catholic background. I just couldn't relate. But the Shinto ritual was so spare that I found it very satisfying aesthetically.

Outside of a Danish fellow who spent some time at Shingu, married a cousin of Hikitsuchi Sensei and went back to Denmark, I was the first foreigner to come and train there. Later I invited other foreigners who were training at Hombu to a *gasshuku* at Shingu that I arranged for them. I think this must have been about 1972 or '73. By that time there were more foreigners training at Hombu, and because I was trying to find foreigners to invite down to Shingu, I met a woman named Kathy Bates from Santa Cruz, who turned out to have Bob Frager as an aikido teacher. That's how I reconnected with Bob after losing contact with him after the first trip to Japan. Later I went to Santa Cruz and gave a slide presentation on Shingu, and out of that, people started coming over to Japan. And I arranged for Linda Holiday, Jack Wada and a man named Dick Ravoir, who did not go on to be a teacher but still trains, to go and train in Shingu, and I joined them the last six months I spent in Japan. Tom Read came over in a group that Bob Frager organized to take to Japan. Visiting and training at Shingu was just part of their overall trip, but Tom and some other people stayed on and trained at Shingu.

At Hombu Dojo, my association with the teachers was fairly limited. I talked with them after class and that was about the degree of social interaction I had with them. Part of their personalities was visible on the mat, but I didn't know them very well off the mat. But I got to know Hikitsuchi Sensei much better. I saw him in association with his wife, his kid and other people in the dojo, and I think because I so strongly desired to have a great teacher, that when I had to admit to myself that he was not perfect, it was a severe disappointment because he didn't fulfill my fantasy of him. And I had a very roller coaster relationship with him, extremely intense, which I would define now as a real, classical addictive, co-addictive, co-dependant relationship.

It was very hard. First of all, he said he had a tenth-degree black belt in aikido. In my naive way, I just assumed that must mean he was the ultimate in all aspects of aikido, and he wasn't; so when I came to realize that, it really shook me up. I thought, "Well, if this is the best that aikido can produce, what's the value of aikido?" It just really rocked my whole world view. It was just quite a few years, really, before I was able to accept him as the human being that he was and to accept the fact that whether he did or did not receive *judan* from O-Sensei—and there's some dispute over that—he was just who he was. And it didn't mean that I had to give up aikido or think less of aikido because he was who he was.

And today when I see teachers who act in a way that seems contrary to the spirit of aikido, it doesn't make me doubt the value of aikido, but it really does make me wonder whether or not they really understood aikido.

I stayed in Japan for six years. There were a number of reasons why I left. One was that through the experience of doing aikido I had changed a great deal as to what type of person I was. When I started aikido, I was really alienated from my own country and culture; I was very introverted, very self-obsessed. I was scared of people. I had difficulty having friends. I was a real loner as a person. And what I discovered happened to me as I trained in aikido was that I opened up more to people and I lost my fear of them. I lost the sense of alienation from my own culture, and I realized that in Japan you never are assimilated into the society; you're always an outsider unless you've been born a Japanese. I also had come to realize that although there were many aspects of Japanese culture that I liked and many people that I had as friends, there were also aspects that I couldn't stand and didn't want to be around. I felt in a way somewhat healed. And I felt drawn to coming back to the States and that it was more appropriate for me to be living in my own country and own culture than it was in Japan.

After meeting Kathy Bates and reestablishing contact with Bob Frager, I got a letter from him saying that he had started an aikido club and class at the University of California in Santa Cruz, and that the person who taught the beginning classes was going to be leaving, and since he'd heard that I was going to come back, would I be interested in teaching it? I think I got that letter just before I left Shingu to go back to the States. The weird thing is that all the years I had trained in Japan it had never occurred to me that I would teach aikido. My desire was to be taken seriously as a student of aikido and I just wanted to be a student of aikido. But shortly before I went back to the States, I was out having dinner with Hikitsuchi Sensei, and he says, "Well, when are you going to open your dojo?" I was completely taken aback. "What?" And I realized that I hadn't actually thought about what I would do when I came back to the States. I thought, "What am I going to do? Am I going to stop doing aikido and become a clerk at JC Penney? What am I going to do?" And I realized that of course I would have to continue aikido and I thought, "My teacher told me that I ought to open a dojo. Yes sir, I'll open a dojo!" And my first question was, "Oh my god, what if some real big man walks in?" Hikitsuchi, being the mystic that he was, says, "Oh, you don't have to ask that question. No matter what happens, you trust the *kami-sama* [gods]." I said, "Oh, of course. Whatever you say, Sensei." And actually, I've never had a problem—so far, knock on wood!

So Bob Frager not only introduced me to aikido; he got me my first teaching job, in Santa Cruz. When I left Japan around Christmas of '73, I went up to Seattle where my mother was, then visited Santa Cruz to check it out and ended up moving there. I started teaching in January or February of '74 in Santa Cruz. Fortunately, Hikitsuchi Sensei had actually prepared me to teach. I mean, he had me teaching classes in Shingu. And he used to take me around and have me explain aikido to people. It was really embarrassing! But he would do that. He'd kind of take me some place and people would ask about aikido and he'd say, "Mary, tell them about aikido." He forced me to deal with talking about aikido in public and to deal with teaching.

Aikido has grown a lot since I started teaching. In fact, I think in some ways aikido has blossomed in America. I think that there are a lot of different strands. I mean, some people are still very technically oriented and other people have kind of gone out into "whooland." But I think on the whole, American culture has given American *aikidoka* freedom to explore the teachings of O-Sensei. And aikido as a spiritual discipline has been emphasized more in the States than it has in Japan. I really think that aikido is more alive in America than in Japan. I mean, there are excellent teachers dotted here and there around Japan, but I really think that the future growth of aikido is not going to occur there; it will occur outside of Japan. Part of the reason for that is that a number of Japanese Sensei feel that it is their work and their duty to try and preserve and keep intact a set of technical skills that they've learned and not to change them, not to evolve or process them at all but to try and keep them the same, like you keep a photo album.

In America we have a number of interesting and important instructors who have helped spread aikido. I think that the work that was done by Frank Doran, Bob Nadeau and later, Bill Witt, in really very actively increasing the number of dojos and the number of people training aikido in the Bay Area is really significant. And you know, not just in the Bay Area—they've gone around and done a lot of teaching in other areas and a lot of people have been drawn to aikido because of their efforts. Of course, they had an earlier set of teachers that I don't really know much about. I know the name

Robert Tann, and obviously, these people were very important. Allen Grow is an important name; Allen Grow started the Oakland aikido dojo, which he gave to his student, Bruce Klickstein. And Allen went up to a place in Oregon, I've forgotten the name of it, but he couldn't make a go of it. After that I don't know what happened to him.

But then there's another generation of students, people like Tom Read. For myself, Tom Read is the most intriguing aikido teacher at the moment, but Terry Dobson, while he was alive, was also right up there. I only met Terry a few years before his death. I didn't meet Terry in Japan. Even in '65 when I first saw aikido, Bob Frager said, "Oh, you know, it's too bad Terry's on a trip somewhere and you won't get to meet him." And when I started, Terry was still in Japan but he told me he wasn't going to the dojo much during that year, after O-Sensei's death; he didn't really feel very connected with the place, so I never ran into him. But he was responsible for the sparking of people's interest in aikido; he was a very charismatic original teacher. Despite the controversies around him, I meet many people who say they took a class from Terry and they'll never forget it; it gave them something that they think about ten or fifteen years later. So I think that he was very important. Also, Terry tried to encode aikido in a way that Westerners could understand better; he felt that it was important to do that in order for O-Sensei's message not to get lost.

As for women instructors, Linda Holiday, formerly Linda Hultgren, has done years of good work in Santa Cruz and she hasn't really achieved much recognition, I don't think. But she really tries to keep alive an ethical spirit in her dojo. She works hard on studying the ethics of human behavior through aikido and on building the dojo as a community and as a family. And I think that she has had a lot of influence. Nowadays there are a lot of women instructors. When I came to the Bay Area in '74, there was a woman named Betsy Hill, I think, a student of Bob Nadeau's, and she did some teaching. I'm not sure if I know of anybody else who was teaching at that time. Now there's a newer generation of teachers, like Pat Hendricks and Wendy Palmer, and in Seattle some of my students are now teaching, like Joanne Veneziano. And Pam Cooper just opened her own dojo. There are teachers that I have met and know of, like Lorraine Deanne. The thing is that they're newer on the scene, men have been around longer, but I think that women are emerging as very significant teachers of aikido because they have had a different experience. I think that they have a lot to offer to the evolution and development of the art.

When I was in Japan, it was clear what it meant to be female: it meant to be weak and less. In terms of who got appreciation, who got strokes, who got teaching attention at Hombu Dojo, those women who trained most like the men, who were physically the strongest and most aggressive and persistent in their training, did get more attention. That was what was stroked, so that's the way that I went in my training. I couldn't even imagine any other way of training at that time. But I feel completely differently about it now.

I was aware that society valued male things, male actions, male behaviors, and did not value female actions and behaviors in the same way. And so I attempted, to the best of my abilities, to imitate the male behavior patterns so I could get the attention I wanted in order to learn aikido. But really, aikido is about universalities. Aikido is about energy. We come in male and female bodies but I'm not sure our beings are male or female necessarily; it's just that I'm in a female body and it has a societal meaning, and it has a physical meaning. But when you do aikido, you are in contact for a moment with something that's much bigger than the fact that this particular species on this particular planet is bipolar in sexuality. So I think that what you need to do is stand aside and let aikido come through. And the degree to which you stand aside is the degree to which your aikido is aikido and it's not female aikido. There is a concept of female aikido in Japan. It was to be graceful, soft, yielding, smooth and completely powerless. Dance.

I think that the progression in my own training has been from feeling valid to the degree that I imitated the strongest males around me, which of course were the teachers and the more senior students, into feeling that my aikido could be valid when done in a way that was much more appropriate to my own body and my own psyche. When I trained at Hombu, I trained quite aggressively, because that was valued, that was what was stroked. And for a long time I didn't even want to train with other women; I always complained that the men didn't want to train with me, but I didn't want to train with the women, either. I had, without being real conscious of it, internalized the male point of view that women weren't worth training with.

I don't know exactly when things changed, but I do remember one day going to Hombu Dojo and suddenly experiencing no interest in strongly throwing my partner down. I had all of a sudden an interest in watching how my partner moved and trying to discern just how the technique actually worked, outside of just "I grab and then I throw him down very strongly." One day my perspective just changed. I started to try and really understand what inner working might be there for doing technique; I wasn't just being strong. I think that a lot of my personal experience of aikido has come out of having the body that I have, one that's usually broken down. And even though I had many injuries and many aftermaths of these injuries, I went and opened a dojo, taught in Santa Cruz, went to Seattle and opened a dojo there. And I frequently found myself in a position of having to educate my students but being barely able to move. I started having to investigate how to get the maximum effect with a minimum of movement, since a minimum of movement was where I was at. And I had to put effort into figuring that out. In Japan I was not a small person. I was kind of an average-sized person in Japan. And I was stronger than a lot of the guys at Hombu Dojo, maybe a third. I could just actually be physically stronger than them because of my size.

When I got back to the States, such was not the case. My experience was that the majority of the men who came through the door were stronger than me, and the aggressive kind of gung-ho, swing-it-through, smash-em-down style aikido didn't necessarily always work. So I had to explore more fully how is this movement actually produced. If I can't rely on strength, I can't rely on speed, I can't even rely on flexibility, what can I rely on? That directed my investigations, and my aikido really started to change a lot from that period of time.

I started to approach the concept of *yin*, which I had always shied away from, because in Japan, *yin* is associated with everything weak. "Oh, you're a woman, you're *yin*; you should be *yin*," meaning, "You should stay home and have babies and cook meals for your husband." Because of my repulsed response to the social connotations of that kind of statement, I didn't want to deal with *yin*, think about it or anything. But I was forced to, because physically I couldn't handle *yang* energy anymore because of what was happening with my body. So I began to explore what it means to yield. My initial interpretation of the word "yield" was the word "defeat." It was "defeat," it was "to be passive, to be done, to be run over and victimized." But looking at it and dealing with it produced the biggest positive change in my aikido. When I started my movement with yield instead of full steam ahead, I started to produce what really felt like aikido to me, at least part of the time. And I had some experiences in my personal life that helped me understand what the concept of *yin* was and also what the concept of *yang* was.

As I explored this, I had at one point an extraordinary experience where I felt myself kind of sink; I sank and I became very, very quiet but it seemed like the boundaries of my body disappeared and I just expanded and expanded and expanded until I realized that I was the size of the universe and that there was a center to me and that this center was like the source of all power. What it felt like was a phrase Bob Nadeau had used in a workshop I went to many years before. He'd asked people to sense what it was like the moment before creation, the moment before the Big Bang. Well, that's what I sensed, that the moment before the Big Bang was *yin*. I realized that was the most powerful moment, when everything is in potential, but there isn't even an everything: there's a nothing, but it's all potential. And then there's everything.

When I had that experience, I suddenly understood that *yin* was not the absence of power. When I understood that, I realized that *yang*, despite its superficial and apparent powerfulness, actually depended upon the existence of *yin* for its existence. Something really changed in me when I grasped that. I mean, not right away. Sometimes you have an insight but the change as the result of the insight takes time. But it did cause a very big change in me. And part of it was that I relaxed about the male-female stuff; I no longer felt that I had to be male in order to be powerful, that I had to look like what is defined by other people as powerful in order to be powerful. I didn't feel that I had to be so pushy all the time. When I went back to Japan in the late '80s, I could really sense the difference; I'd left Japan feeling very frustrated and bitter. I left feeling that I'd never really been accepted or appreciated. When I went back, I found people all over the place who I realized had been my friends, who really loved me and who, to this day, really cared about me. I went back to Shingu as well, which was the locus of much intensely frustrated activity on my part to get Hikitsuchi Sensei to treat women fairly. I felt that if I was asked to go make tea in the middle of a discussion, that this was discrimination, that I was missing out. I was always pushing like that. And when I went back, I just didn't have that feeling anymore. I could just sit demurely and quietly in the corner and not feel any diminishment, which is quite interesting for me.

THE TEACHERS

5

FRANK DORAN

The center of aikido on the American mainland has been the greater San Francisco Bay Area, and the glue that has held the Bay Area aikido growth together has the name Frank Doran. By his own admission, he is the peace-maker, the mediator.

The evolution of aikido in the nineties is in the disciple phase. Doran draws a parallel between aikido and organized religions. Both aikido and most religions maintain vitality by generating numerous sects. However, this dynamic is also the source for endless conflicts among the various schools. One of the pitfalls to aikido is to think that your way or your teacher's way is the way. One of the moments of insight Doran mentions is when he traveled to Japan and saw that there were many great teachers, and they differed in the way they did techniques. "Open up in the time of conflict" is something that is talked about in aikido, but Doran really practices it. However, he also talks about his peace-maker role and how the results have not always been as successful as he might have hoped.

Another area that Doran touches on is the tension between Japanese culture and American culture that emerges when training aikido in the States. Eventually, each American in aikido has to decide how much of Japanese tradition they want to absorb and how much, if any, of the essence of aikido is attributed to the Japanese point of view. Doran speaks personally about his own love/hate relationship with the Japanese qualities of aikido.

Doran mentions that at a time in his aikido career when most were

*moving away from the fundamentals, he went back to basics. In his
teaching, that often means going back to the samurai weapons movement that formed the basics of aikido technique. It's a common experience for those doing a seminar with Frank to see the grandfatherly
drill sergeant persona he often adopts, wooden sword in hand, showing how a precise cutting movement of the sword is somehow the
essence of aikido—a contradiction to ponder for a lifetime.*

*On the other hand, casting for a rainbow trout is Frank Doran,
too.*

I joined the Marine Corps right out of high school. I really wanted
to be a Marine. My mother was so upset about telling my father
that I joined the Marines that she made me promise not to tell
him though I had already been to the recruiting office and joined.
It was two weeks before the bus would take me to boot camp or
something. She made me promise not to tell him until the day I left.
So the morning I left I went in and woke him up. I said "Dad, I'm
leaving." "Yeah okay, well have a good time." "No Dad, I mean I'm
really leaving." "Well, where are you going?" "I joined the Marines."
"The Marines?!" He had spent twenty years in the Navy! So he tried
to give me twenty of his military experiences in minutes. "Sorry
Dad, but I've got to catch the bus."

I was sent to Korea, where I was in combat for a year and eight
days. One of the instructors assigned to us was Sergeant Robert
Tann, a black belt in aikido—an art we had never heard of. Tann
had received his black belt from Koichi Tohei Sensei in Hawaii.
Remember that aikido was first introduced to the United States by
Tohei Sensei in 1953, although technically speaking, Hawaii was a
U.S. territory, not a state at the time. With the addition of Tann to
our section we now had representatives from judo, karate and aikido.
We would generally teach three recruit classes a day, approximately
300 recruits at a time. Training was very severe; brutal would probably be a better word. When we had a break in the training schedule, we still had to be in the dojo, so naturally we cross-trained.

Master Sergeant Carlisle also arranged for ranking Japanese

teachers to come to the base to give our instructor staff private lessons.

It was during this cross-training that I was first introduced to aikido. Shortly thereafter, Tann Sensei began formal aikido classes at the Marine Corps Recruit Depot in San Diego. This was in 1958 or 1959. To my knowledge, that was the first introduction of aikido to the mainland—at least the West Coast.

At first aikido was kind of something to fun around with. When you have six martial artists who live together every day in a dojo, and you have spare time, what are you going to do but martial arts? So we exchanged. But my real interest, even when I was first doing aikido, was judo; aikido was just a toy—I really didn't take it seriously, initially, but I just loved judo. I was heavy into competition. I just loved it. You know, I was *genki* enthusiast then, I was twenty-three, twenty-four, something like that, I was in my early twenties and a Marine D.I. I was in the best physical shape of my life. That was the springtime of my life. That was the time for competitiveness and all that. And I loved it. But over time as I continued to practice aikido, I found there was something there; little by little, my judo time went down and aikido went up until there was a point where I just dropped judo.

When I first saw aikido, I thought it was interesting, but I basically didn't understand it. We had a *shodan* for a teacher and everyone else was brand new. I just basically didn't understand it. So I practiced with Bob Tann for a while and shortly after he started classes, another teacher began teaching. His name was Tokuji Hirata, a Japanese-American from Hawaii. Hirata Sensei was *sandan* or *yondan* at the time, and taught aikido classes out of a judo dojo in San Diego. I trained with Hirata Sensei for three years. Ben Tsuji Sensei, eighth *dan* judo, also taught aikido at a San Diego dojo during those years. I believe he was second *dan* aikido. So within a few years—around 1958 to 1961—several aikido dojo appeared in the San Diego area, as well as Los Angeles.

It's really important to understand that Koichi Tohei Sensei was the chief instructor at World Aikido Headquarters at that time.

O-Sensei was still very much alive and well. And the aikido in the United States was primarily influenced, if not totally influenced, by Tohei Sensei. Even in those early years we all grew up with *Aikido in Daily Life,* which is basically aikido philosophy. His writings all had a very strong philosophical base, so we all grew up with that. Unfortunately, later, after political splits and divisions and stuff, some of the teachers tended to get written out of history, because they're no longer in favor. But the truth of the matter is, history shows that Tohei Sensei, even though he's no longer my teacher, had a tremendous influence on my aikido and on all people training in those early years.

So, I went to Hombu Dojo as a brand-new *shodan* in 1962, seven years before O-Sensei died. And when I went, I was filled with all the stories of Tohei Sensei, because, being an American, all we heard was Tohei, Tohei, Tohei, Tohei. The books were written by Tohei, the people who were teaching us had learned from Tohei. The focus was on Tohei. So when I went to Hombu Dojo, I went to Hombu Dojo with my letter of introduction to Tohei, not to see O-Sensei. Today, I am still embarrassed when I think of my ignorance in traveling to Tokyo to see Tohei Sensei, with no thought of seeing *O-Sensei.* At that time, O-Sensei was just a picture in a book.

There wasn't much talk of O-Sensei. The teachers were all talking about Tohei, which I don't think was a deliberate fault. They all talked with pride about their teacher, who was Tohei. So I went there with this feeling of wanting to see Tohei. And what I saw when I was there was O-Sensei and many other, wonderful teachers. What I saw, for example, was this: there would be five classes a day and I would see maybe Tohei Sensei teach *shiho nage,* and I would see maybe two or three other high-ranking teachers teach *shiho nage,* and I would see that they stylistically were different. This opened up my eyes to see that there wasn't just one way of doing it, and this was okay. Seeing this gave me a tremendous sense of freedom. It wasn't just Tohei; it was just Tohei if you were in the United States.

It was very liberating to see all these different teachers. When you have specifically one teacher, of course you're always trying to move in a certain way, you know, follow exactly, copy, mimic the form of your teacher. But my body was not the same shape as Tohei Sensei's and it was, I think, naturally trying to move in different ways even before I got to Hombu. And what I found when I got there was that some of the ways the other teachers moved were more natural for my body. But it wasn't shameful, it wasn't a bastardization of aikido that Saito Sensei would do *shiho nage,* Tohei would do *shiho nage,* or whoever the other teacher would be, and their bodies looked different, the way they expressed aikido was different. To me this was very freeing. Today I often reflect on that early observation, and have yet to see any of the *shihan* who in their application of teaching look exactly like O-Sensei.

So I think each person talks with pride about their teacher, so if you talk to one individual, you kind of get the idea that their teacher has the true insight into aikido. As I saw people teaching, I had to acknowledge that Hombu Dojo didn't have just Tohei Sensei. Certainly he was a major force in aikido and deserves a tremendous amount of credit. It's like any other pendulum: on one end, people want to wipe him out of history because of things that have happened politically, and so deny that he existed. That's one end of the pendulum; the other end is to idolize him, give him credit for everything. In most cases, if you get rid of both extremes, the truth can be found somewhere more in the center. Just from my view, which has to be looked at with the same jaundiced eye as anybody else's view, because mine is opinionated too, I feel that he was a genius, a brilliant teacher, made a tremendous contribution to aikido. But so have a lot of other people.

There is historical precedent here: When Christ died, what happened to his teaching? His *uchi deshi,* the twelve disciples, could not agree on his teaching and eventually splintered into factions. It shouldn't be surprising to us that on O-Sensei's passing, there was dispute as to his "correct" teaching or form. If we could interview each of Christ's disciples and find out what things they all *agreed* he said, we could get closer to his teaching than focusing on the areas in which they disagreed. You know I am a former police officer and criminal investigator. When you go to a crime scene and interview people, you interview them separately. If you interview five witnesses, you will invariably come up with five different descriptions of the suspect. He was tall, he was short, he had a red mustache, he had no mustache; they all saw something different. If all five agreed that he had dark hair, I'm going to focus on dark hair, and I'm going to throw out the mustache. Unfortunately, the generations coming up today cannot experience O-Sensei's teaching directly. They do, however, have the opportunity to train with *shihan* who were directly exposed to O-Sensei's teaching. My advice to them would be to study with as many of the *shihan* as possible, and focus on their similarities—the principles on which they agree—and not on their differences.

These *shihan* often say, "I was a direct student of O-Sensei ... this is what he taught." It is my feeling that this comes from a very sincere place in the heart. But what we have to bear in mind is that they are sharing what they saw, and what they saw is colored by their own perceptions based on their life experience. Many of them saw O-Sensei during different periods of his life and during different circumstances. It would be nice if the *shihan* said: "This is O-Sensei's teaching as *I* remember, as *I* perceived it."

Sadly, I have no O-Sensei stories. I was at Hombu Dojo for such a short, brief period of time. I have memories of just seeing O-Sensei that are very precious to me now. Just to have had that experience, to see O-Sensei alive, that was something. But people always ask me, "What was it like to take *ukemi* for O-Sensei?" I never took *ukemi* from him. I was a nobody, little Frank Doran down at the far corner of the dojo, so I have no great stories. Never had a conversation with him; I couldn't have, because I don't speak any Japanese.

The first time I laid eyes on O-Sensei was in the old Hombu Dojo; O-Sensei's house was part of the dojo. O-Sensei would come out from the back and this was diagonally across from the office. So the first time I saw him I was participating in a class that some other *shihan* was teaching. And in the middle of the class, O-Sensei wanders out of his house and across the mat right through the middle of the class, He didn't go around. And as soon as he stepped on the mat, everybody dropped. So what I saw was a little old man who looked like all his pictures. I thought it was quite wonderful, really, you know. It was kind of like if you had a football game in progress and somebody gets up from the stands and just walks across the field and all the football players stop playing and wait until this person has left the field before they start playing again. That was what it was like. And when O-Sensei went in the office, everybody started practicing again. That was my very first sight of O-Sensei. Looking back at that moment, it was really quite magical.

It's so easy afterwards to see something that I didn't experience at the time. Everyone is looking for the supernatural or some kind of a godly thing or something. O-Sensei was an extraordinary man on the one hand, and on the other hand, very ordinary. It's after the fact, after his death, that people are trying to make him into a god or something. It's really kind of an injustice because he was very human. And again that's based on what? It's like you coming to my dojo, visiting for a couple of weeks and then twenty years later someone asking you if you saw mystical qualities about me or something. "I don't know, there was this little bald-headed teacher out there, you know, it was a good class." Sorry, I didn't have any out-of-body experiences. If I could see him now, with thirty years' aikido experience under my belt, perhaps I could appreciate what I saw. At that time I was a novice. My eyes were not educated. It was mind-boggling. It was all confusing.

But to get back to Tohei Sensei: Right after I had received *shodan*, I was transferred by the Marine Corps to Guam, and Guam is fairly close to Japan so I took the opportunity to go to Japan. And since my teacher had given me a letter of introduction to Tohei Sensei, I had a direct letter when I went to Hombu Dojo. So when I arrived at Hombu Dojo I knocked on the door. In fact, an interesting little side story: I got out of the cab right at the dojo. I had an address for the *aikikai* and I didn't notice that there was a little sign in Japanese. I couldn't have read it anyway ... there was a path that went up to O-Sensei's house and another path that went to the dojo. Well, I took the wrong path and knocked on the door of O-Sensei's house. I didn't know; I couldn't read the signs; there was nobody with me to guide me. So the door opened and a maid opened the door. I presented her with the letter, she disappeared. I'm standing in the door, and Tohei Sensei who was like the god of aikido to me comes over. He read the letter, was very gracious, had me take off my shoes, and walked me through O-Sensei's house. When I came out Tohei Sensei said, "I'm just about to begin a private lesson. Please come and join." So I walked into the dojo, got dressed, and walked out on the mat.

This was my first experience at Hombu Dojo—the dojo's empty, there's no one in there but Tohei Sensei, tenth *dan,* and this other American student, who was Robert Nadeau. That was our meeting, our first class. I still remember the technique. At the very beginning of the practice, he had Nadeau grab my wrist, told me to throw him *irimi nage,* and I was mortified, my spirit had shrunk up to the size of a pea from being in his presence, being in the Mecca of aikido: There was no dojo filled with people, no place for me to hide. I executed the technique and Tohei Sensei said in this booming voice, "Good, good, very good. Now try this." I've never forgotten that; that was my very first lesson, because one of the things Tohei Sensei always preached was to teach in a very positive way, not to say "wrong," not say "bad." If he had said "wrong" at that time, what would have happened was I would have shriveled up into nothing; there would have been just this *gi.* I would have died, I was so mortified. But by him saying "Good" ... I look back on it now, you know, and obviously, it must not have been good! But whatever a person would do, Tohei would build on that, say "Good, good. Now try this," and he would show you something else—instead of killing your spirit by saying something negative. That was my first lesson, personal lesson from Tohei Sensei, and one I've never forgotten.

Tohei Sensei spoke English very well, you know, broken English, but you could understand him very well. He had a very deep voice and always taught a very positive class. He had what we call "stage presence." He had "command presence." He had a real way about him. He really projected, he was always very positive. He was a natural, born teacher.

Tohei Sensei came to the United States on a very regular basis. And so, looking back in my memory, the period that I was exposed to Tohei Sensei directly was from that first introduction in Hombu Dojo and that was in 1962, until the time that Tohei Sensei formed his own organization and left Hombu Dojo in 1974. So my direct experience with him as a teacher, him being my teacher, was a period of about twelve years. And my exposure to him as a teacher was a result of his periodic visits to the United States.

Whenever Tohei Sensei came to town—town for us being anywhere on the West Coast, almost all *aikidoka* from around the state attended his classes. These were often a whole series of classes, more like camps than short seminars. So for the most part, those of us referred to today as early American "pioneers" did not have daily exposure to a senior teacher. I envy the student of today who has the opportunity to go to the dojo daily and train under the guidance of an experienced teacher, and with a clearly defined structure.

Having been a teacher myself now for a considerable time, and experiencing a lot of good teachers, the thing that I always hone in on with Tohei Sensei is that he was a master teacher. And so that other teachers are not offended by that, it's important to say that there's a distinct difference between someone being very proficient at something and also being very good at teaching. For example, we know many of the world's world-class athletes are not necessarily good coaches. And many of the world's best coaches were never world-class athletes themselves. We're talking two separate arts, the art of teaching and the art of performance. And so, Tohei Sensei, despite the fact that his English wasn't perfect, was still a master in captivating his audience. He was a master teacher, he was a genius. I've listened to many of the *shihan* today who have said the same thing, that he was a genius as a teacher. So apparently, in his own language, he was quite something. It's important to note for Americans too, when he was speaking in English, that we were still captivated by his magnetism; his personal *ki* was very strong.

But of course, another aspect of Tohei Sensei was not having him as a teacher day-to-day in a dojo. This was because he was only in the U.S. for a few weeks a year. So, what happened to me and to many of the other people who were teaching at that time, is that we would be exposed to our teacher for a very brief but intense period of time, and then we would be left on our own, in a sense, to figure it out, you know, and to train and whatever, without being under the guidance of a teacher on a daily basis; this made it very difficult. In my own case, after about twelve or thirteen years of training, I had to go back to school to learn my ABCs. I had no strong background in basics. My aikido lacked substance. During the Tohei years, almost all training was *ki no nagare,* flowing movement. I had no foundation, no concept that there was a solid body of knowledge or basics. It was a bit like the problem in our public schools today: Lots of "fluff" classes and a weakness in basic skills like reading, writing, and arithmetic. It was only in later years that I realized aikido also had a basic framework, like reading, writing, and arithmetic. This framework is logical and clearly defined. I cannot express enough my gratitude to Saito Sensei for the many years of help in familiarizing me with his basic structure. He has taught many seminars in the Bay Area over the past fifteen-plus years.

Anyway, not too long before I went to Guam, Robert Tann got out of the Marine Corps and moved to South San Francisco, where he eventually opened the first dojo in Northern California. That would have been about 1961. I got out of the Marine Corps in '64 and moved up to Northern California because I wanted to train with him. He had, after all, introduced me to aikido and he was also on the force where I was going to become a police officer. The day I was discharged and the day I arrived, Bob told me, "Good timing! We have a Japanese teacher who's coming in today. He's going to teach class and do a demonstration and whatever, so please participate." So I took *ukemi* from Yamada Sensei; that was the day he arrived. He had stopped in San Francisco on his way to New York. And also around that time Robert Nadeau got started. Robert Nadeau started with Bob Tann, which would have been around '61. Unfortunately,

Bob Tann is no longer around. He was a motorcycle officer in the South San Francisco Police Department and he took a bad fall on his bike, was injured and got a medical retirement from the police department, and also retired from aikido at that time. That was probably around '74 or '75.

After I left the Marine Corps, I became a police officer in Northern California in a little town, Brisbane, just south of San Francisco and then, later, in Half Moon Bay. I was on two different police departments. I was a police officer for eight years. I enjoyed it. It was challenging, interesting, exciting at times.

When you join the police department they don't immediately send you out the next day to solve a homicide. You do a lot of street work. And they train you. It was a wonderful educational process and the schooling was outstanding. You study California criminal law, gathering and preservation of evidence. The subjects were very interesting to me. I enjoyed that. Most people have no idea of the knowledge that a police officer has to have to do the basic job.

It was difficult to do police work and aikido because you do work a lot of shift work, a lot of nights. It was very hard. Also I was very successful as a police officer. I had a good career going. I liked police work. But it's a very difficult occupation. You're surrounded with negatives all the time. And it's very easy to be dragged down by those negatives. One of the things I've always felt is, if you line up 100 police officers who have been in the work for ten years, ninety-five of them can't smile anymore. The work hardens you. You have to or you can't handle it. That radio in your car is a monster, it's always dispatching you to a scene where there's some really ugly stuff. You can imagine, even on just a very basic level, what it was like just getting a call or going to the scene of an accident, you're driving along and you're calm and all of a sudden; you get this call: "You have a serious injury accident at the intersection of such and such and such." Right away your foot hits the accelerator, your finger hits the switch on the sirens, and your heart starts pumping in your chest, and you're going from absolute stillness to going 100 percent. And on your way to that scene, you're saying "Oh god, don't let it be kids."

And when you get there, sometimes it is. When you arrive at the scene, people are screaming and there's all this stuff going on. And there has to be one calm mind in a sea of agitated minds. So you have to tell yourself as you're arriving—it's very much like martial arts — "You've got to be calm, you've got to be centered." When you get there, you have to operate, you have to function. You can't be non-functional, you can't let your emotions take over.

In that sense it is very much like martial arts training. You've just got to go on in and do that job. So you get kind of hardened to it. If you think about the fact that the victims are children, you go home and you can't sleep. It's not just accidents. It's other stuff too. It's seeing battered children. It just goes on and on and on. You see that stuff all the time, and if you're too open to it, it just kills you. So at some point you start to sort of clam up, and that's why so many police officers seem hard and cold and impersonal. And they get to the point where they can only relate to other police officers. Other people don't understand them, you know. It's a very difficult kind of occupation, even though I had aikido as a tool to help me think about keeping calm, keeping centered. A lot of people don't even have those images to help them. Still I realize it's like you have to use your mind to recharge your battery—and for me your battery is your psyche—to keep you thinking positive. Otherwise the negatives drag you down, and pretty soon, it kills your humanity. So I was aware of that and seeing what was happening to me, how I was becoming cut off from my emotions.

All during that time as a police officer, I would be doing aikido, I would be aware of "you've got to be centered, you've got to be calm, you've got to harmonize with the situation" and all this kind of stuff. We in aikido talk those words but yet, when something tough happens, what do you do? You stiffen up and all this other stuff comes out. So I just found it was very difficult. And I was on a very small department. There just wasn't any place for me to go, in terms of promotion and stuff like that. I saw that down the line it was limited. And there was just one particular point where I was going through a lot of personal struggle over my love for aikido and wanting to do that full time. I really didn't have many options, it was either police work where there was almost no time to do aikido or just go for it, do aikido full-time. That was very scary because at that time I had family responsibilities and the police work in a sense was like the Marine Corps, you know, I had Big Daddy taking care of me. I had a retirement plan, a medical plan, a good salary, a good career, I had all the security. And to give all that up and go do aikido just to follow my heart was scary, because I think I was about age forty at that point. Just to walk away from your career and have nothing was difficult, because you know what an aikido instructor earns!

What made the decision for me was that somebody reminded me that when you come to a fork in the road, you have to make a choice—which of these two choices is a path of the heart? That made it very clear to me. If I continued down the path of doing police work, what kind of human being was I becoming? When I would go to aikido, I was surrounded by positive people, positive circumstances, we were talking about positive stuff, the essence of aikido. One was uplifting and the other was down-dragging. So I went for it. And fortunately it has worked out for me. I've been able to sustain myself through aikido.

At that time I had been reading *The Teachings of Don Juan* by Carlos Castaneda. I was so profoundly moved by one passage that I wish to pass it on its entirety:

The Path with a Heart

Anything is one of a million paths. Therefore you must always keep in mind that a path is only a path; if you feel you should not follow it, you must not stay with it under any conditions. To have such clarity you must lead a disciplined life. Only then will you know that any path is only a path, and there is no affront, to oneself or to another, in dropping it if that is what your heart tells you to do. But your decision to keep on the path or to leave it must be free of fear or ambition.

I warn you, look at every path closely and deliberately. Try it as many times as you think necessary, Then ask yourself, and yourself alone, one question. This question is one that only a very old man asks. My benefactor told me about it once when I was very young, and my blood was too vigorous for me to understand it. Now I understand it. I will tell you what it is: Does this path have a heart?

All paths are the same: they lead nowhere. They are paths going through the bush, or into the bush. In my own life I could say I have traversed long, long paths, but I am not anywhere. My benefactor's question has meaning now. Does this path have a heart? If it does, the path is good; if it doesn't, it is of no use.

Both paths lead nowhere; but one has a heart; the other doesn't. One makes for a joyful journey; as long as you follow it, you are one with it. The other makes you curse your life. One makes you strong; the other weakens you.

The trouble is that nobody asks the question; and when a man finally realizes that he has taken a path without a heart, the path is ready to kill him. At that point very few men can stop to deliberate, and leave the path.

A path without heart is never enjoyable. You have to work hard even to take it. On the other hand, a path with heart is easy; it does not make you work at liking it.

For me there is only the traveling on paths that have heart, on any path that may have heart. There I travel, and the only worthwhile challenge is to traverse its full length. And there I travel looking, looking, breathlessly.

—Don Juan, A Yaqui Warrior, as told to Carlos Castaneda

When I was on the police department, I had a little dojo in Half Moon Bay. It was a tiny little town. There wasn't really enough population to support a dojo. And I was terribly embarrassed about money and money issues and asking for money. And even though I had a little storefront dojo, of course I had the rent and all that stuff to take care of that everybody understands. But I could just not ask people to pay their dues, there was something inside me that prevented me. In fact, what happened when I never asked people to pay their dues was that many of them just chose not to pay their dues. At the end of the first year I had paid more than $500 out of my own pocket; in other words, I was paying to run the dojo so I could teach. So I just folded the dojo. But during that same time, I started teaching at Stanford University. I've been teaching there ever since. And I also started a little class; it was really the forerunner of Aikido West, our current dojo. We started at a high school and we were in that high school for seven years. And what I did was I built up a following. I built up enough students so that I could quit my job and have enough money to sustain myself. That would have been in '72.

About the same time Aikido of San Francisco came into being. Nadeau Sensei had a class in San Francisco. He was teaching at a church, a Unitarian Church. He had a little group going there, and he asked me to come in and work with him. So the two of us were teaching out of that church though it was primarily his school. And the same thing happened—it began to build and we decided there was a certain time and a certain mass that warranted us having a dojo. So we started the San Francisco dojo. We brought Bill Witt Sensei in with us. The three of us went into partnership and opened the San Francisco dojo. And we operated that dojo—it was a very successful dojo—for thirteen years until finally the lease ran out and we could not afford to stay in there at any cost. They were tripling the rent, that kind of thing. So it dissolved and we all sort of went our separate ways.

Having three separate styles like that has its good points and it has its bad points. It's important that the three people make efforts to try and get along, and you have to be open and okay about somebody else's style, because the three of us are very, very different. I mean, Nadeau Sensei and Witt and myself are just very, very different in many ways. But the students seem to deal with that fine. There were some students, of course, who would only train with a specific teacher, two out of the three or one out of the three. But most of the people came and trained with everyone. And the end result seemed to be fine.

I don't think it's different from any other kind of endeavor. You have different opinions on different things and if you're really rigid in your thinking, that this is the way, then that's never going to work. I felt very strongly in what I was doing, as did the other two instructors, there were certainly things that they would do that I would do differently. But we were okay about allowing the other person to have room to work out his understanding of aikido. Regarding Nadeau, I look at his aikido and I smile and he looks at my aikido and he smiles, but there is a lot of caring for one another. What we're doing is in one sense just miles apart. But it's okay. If people can't do that, how can you have any other kind of relationship? How can you have a relationship with your sweetie or with your boss or whatever, if you can't be okay with somebody else's thinking? And that's of course why we have the stuff we call politics, it's because of people's unwillingness to just be okay with somebody else expressing their aikido.

Of course, there are vast differences among all the instructors in the Bay Area but for most part, we get along. And sometimes we don't get along, either. But isn't that natural too? You grew up with brothers and sisters. You understand that. It's not that you don't really love your brothers and your sisters, that you don't care for them, but there are times when you fight like cats and dogs. We have major disagreements in the Bay Area, we have our conflicts, like anybody else. But by and large everybody is still there and they're still trying. So as long as there's hope, as long as the doors are open and there are people still coming together, even though meetings are painful, political discussions are painful, it's worth making the effort. Of course it would be a lot easier to say "Screw it" and walk away. But inside I think there's some kind of intrinsic knowledge that we have to keep trying. It's like the perfect *ikkyo*, it's elusive. We keep trying and we keep trying. We don't get it right. But we keep coming back to the dojo. I think we have to do that on the so-called political front, too. We have to keep trying. Don't quit.

I really try to be the mediator in the midst of all the conflict. But I have not always always been successful. As I go up and up in rank,

I have more and more responsibility. With that responsibility comes more and more problems that need to be resolved. And I'm just real clear, I don't have the education, I don't have the training, I don't have the wisdom to have an answer for a lot of the stuff we have, the political kind of stuff. So it's very painful not being able to have answers for people. I'd really love to have peace. And I know the people I don't agree with, they're coming from a good place. Even though I don't agree with them and I may fight with them, I know they're of a good heart. It's just that in many cases we're bucking heads. And again, it's like I haven't refined *ikkyo* and I work on that every day, so maybe it's okay that I haven't refined this other stuff.

Well, time heals all wounds. And I sense that some of the people who split away because of how that was handled have had time to really realize that when somebody does something that is that hurtful, there are a whole lot of victims other than the specific victims in that specific event. So the people who split apart, who took sides, then became victims because friendships were broken up. But after time this has settled down and you see a lot of these people coming together again. It's like the situation was abated. But it was very traumatic. I literally was waking up in the middle of the night, getting up and vomiting. I was that sick inside 'cause I couldn't resolve the problem. It was very, very painful for a lot of people.

Things have really changed since I first started. Let's look at my dojo as an example. If you walk into my dojo today, first of all, it looks like a dojo. It's a big mat with a beautifully designed shrine and the flowers and all the stuff that makes it a dojo. You'll see the mat crowded with people, the majority of which are *yudansha,* more like you would find in Japan now. On the mat in my dojo you'll find a couple of fourth *dans,* several *sandans,* a whole army of *nidans* and *shodans.* If you walked into that dojo twenty years ago, what you saw was maybe a *nidan* teaching, everybody in the dojo were white belts; a black belt was rare. So the level of training was vastly different. So there's no comparison. You're comparing a 1964 automobile with a 1996 automobile.

Aikido came from Japan, of course, and I think we Americans

are still struggling with trying to make it our own, because we have all this cultural stuff. And there are things that are Japanese, that as Americans, we're really in love with: there are so many beautiful aspects to the Japanese culture that we're really drawn to, especially the things we're weakest on: courtesy, consideration, things that are being lost with us. There are other things about the Japanese culture that really turn us off. And for the Japanese, I think it's the same thing: there are things that are interesting and that they enjoy about American life, and there are things that are just abhorrent to them. We find things about them that are shocking and vice versa. I don't think that's necessarily bad; that's kind of natural. But there is this kind of love-hate relationship because of all the cultural stuff. The important thing, I think, is to get through all the cultural stuff and see that aikido, per se, as developed by O-Sensei, is something for human consciousness, and human consciousness is not something that is owned by the Japanese; nor can we say that we are going to make it very American.

The principles upon which our art is based, the highest principles and the highest ethics, are things that are shared regardless of cultural stuff. So, how can we make it our own? The way to make it our own is to own that humanness of it and not be distracted by the cultural periphery of trying to "be Japanese." We can do aikido for fifty years and we will never be Japanese. So if you're trying very hard to be Japanese so you can learn aikido, you're on the wrong path. You're never going to make it, even if you study for a thousand years. So you have to be very clear about what it is you're trying to study. You're studying aikido and you're studying these principles, and along the way you're very fortunate as an aside to be able to pick up a part of another culture. But don't misunderstand that that's what you're studying: the culture.

I have a kind of love-hate affair with the Japanese, as I think many Japanese have with American culture. There are things about the culture we have great difficulty with. A very classic example is individuality: our country is based on that. To the Japanese, it's 180 degrees different; if you're an individual, you're pointed out as someone who is not conforming for the betterment of the whole. So it's a different viewpoint of things: the individual spirit has to be more suppressed, more kept within, and everyone contribute to the whole. I'm not making a value judgment on what is "correct," I can only say personally that I grew up in a country where from childhood, independence is highly prized. And so you have this conflict, because the Japanese attitude is very different.

Some of the aspects of the art are definitely Japanese. Three things come to mind right away. We wear Japanese clothes, to start with. We use Japanese words. We practice Japanese courtesy and customs by bowing and by using other formalities—that's just quick, on the face of it, three things that somebody walking in the door on the first day would see. And what's very American? Courtesy is not something that we're very good at. I'm ashamed of the level of it in our society now, but it's something that we haven't been taught. But a handshake is very American and we could do aikido by coming in and shaking hands. We could come in wearing sweatsuits, and we could come in and speak English. There are three things that we could make very American. But, something gets lost. That's where we have to start making the choice: do we want to do that? Do we want to come in and do aikido wearing sweatsuits? Do we want to not learn the Japanese terminology? This is where we have some choices and, where I think some of these Japanese traditions can enhance and better our lives. So I want to steal those things from them. I like the idea of putting on this *gi* that we wear, knowing that way back in the sixteenth century or before, some guy just like you and I put on one of these suits, got down on his knees—his knees were probably hurting just like ours—and faced towards a shrine like the shrines we have in our days, and bowed and got up and went up and down doing the business of martial arts training. And that has been going on for centuries, I think that's very precious; so I want to steal, be a part of that tradition. I don't want my people to wear Levi's and "make it American."

The art we're practicing, the principle of joining your power with that of another, of taking chaos and creating harmony, that does not belong to the Japanese. That does not belong to the Americans. That's improving human consciousness; so that's the point where we come together. That's what we want, not "make American" but "make human." People working together in harmony. What do you see when you walk in the door? You don't see people fighting with people, you see people training their bodies rigorously for the purpose of perfecting themselves. That's the whole concept of *budo*. And again, this concept doesn't have to be Japanese. All through history, you have people from every country of the world, of every nationality, who have gone out and done things that are heroic. Bravery does not belong to the Japanese. On Iwo Jima, Marines died and Japanese soldiers died: bravery was a human quality expressed by both peoples. Courage, human spirit, all of these things are being developed within a dojo. And these are the human qualities that we are talking about.

Aikido also has a lot to teach us about violence. We really have to be aware of the aggression that's inside of us, and that it's easy to talk about harmony. Everybody is right into their aggression mode. They're out there struggling, fighting with one another. So what's the point? What good does it do to talk about, if you're still doing it in practice, in life? So what we have to do in our training is we have to change ourselves. And we do that by giving up our animalistic behavior, our need to be aggressive towards our partner and try things like keeping your posture and opening up your chest, opening up your heart and just going into the center of a person. So if through our practice we can see how aggression keeps coming up and we keep working on it, over a period of time we can effect some change in ourselves. But it's a very long and difficult process.

My whole early life was about violence, all those years in the Marine Corps. A Marine drill instructor is very violent. My time in combat was the absolute epitome of violence, it was absolute horror. And then there was the police work and all the violence I experienced there. I've experienced a lot of violence. I've seen a lot of violence. And I know that there's a lot of violence inside of me, because I was a police officer during all of that period of the '60s.

Frank Doran

The anger comes up in me. The anger is there for all of us. It's just under the surface. And so I needed aikido. I needed a way to channel that and to find a positive way. So for me, my classes tend to be more on the soft side or whatever, and it's primarily because I still have a hard time dealing with the violence. It's so easy for it just to come up in me. So I get really upset when I see violence manifested on the mat. When I see people out there struggling, fighting with one another, it's like I have to calm the whole dojo.

You just have to be aware of when violence comes up inside of you, what it feels like. I mean, it doesn't feel good. We all know what it's like when we lose our temper and when we lose it, period. It's not a pleasant feeling. And people on that mat are human. I mean, there are all different kinds of people there. Sometimes, depending on the training partners you have, the training is just joyful, it's just really terrific. Other times it's like, oh God! You can't wait to bow out from training with that particular person. To try to deny those things is to deny the truth. Those things are there. So we need to look inside and ask, "Why am I reacting this way? Why am I feeling this way?"

The dojo's a very hard training ground. The dojo's a difficult place. It's not always pleasant. But why do we keep coming back? It would be a lot easier to just go bowling than to have all these hassles, right? Imagine if you'd been bowling for thirty years instead of doing aikido for thirty years! It's just that I think that there's a part of us that knows that it's for our own good, that there are some answers there. We talk about "peace" and "world peace," like peace is something out there. Peace does really truly start inside. We have to make peace with ourselves. We have to be comfortable with ourselves. That's very hard, very hard. The dojo brings it out. You go out there and somebody starts swinging at the end of your wrist and if things go well, it's fine, and if they don't, you get angry. But there are restraints in the art, we act responsibly, we work it out, we're trying.

153

6

ROD KOBAYASHI

Kobayashi is one of those people who can make you feel better, relaxed and calm, just by being in his presence. In appearance he is a small man of Japanese/Hawaiian descent. The adage that the training in the dojo mirrors the teacher is certainly true in Kobayashi's case: the movements are big and energetic and the mood is joyous.

Rod's place in American aikido follows the thrust started by Tohei Sensei, and in our book he is intertwined with George Simcox, and most importantly, Tom Crum. He started his own aikido organization and preaches the doctrine of aikido in daily life. The personal drive to advance aikido stems from a singular encounter with O-Sensei in Hawaii. From that moment on, Kobayashi's life mission was set: to advance the growth in aikido.

Of the people we spoke with, he was the most comfortable talking about the elusive notion of ki. Kobayashi likens it to the notion of energy fields used in physics.

As a philosophy or approach to aikido training, Kobayashi separates physical techniques training from what might be called the "aiki attitude." The best developed part of the "aiki attitude" is control over yourself. It is by this self-control that the layers of an energy field become accessible to a person. Kobayashi gives as examples riding through pain, not fighting back immediately, and not having the last word in a verbal argument. The application of aikido principles off the mat seems to be most dear to Rod Kobayashi.

started aikido in Hawaii. I studied under Yamamoto Sensei and Takahashi Sensei. That was in '57. Later I came to L.A. and started practicing under Mito Uyehara, who was the actual founder of *Black Belt*. I trained with him until Takahashi Sensei came from Hawaii around 1960. Takahashi Sensei, who was Japanese-American, has since passed away. I trained with people like Clem Yoshida, who was chief instructor of the Los Angeles Aikikai for some time. He has since retired from teaching.

In the early days of my training there were hardly any explanations of aikido principles. They might tell you "extend your *ki*" and "if you have strong *ki* then you can have harmony of *ki*," or, "*Aiki* is harmony of *ki*." Well, I believed in it and tried it. But later on I found out the most important thing is that we should have basic attitude of harmonizing in the beginning, not after you are able to overcome others or stop others with your strong *ki*. And you don't have to have strong *ki* to be able to blend and control. Even a child with weak *ki* can have the proper attitude to harmonize, to blend with the situation. You don't have to have strong *ki* to do this. The proper usage of *ki*, that is important.

In the beginning we used to have bruises all the time; we had to learn the hard way. We thought, "Oh, develop strong *ki*, strong *ki*, that is the way of *aiki*." But it's not that way. Learning that has been a long process. I would say that when I was in my twenties, I preferred using a lot of strength, physical strength: I thought, "*Ki* has to be stronger." And when I was in my thirties, I realized, "Gee whiz, it doesn't work that way anymore." There are times that I used to get frustrated. When I reached forty, I realized there was a more efficient way of doing things, and when I reached fifty, I realized I didn't have to do a lot of things that I used to do before. You become more efficient. So the proper attitude, the proper movement will lead to efficiency; it's efficiency that's important. And I started looking back and recalling some of the stories people tell about the Founder of aikido, Master Ueshiba, how effective his techniques were. Maybe he was into strength at first. He was pretty strong, too; But he realized that strength was not the important thing. It's your self, how you control yourself, how you win over your self. That's the Founder's teaching. "True victory is victory over oneself." Control yourself, then you are able to control the situation. Then victory is not just for yourself; it's victory, even for the attacker. You don't have to destroy the attacker when you have the right attitude.

Going back to my own history, I was at L.A. Aikikai for a while. Then I started my own Aikido Institute of America. My objective was to train instructors, because there's a lot of people who think the only way you could become a good aikido instructor is by going to Japan. And I realized, no, there are a lot of good instructors here in United States. To train Americans, you have to know the American mind. Instructors can't just force the Japanese way upon American students. I read some articles in magazines quoting some people as saying that the only way you can become good instructor is to go to Aikido Headquarters and to train, and only people who can become good instructors are Japanese. I'm Japanese, but I didn't want to believe in that. So I said, "Well, okay, I'll prove them wrong. We'll start a dojo, we'll have an instructor training center." My objective's to train instructors, then try to send them out to help spread aikido because I believe in aikido principles so much I like to help spread it. In order to do that we must develop good instructors.

I got Tohei Sensei's permission and asked Doshu's permission to start Aikido Institute of America. It was ten years later that Tohei Sensei started his Ki Society. I would say as far as the aikido is concerned, he was the top man—still is. I don't know how often he teaches now, but because of him, I was able to reach this far. He was the one who developed a method of training. The Founder of aikido, Master Ueshiba, might have been the Founder, but to explain aikido, I think nobody can out-do Master Tohei. You just can't beat the way that he explains the principles and the practice of aikido. He really understood and I think he really developed a method of training. The Founder's like an inventor ... but it was Master Tohei who had to develop aikido.

It was a great feeling training under Tohei Sensei. He was able to really help you with his *ki*. Once in '68 I went to Japan to go through *misogi* training which involved chanting for three days. After a while, of course, your legs really hurt, you were suffering through it. He came next to me and started chanting; I didn't feel any pain. "Wow, this is great." I knew he was there next to me, although I didn't open my eyes, I could feel him, I could hear him chanting. I was just riding his *ki*. After he left, the pain came back. "Wow, I have to stay with him, I have to learn how he does that."

To a certain extent, I think I've been quite successful following Tohei Sensei's way. I try to help people, not in a direct way, but by helping people to help themselves. That's the most important thing.

I wanted to develop further what I had learned. So this is why I actually resigned from the Ki Society. Instead of just training they started having contests, of the forms and the techniques. I really wanted to learn how to add depth to aikido teaching, instead of just going through the training and having competitions. I really wanted to develop what I've learned from him, instead of just trying to follow, follow, follow, all of the way. A lot of people, sometimes, only follow without being able to make followers themselves. I gained so much from him that I wanted to really make it a part of myself, just like he did, from the Founder. I wanted to gain, then study and develop a way of teaching the spirit of aikido.

I was forty-nine already when I left the Ki Society. At that time I had many followers who wanted my training, the way I was training. That's why I decided to take further the path that he was teaching.

I just help people to find their path. Tom Crum was my student but I don't really follow so closely what Tom is doing. He's on his way and he's going. There are many people who are applying aikido principles today. We have one of the black belts here, in L.A. His name is Dr. Vince Mobley. He's a psychologist, an educational psychologist at California State, Long Beach, and he has been using quite a bit of what he learned.

It's not my way or path to find out just how successful my students are. I share my knowledge and they go. I don't try to brag about who is successful; it's not my way, it's theirs. It's up to them to develop upon it. If my students communicate with me, I stay in touch. But I don't demand that they do. So Tom is doing what he wants, and there are many people like that.

My teaching is different from most aikido instructors in the L.A. area. The majority of aikido instructors deal with techniques alone. But I go deep into the philosophy and relate the philosophy to the training. For instance, the Founder left a lot of poems, called *doka*. It's in *haiku*, a form of poem. I found that most of the old timers in Japan said, "Oh yes, O-Sensei's *doka* are very fine, but they are very difficult to understand." Whatever I can understand, I try to put into practice. For instance, there's one good one: He says, "If the enemy comes rushing in and tries to attack you, take one step aside and cut immediately." He actually wrote this in terms of swordsmanship. He was probably in his fifties when he wrote this. And he started developing his techniques around these ideas. And what I'm trying to do is put that spirit into the training when I'm teaching aikido.

I explain to the students: "Here. This is where you take one step aside. This is why you have to take a step aside. If you block, you have to be strong. If you take one step aside and then blend, you don't have to be strong. You can utilize that person's momentum, that person's energy. So you can be much more efficient. As the Founder said, "Cut immediately,"—that is, use the simplest, most direct technique.

A lot of people will do fast, long, drawn-out, beautiful, ballet-like aikido movement. I think you have seen that. There are a lot of people like that. For demonstrations, yes, that's good. But is that realistic? How many people will be holding on to your wrist when you're leading them around 360 degrees? Nobody's going to hang on that long. As soon as that person feels you're doing something, then he's going to change it. So that's fine to show people how important the blending is. But to be realistic you have to blend with the simplest technique possible. The point is not to throw somebody, but to lead the person to fall by using that person's *ki*. This is how I try to explain poems within the training. And it's been quite successful. People are beginning to understand these kinds of things. So all my teachers here will be learning how to share aikido principles, not just techniques.

When people say, "Aikido, what kind of martial art is it?" I say it is not a martial art. Because, you see, aikido was called *aiki-budo* before. *Bu* means "martial." In 1942 they took the *bu* out, and started calling it "aikido." That was the middle of the Second World War. That's very interesting—why did they take it out? I'm pretty sure the feeling is "true aikido" is not martial; it's not the purpose of aikido to "destroy the opponent before he destroys you." Yes, it has developed from that, but it's developed into, been refined into a technique to control the situation but not to do violence, to injure or destroy others. You must save yourself; at the same time you must save the life even of the attacker. That's my understanding of aikido, and I'm pretty sure that was the Founder's wish; at the beginning, yes, he had matches, he had to compete against some other people. But when he realized the principles of aikido, he stopped the challenges. It's very, very important that we try to spread the principles of aikido together with the techniques.

In Japan it's all technique. And still to this day, the Japanese teacher might talk about *ki* and harmony, but never really explain how it could be incorporated into technical training. He might say, "Oh, if you blend, you can do a technique," but he never explains it. This is why I say there are better instructors in the United States for Americans, because instructors here try to explain even the techniques.

Through the principles of aikido, you can really change your everyday attitude, attitudes even toward good health or marriage, if you learn how to control yourself, instead of saying the last word. So I say to people, "Never say the last word. Control yourself!" Yes, you want to throw somebody, but control yourself. Blend and control yourself, or try to lead the person, if you need to restrain the person, into position to fall so you can effectively restrain him instead of trying to force him into falling.

Basic attitude is so important. For instance, I tell people if you have to go to a job interview, calm yourself, control yourself, and be able to blend with the situation.

To understand the principles, you have to train, you have to really train, you can't come once or twice and say, "Oh yeah, I understand." To really make it a part of oneself, you have to repeat it over and over and over. This is why training is so important. Some people just want to learn principles without training much. With your mind, you say: "Oh yes, I understand; that's a good idea. Yeah, I believe in it, I'm going to do that from now on." But unless you really put yourself into it and practice the blending, when you have to use it in your everyday life, you may not know how to. This is why training is so important.

The American way is that most students don't want to roll, but they want to throw. In order to learn how to throw effectively, how to be efficient, you still have to do the other part too; you cannot just learn by yourself. You have to work and learn it with others. And a lot of people think, "Oh, if I take an eight-week course, I'll get it." I also teach courses at California State, Long Beach, extension education, and very few people really last eight to ten weeks. Most people last about five weeks and then they just disappear. You think, "Oh, they like it so much," at the beginning. But I guess they want everything to be fed, programmed by us, instead of doing it themselves. But you have to do it; you have to do it and try to make it a part of yourself.

There is value reading about aikido principles in a book, but that alone is not enough to make it part of yourself. You should work with some qualified instructor and get the feeling. 'Cause this is something that you have to do with your mind and body, not just with your mind. Mind alone cannot make it a part of you. Practice the principle and do the technique, then make that part of yourself. Then you don't have to think about it when you have to use it. And later on you say, "Oh, it must have been my aikido training." A lot of people want to be able to say, "Okay, I know it now!" But when it comes to "I'm going to do it," you can't do it unless it's a part of yourself.

Often I tell students when they have problems or they're not very well coordinated—they're having trouble in general—I tell them,

"It's okay. Keep at it! Keep at it! Don't worry. If you can't take good roll in the beginning, that's okay! Just keep at it. Don't overdo it. You can get frustrated. Do it at your pace. Keep at it. And that way, if you keep at it, it's going to be part of you. It's better if it takes longer for you to learn something, as long as you try—keep trying. Then it becomes part of you." There are some people who are so quick in learning and so quick in quitting, too. When they think they know it, they disappear. Sometimes people who have difficulty or are slow are the ones who last longer and they have better understanding of it. So I try to encourage people. "Stay with it, keep doing it, it'll come to you."

We do not tell people what to do, how to lead their lives. Even on the mat, we don't tell people what to do. We help people. We guide them. I have a lot of people coming for my advice. I'm not a counselor, a psychologist. It's very difficult to say, to specify exactly what help they need in their life. But through aikido principles I can train and help people to find their path, help people to find the value of their existence—that's the point.

But training technique alone is not enough. Unless the principle has been taught at the same time the techniques are taught, it won't be part of the picture. So often I tell people "Okay, if you're on the freeway and you're driving, when somebody cuts in front of you, you want to do the same thing to him. But, you must learn to control yourself. Control yourself, settle about two inches below your navel, keep your one-point." This is Master Tohei's teaching. Some people say, "Oh, you take aikido, you're not supposed to get angry." As long as you're human, you will get angry. I have seen the Founder of Aikido get angry, I have seen Master Tohei get angry. The important thing is to control your anger, instead of taking it out on others. So you want to cut back in, but it could endanger other people. So, control yourself. Yes, you're angry, but control yourself. This is what we teach people, how to control themselves. That alone is a big plus to one's daily life, instead of knowing how to throw people around. If they just train how to throw people around, that's exactly what they're going to try to do, cut back in, try to show off to the person that "I can be better than you are." You must control your-self; even if that person was not supposed to do it doesn't mean that you should also do it. It will endanger others.

In beginner's class I try to explain these things, relate them to daily life. So instead of just learning the technique, how to throw, they also know how to relate it to daily life. So I feel that if all aikido instructors try to spread the principles of aikido at the same time they teach a technique, then we can say, "Oh, no matter where you learn, yes, you should get the same result."

A lot of people say, "Keep training and you'll learn about *ki*." Some people may, some people may not. Some people may learn about *ki* but won't realize the principles. Even to this day there are many instructors who are not able to lead the warm-up exercises properly. They lack even that part. We try to emphasize the impor-tance of warm-up exercises. From the very beginning when you lead the exercises, you must have the students' concentration; you have to capture their minds. It starts from the very beginning, not only showing the techniques. It starts with the stretching, doing the exer-cises, *aiki-taiso,* and all that. Then you can learn the techniques. And of course, it's repetitious; you have to repeat things until it really sinks in. So you don't just talk, talk, talk, talk. I tell the instructors, don't be afraid to go back to basics. But don't just stay in the basics. Students will get bored, too. Some people may not like all the talk-ing; sometimes you have to talk, but don't talk all the time. Every-thing in moderation, there has to be a balance. So sometimes I talk, sometimes I don't talk. I try to balance it.

I think Americans are lazy. They don't really want to commit themselves. Many of them don't have that drive, the willingness to continue. This is where I think Americans are losing out to the Japan-ese. Commit yourself and do it. In Japan, they work, they go to work, work for the boss, stay, their loyalty is there, they keep at it, they keep working. The American way is, boom, I want a better job; I want better pay. In Japan, you do that and you don't get a good job.

With *ukemi,* it's important to learn the techniques, and of course, you might some day trip and fall or get thrown off a motorcycle or bicycle, and you're going to be very happy you had aikido training. I have a lot of students who come back and say, "Oh, good thing I had aikido." "I think aikido saved my life, otherwise I would have broken my neck," I hear stories like that all the time.

But I don't want people to train for that purpose. In order to really learn something, you have to know the other side, too. If you have to take a breakfall, can anybody take a breakfall on concrete, in reality? Now, when you're throwing a person, are you going to throw the person to kill them? You can learn how to effectively make a person fall, flip them over and restrain them without injury. But there are a lot of people, you know, who just practice *ukemi* for the sake of being able to practice some very dangerous throw. I don't go for that, because aikido techniques are not for destroying others. *Aiki* is harmony. The technique must be efficient so they do not require a breakfall. Once you learn how to control yourself, you can control your power, how much power you use to throw a person. If you throw a person for the sake of throwing a person, you can injure that person. You should lead the person with harmony, make the person fall. The more efficient you are, the less force is required. The less force is used, the less chance of injury.

If you harmonize with the movement, you use the person's momentum, the person's energy; then as long as you're not in the line of force, you can use very minimal force. But if you're on the line of force, then you're going to have to be stronger. Efficiency means not to have that conflict, not to have all that resistance from the person. Don't give the person a chance or an opportunity to resist you. Then you have efficiency. So in your everyday life, this too will be reflected, because you have the proper attitude.

I think junior and senior students should be the same. It shouldn't be, "Oh, I'm third degree, second degree." Yeah, we have the difference, but I tell students they have the responsibility of helping the lower ranks. That's what the rank stands for. You go to some dojos, they have the highest rank here and then they line up. And it's strict, very strict, very formal, and they have to show respect. To their seniors, respect is something that you have to earn; you don't demand it. All of the instructors work together, and at this dojo, there's no bragging that "so-and-so is higher, so-and-so is lower," they're all the same. But they know they have the responsibility to be a higher rank. Even after the first examination, when we give belts, we tell them, "This indicates responsibility." Each examination, each rank they receive, they have a higher responsibility. They all get along real well: friends, this is how it should be.

Of course, we do weapons training in moderation. Basically, the movements of aikido came from the movements to blend with weapon attacks, so students have to know how to use the weapons. But it's not about how to destroy others with a weapon. It's how to use a weapon to control without injuries.

Master Tohei actually taught me how to use weapons, and I developed quite a bit from that. His way was to teach bang, bang, bang, you know, one, two, three, four, five, and then for the rest I have to go back and try to relate it to what I had already learned from him, and then relate it to movements. But what I do is all in accordance with the principle of the Founder's teaching and with Master Tohei's teaching. And that's what I needed time to develop—my own way based on their teachings. This is why I went independent.

We do meditation as well. Actually, we do chanting once, twice a year. There too, we're not trying to develop something to mystify things, because people can overdo it. It's just like sitting in *seiza* with the pain. This is something that you ride out, just like riding a wave out. Then that teaches people that if you have difficulty right now, don't fight it right now, control yourself, ride it out. That's the purpose of some of this *misogi* training. It's not to find enlightenment. Enlightenment is something that's already with us; you don't have to seek it. You keep training, it's going to come to you. Slowly you realize, "Oh yes, I feel good, oh yes, now I understand." I went through *misogi* training in Japan in '68 and many things came out; I realized many things.

It's very important that all the training you do is to make the basic principles a part of yourself. You go through years and years of practice and you realize, "Now I understand what I went through ten years ago." It's in you; it's in your subconscious, but it takes more training, more work and then it comes out to the surface. "Oh yes, now I understand." It takes time. This is why it's very important that you continue with your training, instead of saying, "Oh yes, I went through that three-day training; now I've got it."

I did have experiences with Master Tohei where I seemed to understand something suddenly. But it was only after I had been doing a lot of training. Once he put on an exhibition in Culver City. He went backstage and we were changing when a city councilman came in. "Master Tohei, is it true that you can't be lifted up?" He did the demonstration and I couldn't lift him up. And Master Tohei said: "Oh yes, it's nothing mystical. Here, would you like to first lift him up?" This guy was huge, you know, he just lifts me up. Master Tohei says, "And now Mr. Kobayashi will calm himself down and then you can try to lift him up." He tried to lift me up, and to my surprise, he couldn't lift me up! I just listened to what my teacher said and it worked. "Did I do it myself? Wait a minute!" It's a good feeling: I thought, "I did it." I had many experiences like that.

Once I was at the Burbank Police Department in a demonstration and I thought, "Wait a minute. I'm going to try something. Maybe as this guy lifts me up, I'll touch him first, instead of letting him touch me, at the moment he tries to touch me I'm going to touch him." So I did the experiment. At first, he was able to lift me up. Next thing, I touched him first, in my mind, and then he wasn't able to lift me. "Hmmm." After thirteen years and all these other experiences I had had, I asked Master Tohei: "Remember all my experiences with you—were you doing something to me?" "Yes, you must control the first movement." And so, what I did by controlling the policeman's mind before he touched me, was the same thing. And it worked. Master Tohei said, "Yes, that's called 'controlling the first move or *shugo seisin*.'" And I thought, "Oh, he's going to teach us all about it." But Master Tohei never did after that. He never mentioned it again. That is one of the reasons why I wanted to study things myself, go deeper into it, study what I had learned from him. And then try to develop from that. And I have done quite a bit. Control the first move. It's a simple thing, but you have to train to make it a part of yourself. Actually, we use that in the training of the techniques. It can be a lot more effective, a lot more efficient if you control the first move.

Master Tohei didn't explore that idea more because from ancient days, Japanese instructors never went beyond a certain point. They keep it to themselves; they don't go beyond. From reading many stories about many different masters, I've learned that they always keep the last or the innermost secret. That's how it is. That's why they don't want to talk. Master Tohei talked, explained a lot of things. Other instructors don't. They keep everything to themselves.

Ki is something like, if you try to shake hands with somebody, that person is reaching for you, sending *ki* out. And we can do experiments like that. Let a person walk by and one person will try to block the way. Then compare the difference with somebody else in front of him: he walks toward that person extending his hand like he's going to shake his hand, and it'll be much more powerful.

Ki is real for anybody who goes through the training. You may not feel *ki* is a part of nature as such. But everything has *ki*. How does a table keep its shape, its form? It's because of its own *ki*. Everything has *ki*. You do not have it only when you train in aikido. No. There are a lot of people using *ki* every day without realizing it. Once you learn how to channel it properly, then you can become very efficient by using *ki*. There has to be *aiki*. This is one of the most important things. It's not just "strong *ki*." *Aiki* makes it efficient. This is why if you train for strong *ki* alone you might just end up using it incorrectly, you might be colliding. Then you have to overcome others with *ki*. But if you can blend, then you don't have to challenge others with *ki*. *Aiki* means "harmony with *ki*." Learn to respect others, everybody.

You can learn about *ki* in various sports. But because I learn it through aikido, that's the way for me to explain it. Of course, in sports, you want to win and that's, you know, not *aiki*. But if your timing is excellent, if you're fielding a grounder, as a second baseman, you'll feel the whole play. That's *aiki*.

I don't recommend that anybody go into this profession as a living, a way of life. I like people to help spread it but you can't make a living; it's not easy to make a living. I would have trouble without my university part-time job. Whenever you think you're trying to make money, you're going to water aikido down. This is what I don't believe in. I have so much to learn yet. It's a lifetime thing. I have no desire to spread my organization, to try to control a big number of followers. What I share with them is theirs; if they want to help me spread my teachings, I appreciate that.

I'm learning a lot from my students. I'm able to develop more things as I'm sharing my knowledge with them. And then I get new ideas from them. They're my teacher. Master Tohei also developed himself in this way. Having good students enabled him to develop himself.

The Founder of aikido, his dream was to have world peace through the growth of aikido. That's what I'm trying to carry out: expand the principles of aikido. I hope that through the principles, we'll have a better place to live.

The first time I saw O-Sensei was in 1968, in Japan. I went to his class. When he started teaching the class, I thought, "Well, I'm going to learn everything I can from him." So I just followed everywhere in the dojo he went, watching and trying to listen to his explanation, whatever he was saying. Then he turned around and looked at me, stared at me. Wow, that was scary, really scary. He stopped me in my tracks. We were not introduced. And afterwards when Master Tohei introduced me in the hallway, he was really nice, just bowed so low. I bowed back and I looked, he was still bowing. I could hardly go any lower. And he said, "I hear you're doing a good job spreading aikido in the United States. Thank you very much. That's really a good thing. Please continue the good work." When the Master tells you that, you can't quit. And that's one of the reasons I want to spread his teachings as long as I live. Even if I'm the last one, I'll still going to be doing it.

At that time, he was eighty-six and not very healthy. When I saw his exhibition at Kubiya Hall, he could hardly stand up by himself;

his legs were weak so two people helped him. And when he started performing, wow, what efficiency! It wasn't because he was so strong; he just harmonized with energy from the attackers. I understood his teachings about the proper usage of *ki*—proper usage, not how strong you are, proper usage of *ki* is important. This is what I emphasize now. Some people say, "Oh, I learned from O-Sensei," you know, bragging about it. It's not important that they trained with him. "Oh, I was the last *uchi deshi* of O-Sensei." I don't think that's important. What they have gained from that, that is what is important. A person could have trained with him for ten, twenty, thirty years. But if the person hasn't gained anything, and can't share his knowledge with other people, it's worthless. What have you gained, what can you show us, what can you share with us? This is important.　•

7

GEORGE SIMCOX

Of all the people in this book, George Simcox is the most enthusias-
tic, almost bubbly, supporter of aikido principles and the aiki *attitude*
that is so prevalent in the Ki Society. Like the other people in this Teach-
ers section, Simcox had a direct experience with O-Sensei. And as the
others perceived, that experience was characterized by the feeling that
O-Sensei was almost a new, advanced species. As Simcox says, O-Sen-
sei seemed to grow bigger as he stepped on the mat.

How Simcox ended up in Ki Society was, as he says, by accident,
but in retrospect, he would have chosen this path regardless. The Ki
Society developed because Tohei Sensei, the heir apparent to O-Sen-
sei, decided in 1974 that he needed to split from the main branch of
aikido. This was after the death of O-Sensei, and since Tohei Sensei
was aikido's main emissary from Japan to the States, it was natural
that many Americans followed him as he set up the Ki Society. Sim-
cox was one of those on the East Coast asked to form a dojo to prac-
tice Ki Society principles.

George is particularly eloquent in explaining the difference between
Ki Society training and the other main divisions of aikido practice.
The big difference, he feels, is that mainstream aikido proceeds from
the premise that continuous, rigorous physical practice will lead in
time to the aiki *attitude. This* aiki *attitude is described as a relaxed/cen-*
tered approach to attacks on the mat and the conflicts of life in gen-
eral. Ki Society's goal, from day one, is to train the aiki *attitude. They*
call it Ki Training.

These techniques of Ki Training, first developed by Tohei Sensei and expanded upon by the Ki Society, are the focus of George's unbounded enthusiasm.

I was born in Elkhart, Indiana, in 1933, May 9th. I moved to California when I was twelve. I was raised in San Francisco and entered the Army when I was in college during the Korean War. I went to the Officers' Candidate School, became an officer, and retired as a Lieutenant Colonel in 1973 after some assignments in Supply and Topography. Now I'm working in a topographical laboratory. I used to be the deputy director. Now I'm working with one of the civilians there. Got two children—one's in California playing music and one's here playing computers, which is not too dissimilar, actually.

I first encountered aikido in Japan, when I was on assignment in the military. This was at Camp Oji, just outside of Ikibakuru in Tokyo. One day a guy by the name of Nelson Fay who ran one of the divisions of the Far East Map Service came up to me and asked if I wanted to take aikido class. I asked, "Why?" "Well, we've got this club, and we've got a real problem here because we're going to lose our instructor if we don't get another student or two. And since you're not going to night school any more, we thought you'd like to join us." So I said, "What's it like?" "Well, it's a little bit like judo but not exactly." Nelson had come from a judo background. And since I was in Japan and had wrestled a little bit in college, I thought I ought to learn something. So sight unseen, I said, "Sure, why not? It's Tuesday and Thursday nights, I can go along with that."

So I showed up one Tuesday night—there was a small gymnasium on the base—and met the *sensei,* whose name was Iwakiri. I found Iwakiri Sensei to be a delightful man. He was, I think, an aikido instructor from Aikikai Headquarters, who also worked as an economist in a bank. He spoke reasonably good English and I think he was as interested in learning English as he was in teaching aikido, because after we'd finish class we would always go out and have a beer together at the officers' club. Well, they had a *gi* for me, which I put on. Then I went out there and did two hours of *nikkyo*. We used old tatami and when you hit them, the dust would come up in your face, you know; if you had allergies, it ruined you. I had ridden the bus to work that day, fortunately, because after I took the bus home and got to our house, I could not hold the door knob to open the door. So I kicked it so my wife would open the door, and she said, "What's the matter, is your hand broken?" And I said, "Very close." That was Tuesday night. Thursday night we did *kote gaeshi* all night long. After that, it was all uphill. They couldn't do anything worse than that.

Shortly after, I picked up a copy of Tohei Sensei's book, *The Art of Aikido,* which he had written earlier. It was for sale in the bookstore; I'd seen it in the PX but never purchased it. I read that and liked it. *Aikido in Daily Life* had come out about the time I started, so I picked up a copy of that, too, and read it. I liked what I read.

We practiced maybe four, five months. The club was sponsored by the Aikikai, and I had an Aikikai membership card as a result of practicing there. Practice back then was, well, we opened up class, we did vigorous exercises, then we immediately went into techniques. One night it was all *kote gaeshi*, one night it was all *nikkyo*. The teacher would demonstrate using one of us as a demonstrator, then we would practice with partners and he would correct us. We always finished with *kokyu dosa.* He never explained how to do *kokyu dosa.* Now Nelson was about 6 ft. 4 in. and weighed about 240 and Iwakiri weighed about 155, was about 5 ft. 7 in., 5 ft. 8 in. All Nelson would ever do was push. He would push mightily with his arms, slide backwards on the tatami, and skin the tops off his toes. And that was all that Nelson ever accomplished in the four months that I watched him do this because he never figured out how to push Iwakiri over. Now, we could push each other over real easy but we never learned how to push Iwakiri Sensei over.

Eventually the club dropped below four students, so we closed up. However, right at the end of that time they had the big 1966 demonstration down in Nakasaka, in Tokyo. And we went down—I think we sat in the third or fourth row of this very large auditorium—

I took that picture of O-Sensei up there on the wall with my small camera at that time. We saw O-Sensei demonstrate, we saw his son demonstrate, Tohei Sensei demonstrated and talked, I haven't a clue as to what he said. Then Iwakiri Sensei took us backstage and we were introduced to each of the three main instructors. So I guess I'm one of the few people left alive lucky enough to have at least met O-Sensei and have a few words with him. I was about thirty, thirty-three, when I met him.

Seeing O-Sensei was interesting. He sort of tottered along, you know, sat over in a corner, didn't say very much. But when it came time for him to get on the mat, he must have grown about eight inches in all directions. It was really a sight to behold, this trans-formation of a rather small, tired, elderly gentleman, stepping on the mat and having a presence that quite outdid what you had seen up until that time. I don't mean to say he wasn't an impressive guy. People who are eighty-six years old are fairly impressive-looking people anyway. But he was just transformed. I don't know how to describe it exactly. It was sort of like watching somebody wake up. Did you ever see somebody kinda sit there and you're talking to them and they're looking at you and you're talking to them and they look at you and all of sudden they understand and something occurs inside that makes them just sort of radiate energy for a while. Or when a kid is learning something new, they're transformed, at least momentarily, into something quite different from what you saw before that. Well, that's about what I saw in O-Sensei. He didn't really get bigger, but you saw something—the little walk changed, the sense of presence changed. It was very interesting.

It was very nice to have been in position to physically meet an individual who had so much influence, particularly in my later life. At the time I realized I was doing something very unusual, some-thing not everybody could do, simply because they weren't in the right place at the right time.

And then we closed up the club. When I moved to Hawaii to join the twenty-ninth Engineer Battalion in July of 1966, I called the Aikikai downtown and asked, "Where can I find aikido?" "Well, I think there's something up there somewhere. Maybe the YMCA can tell you where it's at." Well, I called the YMCA and yeah, they had classes on Tuesday and Thursday nights, which was kind of convenient because I was used to Tuesdays and Thursdays.

So I started taking classes in Hawaii from a fellow named Ishida. He was a very nice instructor. He also taught judo classes in another location. He was Japanese, *nisei*, an elderly gentleman. He was one of the earlier instructors. At the time he was one of the fellows on the board at the Aikikai, I think, in Hawaii. Anyway, I started practicing there. I spent about a week in Hawaii figuring out where this place was, and then I was there twice a week until I left Hawaii.

After I had been there for about a month, Ishida Sensei asked me if I would like to join the advanced class as well as the beginning class. He had an hour-and-a-half beginning class and a two-hour advanced class. There were a couple of [Caucasians] in the advanced class, maybe 10 percent were Hawaiians, and the rest were Japanese-American. There was one other American, a black belt named Dave Tallman; he kind of took me under his wing. I found the Hawaiian and Japanese students were really very delightful people. We got along very well. We were blessed with some Buddhist monks who practiced with us. One elderly gentleman was in his seventies and he was really pleasant to practice with. I got a real opportunity to mix at a very human level in Hawaiian society, which is not something you get to do very often as a military guy.

At that time they had promotions once a year. In February, I believe, I went down to the main dojo and I really thought we were there as a club to demonstrate, but we weren't; the demonstrations were for promotions, though nobody told me that. Different students from different clubs went out on the mat and they called out techniques, which were mainly the eight basic techniques, you know, *katate tori tenkan, shomen uchi ikkyo* and so forth. And then you did *bokken* and then you did *jo*, the two *kata*. This thing went on all day, lots and lots of people were there. And then the black belts got out and they all did *suwariwaza* techniques. Well, about three weeks later I was in the dojo and they started calling out names and hand-ing out yellow belts and blue belts. "What is this all about?" And the guy says, "There were promotions a couple of weeks ago." And I said, "What promotions?" and he says, "You know, we went down to demonstrate? Those demonstrations were promotions!" And they called my name and I went out and they gave me a brown belt; they promoted me to second *kyu*, which was kind of shocking. And the way they promoted you was they called your name out and they handed you the belt. I never saw any certificates or anything like that change hands.

Practice back then was different from what my students are used to now. I don't believe there was much philosophical reflection. If there was, it was lost on me. You know, part of that is the question, what's the student listening to? Ishida Sensei was a good instructor. He would get up, explain the technique a little bit, demonstrate it four or five times, and then he would go practice with somebody. If you were smart, you found somebody who looked like he knew what it was, because you could learn from them. I didn't get any philosophy instruction that I can think of, certainly not like I do here. It was exercise class, it was learning techniques, it was fun stuff to do, nice people to be around.

I think I practiced aikido because I enjoyed learning the kinds of things we were doing; I knew from Tohei Sensei's books that we were learning to go around energy and things like that. And I think that was true for most other people who were practicing. There were some young fellows, who loved to throw people around and to be thrown. They were out there for the sweat and the throwing and so forth.

There were others there for much deeper meanings; there was one fellow in our dojo, for example, who wore a *hakama* but did not have a black belt. One time I said, "That's interesting. Why is that?" And they said, "He has been with us fifteen years and he's never taken a promotion. One day Tohei Sensei said, 'Why doesn't he wear a *hakama*?' 'Well, Sensei, he has never been promoted.' 'Well, he's certainly qualified; tell him to wear one.' So he has been wearing one ever since." The examination wasn't the big issue.

People practiced for a lot of different reasons. Why do people go fish? I don't know. Some fish to eat and most of them go fish for the fun of fishing, and I think these people were there for the fun of being with the people who were there. It's a little bit like the story of the reporter asking the parachuter as he's getting ready to jump out of a C-141, "How are you feeling?" "I'm scared to death." When he asks him why he's scared to death, he says, "I don't like jumping out of airplanes." "Why in the world are you in the Airborne?" "Well, I like being with people who do." I think there were a lot of people who liked being with a lot of people who did these things. There were some older gentlemen in the class, 'cause you had a lot of very senior students there and elderly students, and they would sit around and tell war stories, about things they had seen Tohei Sensei do, things that O-Sensei had done. They'd sort of relive experiences from time to time as you'd stand around and talk. I wasn't aware of any great philosophical sense in these discussions. Now, I found the concept of turning away from the other person's energy appealing because it was kind of how I saw my life anyway. It's the way I had sort of functioned and so it fit a niche for me. I felt comfortable with that.

Anyway, two months after the exam I got put on orders to Vietnam, so I took my family back to the United States and practiced in San Francisco a few times with Bob Tann. Tann was a sheriff or police officer of some kind. He had his little store-front place down in South City; I think I went there three or four times. One night he was teaching people how to face a *shomen uchi* and to step aside, and he got it down fairly well. As a teaching tool, he brought out this thing that looked like a logging chain. He'd whip it over the top of his head and it would come down at you and you were supposed to go either right or left. Well, this one woman tried to go two directions at once. Half of her was going in one direction, half of her was going in the other, and she wasn't stretching at all. Tann saw that the chain was going right for her head, so he pulled the chain in like crazy and it landed on his feet; I think he hurt his foot in the process of getting that chain out of the way, but he never hurt his student, that was important.

While I was there I ran into a guy named Gene Sorensen who is now the Ki Society instructor in Houston. At the time he was the secretary of the Operating Engineers Union Local in the Bay Area. He's about 6 ft. 7 in. and weighed a svelte 270 or something like that. He and I got partnered up and I'm 5 ft. 2 in. and probably weighed 175 at the time. We were doing *kata tori ikkyo,* and I took one look at that big guy and pulled back with my shoulder and blew the whole thing. He proceeded to say, "No, no, no, don't do that." Once he got me to learn not to look at his size, it turned out the technique was rather easy to do. I learned a tremendously valuable lesson; I've always valued Gene's contribution for that one reason alone. He taught me something that I don't know anybody smaller could have taught me.

Several years later, Tohei Sensei started his own organization. Let's see. That happened in '71, as I recall. In '71 I was living in Washington; there was no aikido here. I had one meeting with Tohei Sensei prior to that time. It happened to be over in Hawaii on a government trip, in 1970, I believe. As soon as I got in town, I called up the dojo to see how things were going and went up for Tuesday's class. A guy I knew there, Dave Tallman, says to me, "Hey, Tohei Sensei's in town. We're gonna have dinner tomorrow night, come as my guest." I said, "Great!" So I joined Dave and we went down to the "Inn of the Seventh Happiness." The dinner, which was in honor of Tohei Sensei, was held upstairs. I enjoyed the dinner very much. Afterward, when Dave went over to talk to Tohei Sensei, he took me along and introduced me. Tohei Sensei asked me what I was doing. When I said I was living in Washington, D.C., he said I should start a club. I said, "Gee, Sensei," and Dave said, "Hey, he's second *kyu!*" "I haven't practiced in a while, I'm not really comfortable with that." Tohei Sensei said, "Well, if you do, let me know." Subsequent to that, Tohei Sensei left the Aikikai and founded Ki Society.

My first real back-into-aikido experience occurred in 1974 in November. A gentleman named Kurt Fowler, who now teaches in Arizona, moved to Reston [Virginia] with the Drug Enforcement Administration and he opened an aikido program at a recreation center there. They advertised a demonstration in the paper. My wife saw the ad and told me about it, so we went out to Reston to see this demonstration. It was about twenty-five miles from my place. It was snowing, the first snow of the year. The Fire Department didn't know where the address was. I mean, that's tough, when the Fire Department doesn't know where the address is. But we finally found it. When I went inside, I saw a *ki* symbol and Tohei Sensei's picture and I knew I was in an aikido club that was worthy of being called an aikido club. They had two guest instructors. One was Sumio Toyoda from Chicago, and the other one was Suji Maruyama from Philadelphia. They'd come to help Kurt get his program going. That was the first time I saw *ki* breathing and a couple of other things, so I knew something was a little different, because I hadn't seen that when I was in Hawaii. They asked me if I'd like to take a small mini-lesson and we did *mune tsuki kote gaeshi* . I turned Kurt around, spun him on his head and held him down. He looked up and said, "You've done this before," and I said, "Yes, second *kyu* out of Hawaii." "Are you coming back?" "Yeah, of course." He said, "Thank God." So now I had somebody I could help and I joined in January of 1975.

I didn't know about the split until that summer when I went up to see Tohei Sensei in New York. He was at St. John's University on Long Island. I had a brother-in-law who lived on Staten Island, so it was easy to get a place to stay. Kurt and I and some others went up to attend Tohei Sensei's seminar. The Philadelphia club made all the arrangements. In talking to everybody around the place, I realized that there was a Ki Society and there was an Aikikai; they were different. When you visited one or the other, you didn't seem to see much difference, but our schools all had Tohei Sensei's picture up front and their schools didn't. In a way I didn't actively select Ki Society; I kind of fell into it. Now, had I been given a choice, I would have picked it.

My personal, Simcox view of the world, is that Tohei Sensei is an American creation, that he would never have gone in the direction he did if it had not been for his experience in America from '53 on. Americans did something the Japanese rarely do. A: We're lazy practicers for the most part. B: We ask "Why?" a lot. He just wasn't used to getting questioned why and he found out there were answers to why. His whole teaching mechanism is built up dealing with the whys that he got here in the United States. That's my personal opinion. When I asked Kashiwara Sensei about that he said, "Well, I don't think I disagree with you." He didn't say he agreed with me, there's a difference there. But I feel that his American experience decidedly impacted where he wanted to go with his aikido. His feeling for the art was influenced. And I think that's true of anybody going any place and getting new experiences. That experience is bound to impact them unless they're a terribly rigid personality. And I don't believe Tohei Sensei is a terribly rigid personality. Like everybody, he has his rigidities, I suspect, but he is a marvelously flexible individual as well. I believe that most of what we do here is universal.

Going on, Fowler promoted me to first *kyu* a little bit later. Then he took off to Mexico, got reassigned, and I took over as chief instructor here in Washington, in the Reston program. He and I sat down with Tohei Sensei and talked; I had a seven-day practice session up there, and Tohei Sensei concurred in that judgment. So that's when I became chief instructor.

At the same seminar all the people on the East Coast got together and exchanged information and that was kind of the start of the Ki Society on the East Coast. Suji Murayama in Philadelphia, Mayazumi Sensei up in New York, a couple of people in the Connecticut area, a branch dojo in Philly, and there was Dan Frank and there was our group in Reston.

We also found out about an Aikikai group in our area led by Clyde Takeguchi. I didn't have any problems going over and practicing at Clyde's periodically. In fact, I used to go over there and practice and if he wasn't available, he'd ask me to teach for him. That went on for about a year and a half. Then, finally things started getting different enough that it didn't make sense to do that anymore.

I put up a sign in my dojo yesterday. It says, "We teach attitudes leading to action." In the Ki Society you'll see that we teach *ki* training, we teach mind and body harmony. We're trying to teach an attitudinal situation, and we practice aikido to show that action can reflect that attitude, that there is action that is effective that results from a positive attitude. I think that classic aikido tends to feel that practicing aikido rigorously and in a very dedicated fashion will lead you to an attitudinal change. And I would not fault that argument, except that I don't think it happens very often.

Generally, people learn from something what they intended to learn from it when they went into it, or they drop out fairly soon. If you come in looking to throw some guy across the floor, you may or may not adapt to the fact that gosh, I have to change my way of thinking about things to do this. I see a lot of grunt-and-groan aikido that goes on where you throw your opponent in spite of himself rather than because of himself. My own philosophy is you do a defense *because,* you don't "do a defense." In other words, something is initiated and the defense arises out of that initial action and you probably figure out what it was that happened after it's over, not before. I don't say, "Well, I'm going to throw this guy with a *kote gaeshi.*" I haven't a clue whether the *kote gaeshi* is appropriate until the moment of truth, and it may not be appropriate at all. Learning how to grunt through a technique when it's wrong or when it's inappropriate doesn't teach that what you're looking for is an attitude of not grunting through a technique when it's wrong. I think you have to say that up front. I've seen a lot of instructors spend a lot of time trying to teach a guy how to make a technique work. I don't think good technique is "made to work." Now, if you're trying to teach the guy good form so that the technique is easy to do, it's probably appropriate, but rarely do you hear it articulated that way. Instead it's, "Now throw your hand this way and you can really get on this guy." To me, that's not what we're trying to do, in the Ki Society, certainly. Tohei Sensei talks a lot about a happier, more pleasant, more gentle world and he wants to use his system to try to create that. He not only talks about doing that, but the classes are set up in a way intended to do that. Others talk a lot about love and happiness and harmony, and then you watch them practice and you

wonder where it all went. It certainly doesn't look like a loving, harmonious bunch of people out there.

One of the things that pleases me about our dojo is that for the
most part people walk in as visitors and regardless of why they're
here, they'll sit down and look and they'll say, "What a harmonious-
looking group of people. Everybody seems to be out there doing nice
collective things." And even if they think, "This is not going to teach
me how to kick butt, so I'm not going to take this," well, that's okay.
If you really want to know how to do that, we're probably not the
place to be. We're not going to help you learn that here. In fact, when
people say, "I want to learn self-defense," I'll say, "What do you mean
by self-defense?" and they'll say, "What do you mean by 'what do
you mean?'" And I'll say, "If you've defended yourself, what does
your opponent look like?" If he's a bloody pile of trash at your feet,
this is not the place you want to come, because we won't teach you
how to do that.

That sort of attitude has been there all along if you cared to look
for it. Westbrook and Raitti wrote about it when they wrote *Aikido
and the Dynamic Sphere* and talked about the four levels of violence
with aikido at the highest level, where you put the attacker down
and walk away as opposed to picking a fight and then stomping the
guy. So I think that it was conceptually available and understandable. I'm not sure that a lot of people practiced for that reason. I
don't know. I don't know that I was into looking at why people practiced. I'm not sure that when I first started teaching that I was into
that issue as much. I mean, I think I followed the forms that Ki Society proscribes. I'm not sure I had a philosophy of my own yet that
exactly coincided with what Tokyo was trying to do. I spent a lot of
time trying to learn techniques instead of learning the why of techniques, trying to learn the what.

First we go through a what process, and pretty soon we go
through a why process. And then pretty soon you think, "Gee, this
is interesting." The most interesting things that take place have
absolutely nothing to do with what we overtly do on the mat. I had
a guy telling me yesterday, "George, this is marvelous. Yesterday, I

walked into our accounting department and I hear this woman screaming through a telephone. I talked to her for a few minutes, took care of her problem, and, you know, used *ki* principles in talking to her, relaxed her and so forth. I walked in on Friday and a florist had shown up delivering some flowers from her because she was apologizing for her attitude. And here I was wondering what I had done. All I did was apply the principles that I've learned here. I came here to learn aikido. I still like it, it's fun. But gosh, I use these other things all the time, keeping one-point, relaxing completely, taking a broad look at a problem instead of taking a very narrow view of a problem."

One of the students here is a lawyer, a state attorney for the Commonwealth of Virginia. He was telling me of a case where he was on the Commonwealth's side, a personal injury case of some sort. The particulars aren't very important, but after the defendant finished his testimony about this devastating situation that happened, he turned around and blithely waltzed back to the table. The lawyer says, "I was watching him walk back and I suddenly realized that he was walking like nothing was wrong with him at all. So I stood up and said, 'Your Honor, I certainly appreciate the testimony of the defendant in this particular case. I want to call the jury's attention to his total testimony, not only what he said but to that delightful little walk that he had all the way back to his desk.'" He said the defense attorney looked up, rolled his eyes, and that was the end of that case. And my student said, "I would never have been in a position to make that observation if I hadn't taken training here at the club, because I would have been so busy trying to think of what I was going to do next that the reality of the opening would have never been apparent to me. One of the things I've learned here is that as a lawyer, I have to not only deal with my perception of what's going on but I also have to step back and see what's going on, because there are many things going on simultaneously; and when you focus too narrowly on something, you miss the rest of it and your chance to do something important may be gone."

We have a lot of people who seem to think that the way to get out of a problem is to walk straight through it. Now we all know that if we work in buildings, we look for the doors. But if we have personal problems, we don't look for the doors, we crash through.

Tohei Sensei's idea is you want calmness in the mind as well as calmness in the body. We can't really test the calmness in the mind very well but we can test the body. And if the body is calm and the mind and body are one, then the mind should be calm as well. There are Ki Society tests where you stand with mind and body coordinated and somebody applies pressure to your chest to see whether he meets resistance or not. There's a real art in how to do that, because it's very easy to attack a person's chest, which is quite different from touching a person's chest for evaluation. So we try to emphasize in Ki Society that we are testing to evaluate and to help the person progressively move ahead. We're not testing to defeat the person, to prove that they can't do something, but to rather help them learn that they can do something. I've seen that done in a few other places, but not very often.

Yesterday I had an instructor's group in my dojo, and we were chatting, and one of my guys who is studying to be an instructor— he's a professional school teacher—says, "You know, George, we did something last night. It was really very interesting. You had us practice the number of ways in which we could fail a particular test. I've never seen that done before and it was marvelous. I learned more about this whole process sitting there playing with ways to fail than I ever would have learned just passing the test. It was delightful. I've gotta try to figure out how to use that on my school work, except I'll drive the people in the school system nuts if I run around talking to them about how to fail things." And yet sometimes, if you want a good scientific experiment, you have to fail a lot of times before you find the true path. What we do here is look for ways of trying to move people forward in some fashion.

We can guide people in how to use continuous projections of energy to accomplish anything. One of Clyde's students works over in the mail distribution center in Landover and he was having trouble pushing these big mail carts around, 'cause he's a little guy, kind of a thin, elderly fellow. I gave him a class on mind and body coordination and he went wild. This was one of the last classes I gave before I stopped teaching over there. I saw him a few months later and he said, "Wow, I haven't had a bad day pushing those things around since. Now I just take a hold of the mail cart, get my one-point and move out."

That's what I mean by improving. So I use "unbendable arm" not as a trick, that's not the value of it; the unbendable arm is valuable because it helps you to redirect energy very efficiently. We help students try to understand that, let pressure build up to the point where it's getting very massive, and then suddenly turn everything off. It's tantamount to walking up the stairway, pulling yourself up by the handrail and suddenly, the handrail gives way and you collapse in a pile.

An important point is that Ki Society techniques have evolved. We're doing new things all the time. Friday night we had negative instruction, we explored how many ways you can fail. That's the first time we've ever done that. We probably do one or two new things a week. It's really old wine in new bottles, it's different ways of looking at something from another perspective. You can take forty pictures of the same mountain, and you can make them look like forty different mountains if you take them from different perspectives. That's a lot of what goes on in Ki Society. I find as you teach, you'll open your mouth and say things, and sometimes you wonder why you said them, and if you follow them far enough, you'll know by the end of the evening why. I've never had it happen yet that it wasn't a very positive thing that occurred.

Some people think that if you don't have a core of intense physical training, somehow something's missing. Well, somehow, something's missing to be true—the question is, is the something that's missing something that you need? To train hard to become soft is a little difficult and a contradiction in terms. You have to train soft. Should you train vigorously? I think so. But in the end, it isn't the vigor that's important, unless you're trying to take on eight attackers somewhere in a dark alley. And if you're damn fool enough to be in an alley with eight attackers, there probably isn't any hope for you anyway.

I think hard physical training can make you confident. Confidence can help you become calm. But I think that you have to understand what calmness is. There's a calmness that comes from meditation, where you sit in a corner and meditate or you go to some place and you learn how to meditate. The difficulty with that kind of calmness is that when you walk away from the place where you are, it also tends to go away. Tohei Sensei likes to talk about the monk who goes and sits under the waterfall for four years. Well, eventually he gets enlightened and comes back down. But when he steps into the street, a great big Isuzu truck goes by with the air horns blaring and the guy yells, he loses it all and goes back up to the waterfall again. You get very clean that way, but you know, you can't live like that. We're teaching an activity for learning, and one way to teach calmness is to point out that calmness is an active thing. If you ask an American to relax, the first thing that they'll do is they'll slump. I say, "That is not relaxation, that is collapsing." The opposite of collapsing is tension, and a lot of Americans will get tense. Sometimes we're tense and we know we're tense; sometimes we're tense and we don't know it. Usually, if you're driving down the road and you get caught in a traffic jam, you get tense and don't know it. Suddenly you find your shoulders are up, your neck is hurting, and you realize you're tense. And once you understand that you can relax.

What I try to do here and what the Ki Society tries to do is to teach that there is collapse on the one hand, and there's rigidity and tension on the other, and in between is this thing that we call "calm." Calm is a living state, it is a dynamic state. It's the calmness of the rapidly spinning top, not the calmness of the top that has lost all of its energy and fallen over. It's the calmness that makes the unbendable arm an unbendable arm. I can stiffen my arm out and make it act like an unbendable arm, and I get all sorts of terrible things happening to my elbow joint when I do that. But if I relax all the muscles and fill myself with energy, my arm is unbendable and I'm calm. The other example I like to think of is that tension is like the power of the pipe, but calmness is like the power of the water flowing through the pipe. The power of the water that washes through the pipe is the power that allows you to get out the gold. You can take the pipes out and beat on the rocks all day long and not find the gold, but allowing the water to sluice out and hit that mountain and wash the dirt down and help you sluice the gold is a very effective way of doing it, lousy for the ecology, but it's an effective way of mining gold.

I read a book one time where the author made the observation that aikido was the one of the most aggressive arts there is. It's tremendously aggressive because we get the attacker doing what we want him to do and then we clean his clock. And when you can make a guy do what you want him to do and then clean his clock, you're working with an aggressive bunch of people. Well, it isn't quite that way. But we do elicit behavior, because in offering the hand in a particular way, you can encourage behavior. In offering it a different way, you can encourage other behavior. So we try to teach the student in his learning a technique how as a *nage* he makes his offering. We try to teach that this technique is effective against this kind of a *ki* on the part of your attacker; whether he knows he has *ki* or not, he does, and he's attacking in a particular way. This technique is for that kind of *ki* in this kind of condition. If you change the *ki*, then the conditions have changed and I have to change the defense. Teaching you how to defend against the wrong *ki* is not doing you any favors. I owe you an opportunity to learn how to defend against that particular *ki*.

The reason that classes get a little wild once in a while is because we'll run into a bunch of students defending in a different fashion, you know, the *nages* or the *ukes* will be behaving a little strange that night, so then we'll go into teaching how to deal with the strangeness you encounter. It doesn't do any good to tell a student here that we're teaching how to deal with life in general and then say, "No, no, no, you're not attacking right," because they are going to attack that way. Our purpose is to help the students learn to become more confident individuals. You don't make a guy become a more confident, relaxed individual by saying, "No, no, no, don't attack that way." So, as a local instructor, one of my jobs is to try and encourage my students to understand how to be relaxed, how to be calm, and when facing a weird technique, not to say, "No, no, no, that's wrong. Do this," but to say "Okay. I have this. Now I have the opportunity to do that. Thank you very much for bringing that in."

Kashiwara Sensei, an important Ki Society teacher, made an observation to me while he was visiting my dojo. He said somebody had studied with me a little bit. This student said one of the things he liked about what I did was that I did all this in a very American way. I don't do any stuff Japanese. When we bow in, I don't have people giving the Japanese sign for bowing in, *Onegaeshimasu*, we don't do that. I'm not into that. I don't set the dojo up with a lot of oriental trappings. Most of the calligraphy you see were given to us and those are revered gifts. They're there because they are very real things to the dojo as presents and things. Otherwise, it's a very unJapanese facility. And I believe aikido can be very American, that Ki Society can do very well in the American culture. But we have to find the tools, the things that appeal to Americans. They may not necessarily be those that appeal to the Japanese.

The motto I put up in the dojo, the one I mentioned earlier, "We teach attitude leading to action, not action," this is a kick I've been on lately. In fact, in our instructors' group yesterday, we spent an hour and a quarter talking about that and twenty minutes practicing technique because they know technique. I've been working on how we can make this program more useful to the students. How can we help the students to more easily learn the daily living aspects of what we're teaching? And how can we teach them to be comfortable with those things, because sometimes people learn this stuff, but they're not comfortable doing it 'cause it feels kind of mystical. How do you make them feel more comfortable in dealing with the spiritual side of aikido so they can talk about it amongst themselves outside of the facility? I'm not trying to create a bunch of evangelists, in that sense, but I want them to be very comfortable with what they're doing and why they're doing it and to share their experiences, because in sharing your experiences, you find that you're not alone.

THE INNOVATORS

8

TOM CRUM

Tom Crum has done more than anyone, except perhaps George Leonard, to bring an awareness of aikido principles to the general public. Aiki Works takes him all over the world leading seminars and training workshops. His book, The Magic of Conflict, *has become a bible to many managers in American industry, government, and labor.*

Crum is a handsome man in the mold of Robert Redford. They share the same sandy-red hair. It is doubtful, however, that Redford could do fifty one-handed push ups or throw an attacker twice his size with big, effortless motions like Crum does.

Crum's aikido roots extend back through the Rod Kobayashi/Tohei Sensei line. A characteristic of this line has always been the effort to integrate aikido principles into daily life.

Many Americans who saw O-Sensei or studied his life and thoughts have concluded that he created something new. In terms of conflict, first there was the animalistic tooth-and-claw approach, then over time the broader concept of the warrior emerged—the one who fights and defends for a greater cause—and now there is aikido, a new archetype in the conflict arena. It is to this wider meaning of aikido that Tom has devoted his energy.

Tom relates a personal experience when he first felt the kind of power that comes from moving from the center. Much of what he has to say here is a further exploration and expansion of the possibility of moving from center. Operating out of center is the most important training principle in aikido and Tom builds on it in three ways. One, he points out that in a physical sense, it is the antithesis of being closed, holding onto your old ground, being tense and weak, with shallow breathing. Two, he connects operating from your center to what others, like Joseph Campbell, have called following your bliss. Three, and probably the most interesting idea Crum presents, is relating the obsessive need we feel to be right and all the painful psychological baggage that goes with it to the desire to win in a fight or conflict.

It is the goal of aikido training to replace the necessity to kill or beat the opponent with the experience of operating from the center, where both the aggressor and the victim come out safe and well.

Tom is on a mission to bring the Aiki message to as many people as possible. With his classic good looks and booming voice, he seems well suited to his own bliss.

I grew up in Washington, D.C., in a little town called Tacoma Park, which is half in D.C., half in Maryland. So I lived in a very ethnically diverse area and loved the martial arts from when I was very little, starting with John Wayne movies, into anything that seemed to have a certain amount of combat to them. My father got me my first set of boxing gloves when I was eight years old. They were like gigantic pillows you strapped to your wrist. That was a great experience to have my father bring home these big gloves to a little kid. And so my first awareness of getting actively involved was having kids in the neighborhood come to our fenced-in backyard, and we'd take a big pot from the kitchen and hit it with a big spoon, that signaled round one. And the only way to get out of the ring or the fenced-in area was to bleed, feign death or cry. So we learned how to do all of those things.

I didn't have any brothers. I had a sister, an older sister. But I had cousins who lived right up the street. And seeing how it was a fairly dense neighborhood of folks, there were kids all over the place, so it was very easy to find camaraderie in the neighborhood. At any rate, we had all these kids come down, we'd hit the "bell" and that was it. It taught me some things about conflict that I'm still trying to unlearn to this day! But I really loved it, I immediately fell in love with anything that had to do with physical combat.

In high school I did boxing, wrestling and then a great American sport called football, which was definitely a martial art. Then after my teenage years I got more formally involved with karate, t'ai chi ch'uan and kung fu, prior to learning aikido. I got real beat up in those kinds of activities, particularly football. The physical abuse left me, by the time I was in my early twenties, pretty beat up. I had a couple of serious back injuries where the doctors declared I would not be able to do anything again, and knee operations where the doctors again wrote me off. It was one of the great opportunities of my life to experience the fact that the medical community is limited in its knowledge as to what real healing is about, to what the power of the mind and the body working together can accomplish. I mean, I can remember lying on the hospital bed after an operation just wanting to know when I could play ball again, and the doctor walked away saying, "You'll never be able to do anything again other than a light game of golf." And that's pretty intimidating, pretty devastating to a young person.

You know, we've tended to treat physicians as gods ever since the days of penicillin. Right after penicillin there was a major shift in the way we viewed the local guy in the neighborhood who you trusted to support you in certain ways. All of a sudden we had a miracle man who could prescribe a pill, which could heal from diseases people normally died from. Penicillin ushered in a whole different way of being treated by the medical community.

So since I grew up in that post-penicillin world, when a doctor said something like that, I tended to believe him. And, of course, we experience what we believe in this world, not the other way around. So I had this incredibly negative diagnosis about my health, and if I didn't have some very powerful people around me and also some prior knowledge—looking at different philosophies, looking at different attitudes—I think I would have bought into that belief system and I'm sure I would have validated or verified it. But I had some real supportive people around me who said, "Maybe this is the best opportunity you've ever had, maybe this is the best opportunity for you to look at what's below this tip of the iceberg called the physical body." They said, "Maybe these mind, spirit, and body integration philosophies and disciplines are real, maybe there's some reality to them, maybe that's what you're supposed to do, maybe that's why you injured yourself because now you get to walk your talk." So it put me on a massive search and I had to dramatically change how I lived my life.

As I say, I grew up athletic and participated actively in boxing, wrestling, football, anything that had to do with combat, if you will. That was my real love. And yet I found myself extremely spiritual by nature. I didn't have a real formal religious training. There wasn't any pressure for me to get involved in religious activities, and maybe that's the reason I began to study religion on my own. I got very sick when I was in eighth grade, ninth grade. In ninth grade I broke a number of bones in sequence; I broke one, healed that, I broke another, healed that. Then I got very sick with pneumonia and I became very anemic after that. So here I was, only in ninth grade, this very, very active person who could hardly walk a block before I had to sit down and rest. So I picked up the Bible, by myself. Usually, that sort of thing works the other way around. The more pressure you have on some kind of religious training, the stronger your inclination to run away from it. But for me, I just said, "Hey, I've heard this is a great book," so I started reading it on my own. And then my health started to return, and things started to happen in a real powerful way, and I got very much involved in philosophical, spiritual thought. I instituted grace in my own home—how many fourteen-, fifteen-year-old boys come down and declare to their family that they'd like to say grace? It's not the usual thing we do.

This was an era when we didn't have the new-born Christianity or the whatever it was in the '50s. And yet I loved everything that I ever picked up that had that philosophical-spiritual context, from *Siddhartha* to Christianity to a kind of oriental, samurai philosophy. Like a magnet I was drawn to it all. And that just sort of stood in juxtaposition to this wonderful physical activity. I just loved to go out and run into things. So it was interesting, I guess you could say it was a split, but in my mind it never was. I can remember in high school when I was captain of the football team, I'd go before games into a church to meditate. It wasn't a church that I ever attended, it was a Catholic church that was open. Pretty soon I had a lot of the ball players go with me and we'd just go and sit quietly before a game. This was in the early '60s—I mean, this was really strange stuff to see in those days. But it was really where my inclination naturally led me. And so I'm sort of thankful that I didn't have a strong religious training. In my family, religion was one of those things where you should go to Sunday School or church for a while, and then when you're older you play golf instead of going to church. So there was a lack of strong rigor and discipline around any religious training, and as a consequence, I think I grew naturally toward it. It was fascinating how so many people ran away from it.

But there was this split. I can remember distinctly disliking bullies when I was very young. This was before I had any kind of religious training whatsoever. I really felt bad in school when I found people getting abused. I was one of those naturally athletic, smart, good-looking kinds of people, so it wasn't that I was getting abused that made me so angry with it. There was just a gut-level feeling of empathy for people who got picked on because of their size, intellect or skill level. There was this intense dislike for bullies. It was also, I can remember, a very real part of my upbringing. And negotiating, reconciling people, resolving fights was always a particular natural skill that I had when I was very young. Even in elementary school I was breaking up fights. So although I loved physical combat, football, boxing, wrestling, martial arts, it was the challenge of it, not the anger in me that caused me to go with that.

I went to college at Bucknell University in Pennsylvania and played football all four years as a defensive back and kick-off/punt return person. I graduated with a degree in mathematics and got a job working as a systems analyst for a multi-national company down in Houston, Texas. Being down there, I really felt that the rug had been pulled out from under me, on all levels. I had had a child. Of course, I had been in a relationship three years prior to having a child, but I didn't expect a child and marriage and all of that to happen at that rate that it did. Suddenly, I found myself with responsibility, a job I didn't like in a geographic, political climate that wasn't what I would have chosen. All this wonderful physical stuff was suddenly taken away. I couldn't run, I couldn't do any of this stuff I was able to do. So I was in this massive depression on a variety of levels. I was so far down that I really turned once more to real spiritual seeking, and I just started opening myself up to prayer and to meditation. And I found some very supportive people who helped me through that significant time.

So, anyway, that was a shift, a major shift. From that moment, it was step by step. There wasn't any miraculous healing. It took, I'd say, three years from that point to get into what I would call full recovery or the transformation into a new me. So drop by drop, I changed the way I ate, my work-out patterns. I became more involved with meditation and more involved in my own disciplines, lapping up everything around me in terms of the physical arts, the martial arts. I got into arts like shotokan, kung fu and t'ai chi ch'uan, which was the first of the martial arts that I saw had a little different perspective than just fighting. Again, for me, the fighting aspect did something internally that made me feel more vital. But always I wanted to use it somehow in a Superman or Robin Hood way to protect the innocent. It was the classic warrior mentality.

From t'ai chi I got the first inkling of the idea that there was another way in the physical arts besides the fist-versus-fist approach, there was a whole other approach. But studying t'ai chi and teaching t'ai chi, I found that for me it was a little too nebulous, a little too ambiguous. I didn't have a real feedback mechanism to give me tangible, measurable feedback, and that's what aikido had. It's a little more powerful.

So I left Houston. I came here to Aspen, Colorado, in 1970. I realized that so much of my dilemma had to do with the fact that I never really followed my heart. I always sort of lived out of the approval box, getting someone's approval, whether it was from parents, teachers or friends. So I made a major commitment to follow my heart.

My life didn't work the other way around, and I had had the rug sufficiently pulled out from under me that I had a lot of motivation and
courage to take a new stand, a new stand for life. I wrote a letter to
my folks and I basically said I trust that you think that I have a good
heart and that you love and trust me, and I want you to know that
from this day forward I am going to follow my heart. That's something that I haven't done, and it's going to take a lot of courage on
my part and your part to let me do that. If you trust that I have a
good heart, then you'll trust me when I follow it and there won't be
any pressure from you to do it the way you wanted me to do or the
way that you think it should be done. Basically, it was a divorce
notice saying I wanted to move out of any parental approval box
that I was in, consciously or unconsciously, and I wanted to step
forward in life in a dramatic and new way. I sent that letter off at a
very dramatic time in my life. And to this day I have not received a
reply to that letter. To this day.

At any rate, I sold everything, quit my job, got a VW van—it was
the '60s, right? —and piled everybody in it and went to the mountains. I proceeded to follow my heart by devoting myself first to my
own training, which happened to be in the mind-body disciplines,
whether it was martial arts or yoga or meditation. All of it was starting to fall into a very focused discovery of who I was and an integration of body and spirit, whether that had to be with nutrition or
whether it had to be with meditation or whether it had to be with
martial arts.

It was in the summer of '73 that we created the Aspen Academy
of Martial and Healing Arts. I joined with Marshall Ho, who was a
t'ai chi master and Bob Bishop, who had his Ph.D. in regional planning and was also a martial artist. We were very interested in creating an academy that brought together for the first time a variety
of arts. In the late '60s, early '70s, it was still a very isolated, terri-
torial imperative kind of system in the martial arts. If you studied
one martial art, that's all you studied. You never went outside of
your dojo. Other arts were available, but not to you. You chose one
and that was it. You found one teacher and that was it. There was

this very archaic system in the martial arts. We felt that the United States, being the great synthesizer, was the place where we could bring together arts from five countries—the Philippines, Japan, China, the United States and Korea. We felt that we could bring them together in such a way that the students and teachers would really begin to discover some common threads while the students were still nurtured in the art that was best for them rather than in the one that they happened to find in their own neighborhood. And we proceeded to do that.

We started an academy and would bring in 100–200 students for a four- to eight-week period. It was very interesting to have Koreans, Japanese, Americans, Filipinos and Chinese all together under one roof sharing training. It was a very dramatic, highly progressive learning time for all of us. And we didn't just do techniques; we'd talk about what you do in your art, how does it work, what's the common ground, what's the thread here—which in the early '70s, I mean, this was very far-out stuff. Everyone knew about other martial arts, but to actively come together and say this is what I do, what do you do, what's the common thread, that was unique. That's when I realized at a very deep level that there was something going on here that I was learning that could be useful to the world at large and it had to do with bringing people together to find common ground. We were bringing people together who were isolated and often very competitive with one another—I mean, even though they might not have spoken it, they were isolated and competitive and opinionated. To bring these people together and start working out common ground and have it be productive was a fascinating experience for what's possible in terms of resolving differences.

And then, of course, as I started to work more with aikido, that was just a revelation. Obviously, at the academy, one of the arts that we had was aikido, which was an art that I had read about but never participated in. Rod Kobayashi was the first aikido instructor we had here that very first summer. I was just really impressed with his being, his way of being and his way of moving. And although I was studying the art, I had a lot of other arts in my mind and in my body.

So it was just sort of another thing to add to my bag of tricks, until one day, at the end of the day, there was Mr. Kobayashi and he was working out with this big guy, maybe 6 ft. 2 in., 210 pounds, throwing him all over the mat, and I was watching this. Of course, I'd been practicing it, but as I watched it, I just saw it differently. I saw the movements, but I saw something else. I saw it as a metaphor, a distinct metaphor for living in the world; and yet, nothing really fit at that moment or clicked at that moment until they got down on their knees and did *kokyu dosa*. The student grabbed Rod by the forearms and Rod moved so easily, throwing him over, over and over again. And finally Rod looked up at me and said, "Would you like to play? Would you like to participate?"

Of course, in my mind, "play" meant "win," so metaphorically, I put on my helmet and my mouthpiece and buttoned my chin strap and I went for the win. I went over there and got down and grabbed him by the forearms, ready to win. But when I grabbed him by the forearms, there was that soft but powerful feeling: It wasn't like wood or steel, like when you wrestle with a person; it had a very soft, pliable feel but very, very powerful, full of *ki*, full of *chi*, but in my mind, it was just so distinctly different from what I felt power was that it was alarming. But of course, I immediately forgot about that and went back into the push. So I'm down pushing and struggling and straining, face all clenched up and muscles bulging. And in my frustration, because it was literally like pushing a mountain, nothing was moving, my eyes went up his chest to his face and there he is, big smile, eyes beaming, very relaxed, and as soon as our eyes met, he said *domo arigato*, "thank you very much," and I was on my back.

So I got right back up again and the first thing out of my mouth was that I wasn't trying, right? That's what I said, I wasn't trying 'cause that's usually what we do: when your belief system gets shattered sufficiently, you go into denial. So for me, in my mind, I must have not been trying. So I went back and accessed my martial arts bag of tricks and realized, maybe I needed a lower leverage point. So I got my center much lower and watched my breathing —maybe he caught me on an inhalation, because that's physiologically weaker than exhalation. Maybe it was the way he looked me in the eyes 'cause there's a moment of paralysis when you catch a person in the eyes. So I'm watching all of this stuff and accessing all of my strategies and techniques. I'm struggling; he's relaxed; I'm on my back! And it only took three or four times for this, and I'm sufficiently dense that it takes at least three or four times, sometimes more of something happening to me before I say maybe I can learn something here. It was a real small moment in time, but a really big moment in that something really crystallized in my body.

For all the previous years of training, there was always a seeming break between what I held philosophically and spiritually and what the world actually looked like in the streets. One didn't fit the other. There were of course the Buddhas and the Jesus Christs and Mahatma Gandhis who walked the planet but they were very special people, not ordinary folks like you and me, and therefore there was still a break between philosophical, spiritual understanding and in-the-street what we do. But for the first time I guess it all came together in a real powerful way where I realized that there's something here that in a direct physical confrontation was easy to see, there's another kind of power. It all fit, the spiritual, philosophical and the physical connections suddenly became all one in that feeling. That was just one little moment. But it was a moment that shifted me mentally in such a way that I made a decision, a commitment, that I would really take a look, not just at the common threads of all these martial arts, but I would specifically begin to look at the thread of *aiki* or this willingness to blend, this ability to blend that existed in all these arts, as well as in what I was doing in my daily life.

So out of all the common threads in the martial arts, I focused on the common thread called *aiki* that was in every aspect of my life. And that's when I just started to collect data and write it down and use it in my training. I asked myself what's going on, what is t'ai chi doing? What is karate doing? What is kung fu, what is aikido? And where in parenting, education, sports, does this occur, where fist-versus-fist is not the real powerful way? Getting run over and acquiescing is obviously not powerful; it could be powerful if you were real manipulative and good at that, and a fist can be powerful if you're able to rape, pillage and plunder—if you have that kind of force and you use that predominantly, successfully, you can have power. But the rape-pillage-plunder and the manipulative approach to life clearly weren't the only ways, and when I experienced all three, this third way was distinctly more powerful and of much more service and relevance to where the world is right now.

Then I started training aikido on a regular basis at the academy. We started at seven in the morning and would go until ten at night; that's intensive training. But although I was still studying and working with three major arts at the same time, I had a focus on *aiki*, even though it wasn't just from aikido. The Philippine art of *escrima* had *aiki*, *kali* had *aiki*, and the karate had *aiki* in it. So I just intensively focused all day long on the arts, though aikido became the main art, because *aiki* was its philosophy and purpose. But I didn't want to give up other disciplines, and that's really where a lot of the value of what I have today comes from: I was willing to look at other disciplines rather than devote myself fully to one. I would just study every day and travel whenever I could to study with various people.

At the academy we had a wonderful opportunity to bring in people every year who taught aiki-jujutsu, taught the various styles of aikido. It wasn't limited to one style. For the first few years, though, it was locked into people of the Ki Society orientation—we had Koichi Tohei and Kobayashi. I thought Tohei was a wonderful man. I was very impressed. This was during the time when he was leaving Hombu. That's when I met him. We'd take a drive up to Maroon Bells and he was literally in tears over the difficulty of the split, how it was necessary for him to do that. Kobayashi, Tohei and I would go up into Independence Pass, go up to Maroon Bells, and a lot of the conversation had to do with this impending split, the big decision.

From my perspective, it felt as if the reason for the split was a real ego clash between Doshu and Tohei around teaching methods and keeping the teaching methodologies as O-Sensei had. Tohei was a very creative, independent person with a very strong ego and a tremendous amount of ability and charisma and the ability to teach. He felt stifled in not being able to use many of the teaching methods that he developed, because it was somehow a little different or took a different emphasis, maybe. I mean, I think it was definitely an ego clash. I guess—what I arrogantly say from where I sit now— is that if they had had some of the real applicable skills of negotiating and conciliation, I think that they could have resolved their differences.

I absolutely believe that the world needs to have the *aiki* approach utilized in every aspect, and *aikidoka* did not use it in this case. It was clearly evident that Koichi Tohei was a brilliant *aikidoka* who had the power and the teaching ability and the understanding at a very deep level and yet, when it came to his own political life within the organization, the skills weren't used or understood at that level.

One of the main things that I'm doing in my work is trying to take the principles of aikido off the mat so they are really directly applicable in family and parenting. The traditional approach is that over many, many years, you integrate a pattern of movement in such a way that it somehow spontaneously emerges in other aspects of your life. I think that also works, I think that definitely happens, but not all the time for everyone. In terms of learning martial arts technique, in terms of learning the technique of aikido, I would say that if you fall down enough times and just continue training long enough, you're going to re-pattern those movements. But that is not to say that re-patterning those physical movements is going to necessarily translate into dealing with your daily life, because our pattern reaction around becoming angry and fighting or becoming acquiescent and fleeing, those patterns are awfully deep and we often don't see the immediate translation. That's not to say that some people won't have a transformation in every aspect of their life, but I don't think that can be a general rule. In fact, I think that in most instances it's not.

I also think that we have learned something about communicating and learning technologies at a higher level than ever before, and one of the things that we've learned is that all modalities are useful—the kinesthetic, the auditory, the visual—they're all useful in the learning mode. And to focus on one simply because it has always been done that way is, to me, not emptying our cup, not opening to what's possible. And boy, I think that is a real critical thing that the world needs to learn—that all of our learning technologies have been limited. The Westerners may have a tendency to articulate too much, to be too digital-auditory, to be too in the brain, in the mind, in the intellect. And the Easterners maybe have had a tendency to just do, do, do as I do, let's not talk about it, no explanation needed. But that also has its limits. That's one of the reasons we started the academy together, because we realized that we all can learn something from each other, and there are different learning tools and teaching methods and all can be integrated and useful. And the bigger your bag of tricks for bringing out learning technologies, the more you'll reach more people more often. So I think that the Eastern way has been extremely limited in its approach to learning of the martial arts, at any rate. The evidence from most of the people I know who study aikido shows that the average person who studies a number of years has made some inroads in repatterning in his general life but not substantial ones, not overly substantial ones. They're leaving the mat feeling very happy, but the minute they're in rush-hour traffic, they're still doing their same old stuff. I think that the general principle of openness, of the discovery domain versus the perfection domain, is not prevalent in the martial arts.

I think that we have deep, deep patterns that we unconsciously operate out of, growing up in our families, at whatever level of dysfunction was in our upbringing. The way we've learned about conflict in our life is by watching our parents, who watched their parents, or by going and watching our buddies in the schoolyard or by watching Rambo movies or John Wayne movies. There is a tendency to acquire some basic conditioning, and you add that to the lack of self-esteem so many of us have that gets anchored in very early and then when trauma hits us in our own daily life, our tendency is to operate unconsciously from those patterns. So to integrate new skills in dealing with conflict, internal and personal conflict in daily life, takes just as much training as learning techniques on the mat.

Aikido and daily life are not identical. You know, aikido is a powerful metaphor, to experience a new level of power and to understand that harmonizing with an opponent is effective, but it doesn't naturally translate into daily life without some nurturing.

Most of our suffering as individuals has come not because we are evil people, but because we've wanted to be perfect all of our lives. And that desire to be perfect creates in us a self-esteem which is based primarily on performance or a model. And in that domain, having to be a certain way or be like someone else exactly, we start to look at everything as either being right or wrong. And most martial artists, if you go in their dojo, even though they might preach that it's very important to be open, basically you're either doing it right or you're doing it wrong. And there's a connotation that wrong is bad, because we're brought up to be perfect. We want to be perfect. We want to do it as that person did it or perform at a certain level. And so we start to judge everything as right or wrong. Wrong is bad, and that means failure and a damaging blow to your self-esteem, because your self-esteem in perfection, remember, is built on performance or a model.

So now you've developed an incredible fear of failure. As you get older in the art, you're really afraid to fall down because you have so much at stake. So you develop this need to control, because you have to limit the amount of risk so the possibility of failure is lessened. And out of that need to control, you become very judgmental. And then you enter the great sin of every religion, which is judgment. You begin to judge most harshly yourself and others. And in that domain, everything becomes work rather than play. And that's why you can become a very hard-working student and start to perform at a very, very high level, masterful level, and even begin to look like the person that you had imaged. And yet your life is work, your life is stressful, your life is suffering. You take on a very stoic, angry, authoritative demeanor, all under the guise of something you may profess is very beautiful. But the game plan under which you learned that very beautiful art left you feeling like it was all work.

Another approach is through discovery. Discovery is the domain in which your self-esteem is based on inquiry; it's based on creativity. Well, if your basic self-esteem is based on inquiry and creativity, then there's really no right or wrong. That's not the predominant question. If there's no real right or wrong, you don't have failure. You simply have outcome. I mean, you do have goals, you do have visions, you do have expectations, but without the emphasis on performance and a model as the basis of your self-esteem. Instead it's creativity and inquiry. What happens is when your expectations don't get met, instead of having a failure, you just have an outcome. So you're willing to look at that; you're like a little child and you learn at a really rapid level like children learning to walk or talk. They don't mind falling down 'cause they don't call it pass-fail. So, from that you have more willingness to risk rather than less willingness to risk, as you do in perfection; you're far less judging; you're far more accepting. You don't have a controlling attitude; you have much more of a spontaneous attitude, so work becomes play and it's very child-like. And I think the essence of the art of aikido should be discovery and a child-like innocence.

I think that we have to honor the fact that the perfection game, the perfection domain, is so patterned into every other aspect of our life, that even though we may not be trying to do it in aikido, the normative system in life pulls us back into trying to be perfect. So before you know it, we're trying to do our techniques perfectly, and we're trying to do it exactly like that person did it. And, if we only study with one particular person or style, we end up saying "that's right, that's wrong." And before you know it, it's all the same game. Even though the teachings may talk about being flexible, being open, trusting the universe, being centered in the universe, there are no enemies, if you operate from perfection, there's always an enemy. The enemy is being wrong. The enemy is failure. So trying to acquire and integrate this wonderful philosophy of there being no enemies, if you're dealing with energy and trying to be centered

in this wonderful flow of energy, but coming from a place of perfection, of a right or wrong, you end up with an enemy. And the partner is right or wrong, my technique is right or wrong, my statements
are right or wrong. And thus, those patterns are set so very, very
deep that just going and rolling around the mat twice a week or
three times a week, I'm not sure that you can break the normative
system. I think you need more training. I think people need to really
look at the dynamics of relationship; I think they need to go back
to the source of their childhood.

I think that we have to recognize that *aikidoka* aren't the master
teachers in those areas. We have to be open to get it from all over;
we have to just keep emptying our cups. And there's a tendency, I
think, in all disciplines to believe that our own approach handles
everything. Study this and everything else will fall into place. I think
we have to be open to the various ideas and thoughts and teachings
from other disciplines. Meditation doesn't necessarily negate the
need for psychological analysis. Psychological analysis doesn't negate
the need to sit down quietly. In my book, *The Magic of Conflict*, I
love the quote that says, "All of man's miseries derive from his inability to sit quietly in a room alone." That's the quote from Pascal. That
is such a beautiful statement. Our inability to sit quietly is something that we need to learn about. At the same time I think we need
to have a little bit of rigor in looking at our families, looking at the
dysfunction inherent in them, looking at our relationships, looking
at our skills in resolving conflict and knowing that there are real
strategies that can be implemented to help us do that.

I'd like to give you my definition of a true warrior, because I think
that what all of us as practicing *aikidoka* are about is warriorship.
My definition of a true warrior is this: "A true warrior cuts through
his story each moment and steps forth from his vision." What that
means is that we've got a great story; all of us have this wonderful,
wonderful story. And that story, whether it's our dysfunctional family or our alcoholic parents or a hippopotamus rolled over us when
we were four or we caught a cold yesterday and that's why we can't
do it, those stories are the legitimate reasons that keep us from liv-

ing our vision. We have to be able to cut through those stories, to acknowledge them, to be open to them but not to operate out of them.

I think one of the biggest catches is that most people now are beginning to recognize that they need to get a clear vision and move from that place; but what they do is they're usually moving unconsciously out of their story. They say, "There's my wonderful vision of how it should be in the world," and they begin to try to get there from their story. Their story is all those legitimate reasons, all those things that happened to them, and there's very little power in that. I do physical exercises where a person is holding me behind the back and I cannot move forward if I operate from where they're holding. I need to step back, if they're pulling me backwards, get centered, bring the story—or in other words in this case, their physical arms around me—into my center and move from that place, and then I can walk them right across the room. There's such a dramatic difference, people begin to experience it on a physical level. We're going to have to give up our knowledge, which is basically our story, and our opinions and our skills, which are all part of our story—we've got to quit holding on to all of that and be able to constantly break through that so we can be open to really moving from our hearts and center. And I think the only stability in the world, true stability, is to be absolutely vulnerable. That's the old tradition, the old samurai tradition: to die is to live, which to me means to be willing to let go of your story, your ego, your opinions, your knowledge, your expectations, long enough to get some presence and move from a different place inside yourself.

I think it's terrifying to begin the process of letting go. I think it's terrifying to cut through your story because your story has in a sense held you up. It has given you all the reasons to still be okay even though you've been falling down a lot. And to cut through that and be willing to fall on your face and be fascinated by it rather than frustrated by it is such a major breakthrough that it's terrifying to do that. And yet, going through the fear, being present in the fear, breathing it, acknowledging it, allows you to turn the fear into power so that you move forward from your center. And that's exhilarating, so I think the pain and the tears and the laughter all happen in the process. One is not the end result of the other. They're just part of the whole process. It's a moment-by-moment experience. There are many moments in the day where I let my fear paralyze me and I stay in my story. And then at other moments I cut through and I go forward. And it's all those little things where the training is: it's talking to your child and being with your spouse or the other person in the office in a way in which you maybe hear them for the first time and you let them in, without belittling them or making them wrong. In other words, the training is being rigorous about being centered and changing language and being open to learning, rather than being right. All of that, all of those little, daily events are where the training is, rather than waiting for the big event in your life to do it, where it's often too difficult. When you're really injured or really sick or there's trauma in your family, there's a sudden divorce or whatever, those of course are times when you turn for support or help, but I think it builds on a day-to-day basis far more profoundly, which again is why I wouldn't want to trust one single physical method on the mats to teach me all of that.

Lots of people have influenced me in aikido. There is no one way. For every technique we do in aikido, I found at least, through the academy, six to ten people doing it an entirely different way, very efficiently and proficiently. That's got to open your mind. It's like watching one guy stand like Rod Carew and hit a ball over the fence and another guy stand on the opposite side of the plate with a stance that looks absolutely different, and yet he hits it over the fence with just as much power. You realize there are some principles there that are the same, but the overall look can be very, very different.

I think that every martial artist who has studied for five years or more recognizes that techniques don't do anything for you when it actually happens to you. The study of the techniques sets you into a pattern of movement that can be spontaneous, but in the moment of physical confrontation, you're not thinking technique or if you are, you're too late. You need to be responding from a place of the energy given. And what that technique ends up looking like can be almost anything. If your intent, for instance, is to protect yourself, to disarm the other person or their ability to harm you without harming them, it could look like almost anything. You could take a pillowcase and put it over the top of their head and that would be a very effective technique, far superior than going for your perfect *sankyo*, when the fact is this big sheet is so much easier to pull over their head and tie them up with. The appropriateness of the technique is directly related to the energy of the moment.

That's why I think people need to constantly vary their training. They need to constantly vary the speed in which they deal with the attack, from slow-motion, exquisitely slow movement, to very, very fast movement, to multiple attacks, to doing it blind-folded, to doing it in a variety of settings. Danny Inosanto used to come to the academy. He taught the Filipino arts but he also taught jeet kune do, which was Bruce Lee's art, and of course, his practice partner was Bruce Lee. He told me that when he trained with Bruce Lee, they used to train in whatever they wore to work. It was ludicrous, as Bruce Lee would say, to come in wearing light, flowing pants and do high kicks when what you wore to work were tight blue jeans or a suit. If you wore a suit to work, if you wore blue jeans when you went out at night, that's what you needed to train in. So come in your suit, come in your blue jeans, and then we'll learn real martial arts that are practical. And I think that has a lot of bearing. People should notice the different settings in their daily life. Where do they end up in daily life? Is it in a subway? If you ride a subway a lot and are interested in dealing with energy that happens around a subway, maybe physical-confrontative techniques, you should do subway techniques. You should create a training environment that looks like a subway and you can deal with the emotional, mental aikido, prior to ever getting in a situation.

Aikidoka don't train that way very much right now. Look at kneeling, the *seiza* position, and doing *suwariwaza*. You know, you do that a lot in aikido practice, but do Westerners sit like that? Rarely. You'll be attacked on a barstool or maybe a chair before you're attacked like that unless that's how your office is set up. So where are the chair techniques? I think it's good to practice chair techniques, sitting in a chair, sitting on a barstool. The reason that suwari-waza is practiced in Japan is that is how they sat. That's how they were. I'm sure if they had been sitting in chairs for all of those generations, that is not how they would be practicing. They would have chair practice. And I think that people have to be open enough and willing enough and adaptable enough to look at their lives right now. I don't do a lot of subway techniques because there isn't a subway out here in the mountains, but I think you could set that up in an inner-city situation, and probably should. And I also think that is where you would come up with much more real, practical applications, because most of the stuff that happens in the subway is not physical. Most of the stuff that happens in your daily life is not physical. And the aikido can be learned in that way—how would you use *irimi* or *tenkan* when your child comes to you with "I don't want to do the dishes,"—that's where it happens. And that's of course so much the nature of my work in the world. People who aren't interested in aikido, the martial art, are certainly interested in the principles if they work in daily life.

Even with these people, who only want to use the principles in daily life, I think they need to train physically. I don't think you can take it very far at all without training physically, but the physical training will look different. In other words, I think that people have to have a real concept of center and know that whatever goes on mentally and emotionally shows up in the body. So your physical training, whether you're doing on-the-mat techniques or not, needs to be there, which means you have to have an awareness of where you're tense, where your movement is limited, where you're holding your position. Even in a mental and emotional stance, it shows up physically. Anybody who's really fighting about being right and holding their position, if you look at them physically, they're holding their position physically. So I think the training is physical and needs to be physical; it just doesn't have to look like *katate-tori nikkyo irimi*. So that's where I think people misunderstand the question. They say, "Well, don't you need physical training to embody this work?" I say "yes," but the physical training isn't necessarily on the mat doing *nikkyo*. It's physical training. It's being aware constantly— are you moving from center, are your movements flowing, are you tense, where are your feelings right now, are you feeling angry, where does it show up in the body? That physical training is extremely important. I certainly think that there is a benefit to training in the aikido, a very strong benefit in the technical training of aikido because you really do learn on a very real physical level that tension and rigidity do not create appropriate or effective techniques. Limpness does not create appropriate or effective techniques. Flowing, centered movement in which you are connecting center to center does. And that has a real ability to shift one's motivation and one's commitment in daily life practice.

Now I spend much of my time doing what I call *aiki* work. I have eight people that I specifically trained over a period of averaging somewhere between eight and ten years who work with me in doing my *aiki* work. Of course they all train in aikido. They're all brown belt, black belt, and up, so they do the aikido training also. But they're working on directly applying this stuff in daily life, supporting people in applying it in daily life. So I'm really excited about having it grow. This stuff is, I think, leverageable, it's learnable, it's applicable.

I have a whole staff now that goes out when I work with businesses, educational organizations, and organizations in general. What I call "the magic of conflict" can be learned by anyone. But you need people who embody it to teach it, that's for sure. It's real difficult to teach it when a person doesn't have the physical exercises or hasn't put it into the body, and it's real hard to communicate it when a person hasn't embodied it at that level. That's why it seems to take a certain amount of training in the physical art as well as facilitation skills. You have to come from a place that has real credibility to really communicate, because otherwise it's "Yes, oh this is very interesting." But what that really means is it's left in the intellect. "Nice thought, nice idea. Of course I'll be loving and more patient and more flexible in my next conflict." And then of course when the conflict hits, I'm too busy being right, I'm too angry and too upset to use any of that. So I have to first learn what's going on in my body. This feels like my rigidity, tension, holding my position, or I-want-to-fight or I-want-to-flee feeling, then I can shift that. And when I work on myself, then I can start using my skills, when I can take a moment to get centered and calm. That's the difference.

Right now my life is very successful. I mean, I get up every morning and do my share of falling down and being uncentered and all the other stuff, but I really do have a deep, deep love for this work. It is who I am. I'm out practicing what my life is about. My work is practicing what my life is about, and I don't see how you can not be successful when you operate from that level. I'm always learning. I'm training. I'm real disciplined in that sense. It comes from a level of that's what I would do if I wasn't getting paid for it. If I had to go out and work in order to earn money to do this, I would do that. But luckily I'm able to do what I do and get paid for it. It comes from following your heart. I'm convinced that if you follow your bliss, if you're really committed to taking a look at what moves you, what you want to do in your life, I think life supports you in fascinating, miraculous ways, constantly. And I think most of us who look at our lives and see that it's a mess, well, those are the signals and guideposts saying that that's not the direction. So we try harder. Usually we try harder, producing the same old patterns, the same old results, rather than saying, "Where is the opportunity here?" If you really believe in the practice of following your bliss, and working from your center, you'll get supported for that; then if you're not getting supported, you're probably going the wrong direction.

My point is that obviously there is a reason that we're here. So in a sense that is predestined. But that's just one variable. I think that life is constantly shifting, constantly moving us forward, constantly motivating us to evolve. It's not pre-determined. And yet there's obviously some variable in there. Your genetics are predetermining but that doesn't mean your genetics are going to dictate your life.

I think that the guru thing is one of the big traps for anybody out there, really willing to be out there and share some valuable things. People tend to become dependent. And that's the last thing that we need, another co-dependent relationship. One thing that I think I'm constantly encouraging in this work is that everyone should make choices, everyone should constantly create their own life in a real independent way, from a centered place, rather than a co-dependent way. I mean, the whole teaching of centeredness negates the context of a co-dependent relationship. It negates that whole context. So you would think that would never be a problem in aikido. But because people do have addictive tendencies, co-dependent tendencies, it's certainly something that everybody has to be aware of who is involved in teaching personal work where they're really out in the world. I also think it's one of the biggest obstacles we all have —to opening our own hearts to compassion and letting ego have its place, not being in control of things. It's a real trap.

I feel that we all have to be aware of who we are and how we present ourselves, that we have to be very rigorous about whether or not we're manipulating in some way, shape or form, whether or not we're using our skills to influence in a way that doesn't allow others to have conscious choice. I think that's something we all have to be aware of and more rigorous about than the average individual— every teacher has to have that, every teacher.

I don't think aikido has even come close to its limits yet. I think, whether it's classical aikido or the principles used in daily life, we haven't even begun to touch what's possible in educating, opening up a whole new discovery mode. We have the ability to support a world that really does work. The major issues that we have right now around the environment, around economics and around international politics, are so big and so serious that it is obvious that things need to be done in an entirely new way. I think there's a big opportunity here. I think the 1990s can be an incredible decade for issuing in a new order of thinking around conflict, around dealing with one another. And I think aikido and the principles inherent in the art speak to that, speak to turning it all around. So I'm really excited by the possibilities; getting humans to be really conscious and bonded to the planet, getting humans to see that war is now obsolete because of the technological development of weapons. There are no spoils to the winners anymore; there are no winners and losers in that kind of war any longer. And pulling us together just as a world of people, rather than as individual nations hiding from one another, that's the opportunity we have right now. I can't think of a better place to be working in than in aikido.

I feel very much in communion with the aikido community. And I love living here in the mountains and not being affiliated with any particular segment of it. I'm able to travel all over the world and everywhere I go, inevitably the question is, where can I study aikido? So I always send them to wherever aikido's located in their environment. And I recommend that they go in there with an open heart. I tell them there's stuff to be learned there that's of value, and there are things to be let go of because they're not what you need. But you can get some very wonderful things from the art of aikido. I always encourage people to get it wherever it is. I really support the aikido community, and I can do that in a much more universal way because I'm not affiliated. I think if I were affiliated I would have a little bit of an ethical problem about encouraging people to study at certain places that weren't viewed as part of our team or our organization. So I like the non-affiliated place but yet feel I really contribute to getting the word of aikido out to people in many different ways.

9

GEORGE LEONARD

No one has written more words in the English language about aikido than George Leonard. His championing of aikido has brought more Americans to aikido dojo than anyone else alive. In books such as The Ultimate Athlete *and* Mastery *as well as his numerous* Esquire *articles, Leonard has written prolifically about the magic of aikido and its ability to transform people's lives.*

Leonard also teaches workshops around the country called L.E.T.: Leonard Energy Training. The premise is that we all have available to us remarkable resources of energy which are largely untapped. Every beginning student in aikido is quickly amazed by the unbendable arm demonstration or the instructor that ten strong men are unable to pick up. There is a side to aikido, the magician side, the secret power, the manipulation of energy, that fascinated Leonard since the first day he stepped on the mat.

Related to L.E.T. is Leonard's famous "Samurai Game." Anyone who has the chance should play the game, especially with Leonard in the role of a god, admirably demonstrating that the gods are at their capricious best in war.

In this chapter, Leonard chronicles the evolution of Aikido of Tamalpais and describes what it's like to be part of a dojo without one instructor.

Leonard also talks about one of the big pitfalls in aikido, carried over from life—the obsession with being right or the drive to be perfect. Once that mode takes control, it sets up conflict, violence, and

*denial of what Leonard calls the "dark side." As Leonard says, "Aikido
is not the denial of violence, but the refusal of violence."*

*Leonard believes that aikido has the capacity of a religion. He says
it's big enough to include the devil and "big enough to be non-Japanese." In psychological language, aikido is archetypal. The American
experience of aikido has been fundamental in sensing these possibilities, and Leonard's writings have been instrumental in bringing public awareness to the potential of aikido to transform people and society.*

I had just resigned, after seventeen wonderful years, from *Look*
magazine because I wanted to write *The Transformation*. I was
facing the most intense and extensive mental work of my life—a
lot of studying, reading, research and writing. Mental work of that
sort, I think, is a most unnatural act. And I'm a rather wired person. Fast reflexes—that's the upside. The downside is that my
autonomous nervous system is always going full blast. To stay balanced I need a bit of exercise. So I rejoined my tennis club. I had
let my membership lapse, so I had to repay a rather fat initiation
fee. I was planning on a regular tennis schedule. But something
unexpected happened and as it turned out, I never again even visited my tennis club.

Now bear in mind that as of this point I had never in my life considered being in the martial arts. It wasn't a question of considering it and saying "yes" or "no." I had never even *thought* about it.
The martial arts were totally outside of my realm of existence and
conception.

So, right after I sent my check to the tennis club, late October of
1970, I got a phone call from Michael Murphy, co-founder of Esalen
Institute and a close friend. Michael started talking about a martial
art called aikido. I'd never heard of it. He said it was one of the most
effective of the martial arts. It also had a great philosophy behind
it, with mystical and transcendent possibilities within it. Michael
can make anything sound fascinating. With one phone call he can
change your life. I was bug-eyed. "Is that right? What? *What?*"

Then Michael went on to tell me he had discovered this remarkable teacher, Robert Nadeau, who was teaching down on the peninsula, at Mountain View. "What I've decided to do," Michael told me, "is to bring Nadeau up to San Francisco twice a week to do an experimental class for the Esalen San Francisco office staff. We can find out if aikido is all that it's cracked up to be. Maybe it's something we can add to the Esalen program. And it will be good for the office staff. We'll have classes on Tuesday and Thursday afternoons from four to six. Esalen will pay part of the expense of getting him up here. The amount the individual student will have to pay will be nominal."

Now this—Nadeau coming to San Francisco—turned out to be a very important step in the subsequent development of aikido in northern California. A lot of aikido history stemmed from that move.

Anyhow, Michael said, "George, how about joining?" I wasn't a member of the office staff nor was I in any way a member, officially, of Esalen, even though I've been a friend of Esalen. "You and Lillie join. Dulce and I are going. Let's go all the way to black belt. Let's do it, George. Let's do it."

I said, "Sure, anything you say, Mike." So, knowing nothing whatever about it, on November 11, 1970, I went to my first aikido class. We didn't have a dojo. We had to have aikido in a living room of Betsy Carter, who had a nice place out near Twin Peaks in San Francisco. So here comes this physically rag-tag Esalen group. A lot of them were very much out of shape. Some were considerably overweight. We all gathered there in Betsy Carter's house. And in walks Nadeau, a strange kind of *sensei*. He was wearing a leather jacket. He had that whole aspect about him—a different sort of person. And with him he had this angel named Betsy Hill. Betsy was just beautiful: ethereal, long black hair that hung way down her back. Anything Nadeau said, she hung on his every word. The class began and pretty soon he shows us this energy arm, this "unbendable arm." "Wow. This is great stuff." We did the class. I was entranced. I thought Nadeau was a really remarkable person, strangely eloquent. He had a wonderful way of expressing himself. By the third class I was hooked.

I think this represented a very special opportunity for Bob, because his secret dream—he actually told us at the time—was to take aikido outside of just the martial arts audience. He had already started teaching what he called "non-falling aikido." He had a class— my understanding is—down on the peninsula where older people, people who were not in good shape, could learn some of the principles of aikido, some of the moves. He was quite ingenious in developing a lot of these exercises. And then he began calling it "energy awareness." The Esalen group, these were probably more what he would call "intellectual people" than the people he was used to teaching. They were all most interested in things like "energy." Nadeau did not use the word *ki*. He said, "We are not Japanese, we're Yankees." He wanted to Americanize it all. He did not use the term *ki*. He did not use the word *hara;* he used the word "center." Also, no bowing. We didn't have any bowing. I think he really looked at it more as an opportunity to teach energy.

We had a hard time finding a place to practice. We tried a garage on Union Street but that didn't work out. We finally found this absolutely wonderful place, the Unitarian Church on Geary and Franklin. The Unitarian Church is a real urban center, one of those very busy, bustling urban centers where all sorts of things are going on. They had an octagonal chapel with a very high ceiling. At every other octagonal place there was stained glass, so the afternoon sun would pour in in different colors. And we got the traveling mats, and kept them in a little balcony in this octagonal chapel. We later referred to this time as "the period of the church." Everyone said "Remember the church?" because that was a very bizarre period.

Nadeau seemed strangely reluctant to put the mats down. At that time we really wanted to get some aikido: "Come on, let's put the mats down." We didn't call him *sensei,* he didn't want us to call him *sensei,* just "Bob." He would generally bring with him Betsy, Tom Everett, Harvey Moskowitz. At any given time there would be at least two brown belts. So those classes were most interesting. When we learned falls he put down only one mat. It was like landing on an aircraft carrier. Now we teach it from *seiza*. But at the church we had to fling ourselves down and over. It was really compact. I don't think he was so interested in that part of it. He was very interested in energy. He loved it. But gradually it became an aikido class. Everybody kind of wandered around. Everybody was talking, there was no discipline. But Bob was fascinated. He was teaching. I really liked it. I think I could see the man's genius.

I'll say right now that Nadeau has a certain genius. He can tune into unexpected areas of thought. He doesn't just go down the straight line. He comes up with really original things. Many of these energy awareness things, as perhaps you know, I've used and adapted and changed and I've created many of my own. But that's really where I got my training in energy awareness. Anyway, these classes gradually began to dwindle. I was disgusted. Not so much disgusted, it's just that "How could anybody fail to enjoy this incredible thing we were getting here?" But people began to kind of ... well, they were kind of busy. They had to work back at the Esalen office.

Then we brought in another friend of mine, Leo Litwak, who had nothing to do with Esalen. He's a very close friend of mine, my age—a philosopher and writer. We became very good *aiki* buddies from the first. Did you read my piece on getting a black belt at the age of fifty-two? It's in Richard's book. It was a very, very rich and powerful time in my life. There was one time when I was being Rolfed. I'd get Rolfed on Tuesdays and Thursdays and go straight from there to aikido, drive into the city to the church. I really loved it without any equivocation on my part. Leo also loved it. Finally the only people left were me and Leo and Dulce, who later married Michael Murphy. After four or five months, even Michael quit. Everybody quit. Finally Dulce quit, and there were only two of us left. And there would be three teachers, Nadeau and two brown belts. Now I did not go into aikido to get a black belt. That never entered my mind. I never thought that I would ever get any rank because we didn't ever see any other black belts—Bob was the only one. At that time there weren't many around.

That lasted one year with the Esalen group; it lasted longer at the church. Meanwhile the class continued to dwindle, as it will.

219

There was one woman, she weighed about 280 pounds, she left very quickly. She got up off the mat several times, that was it. Other people didn't like the feeling of their wrist being twisted. They weren't getting it, they just couldn't get it. Later I found out that was about typical. Aikido's dropout rate is fairly spectacular. But I didn't understand it at the time. We'd come in, and there'd be Nadeau and two brown belts and we'd work with them. So for a long time I had the privilege of working closely with people who were pretty good at aikido. And we continued doing some energy stuff. For example, Nadeau would sit in a chair across from me and tune into me and tell me what my energy was. It was amazingly accurate. It blew my mind. He'd say, "Now, your energy is too much up in your head. Let it go down." My eyes were closed. Pretty soon I'd feel it surging down, I'd feel a little surge in my chest. He'd say, "Good. Now it's in your chest." "How do you know that?" But I later found out we can all do it if we just open ourselves. Nadeau used to say to me, "I'd really rather be thought of as a meditation teacher than an aikido teacher." He really had great hopes for that, spreading his thing to the masses.

Meanwhile everybody was dropping out. But also meanwhile, since he was driving all the way from Mountain View with his two brown belts, why not open a public class? So a public class opened at seven. Our class was from four to six. Sometimes I'd stay late and I'd see the public class begin to drift in. And this was a strange bunch. Don't forget this was in the late hippie era. All sorts of people would come in—rock musicians, strange types dressed in all sorts of weird clothing.

I'd been doing aikido for seven, eight months, and we'd go out and have coffee afterwards with Nadeau—standard procedure. One day he said, "Hey, let's go over to the Oakland dojo." I'd never seen a dojo. I said, "Great!" So we got in the car and drove over to what later became the Aikido Institute. At that time Alan Gnow was the teacher. He was, I think, Nadeau's first or second black belt. Bright lights. I could see these people doing falls, I could see them doing techniques way beyond what we were doing. I confess that if I had gone straight to a dojo, I would probably just have turned around and run in the other direction. It was way too much. I took several wild falls and came up kind of bruised. But by then I was hooked, it was too late. No way I was going to leave, ever.

So after a year, precisely a year, Esalen's treasurer began looking at the accounts and said, "What the hell are we doing? We're subsidizing an aikido class for George Leonard." So they decided to cut off the funds for the afternoon class. But by then Bob must have had about fifteen regular students in his evening class. We had a big celebration the last night, a big crowd. All the Esalen people came back. Mike Murphy came back. He took some strange falls. One time Dulce put a *nikkyo* on him, and Mike let out a big scream. He reeled backwards and crashed into all of these folding chairs that were stacked against the wall, and they all fell down on him. The whole thing was not the kind of aikido class you're used to seeing. At the end of class Nadeau presented Leo and me with blue belts. I mean, that was an amazing thing to me. A blue belt! I thought, my god!—you're a king if you're a blue belt. Wow! So anyway, then I joined the public class. And that was quite an experience.

The public class went on right there in the church. This was the forerunner of what became Aikido of San Francisco. Michael Murphy got Nadeau to come teach the Esalen class and because of that, Nadeau started the evening class. The evening class then became the nucleus out of which was created Aikido of San Francisco, out of which came dozens of dojos.

Now don't forget we had started very late in 1970 with the Esalen class. We really didn't start in the church until the beginning of '71. It was one year after that they closed the afternoon class, the Esalen class, our private class with a spectacular student-teacher ratio of three to two. Then we had to join the public, the great unwashed public. That lasted a year and a half before we started Aikido of San Francisco at the Turk Street dojo.

One more thing happened. When he started the public class, Bob also had a Saturday class, and he brought up from Half Moon Bay a police officer named Frank Doran. Frank had been teaching, I understand, a few students in a little garage dojo. But now he was teaching the Saturday class. He has changed over the years. He was more of a policeman at that time. Then I started on the Saturday class, too.

Just let me say a little bit about the group we had in the church. As I said, it was an urban center with all these street people sort of wandering in. And a lot of times they'd just wander into the aikido class. They'd take the class, pay whatever they had to pay, a couple of dollars, whatever was being charged at the time. They'd be stoned out of their head or drunk. We had these strange characters come through. Two guys came in one night and they were both wearing harem pants, I don't know why. That was still the late '60s, you might say. Later they were just kind of working out together and both of them were kicking each other in the shins as hard as they could with great anger. There was one strange Japanese who came in with a putative brown belt from Tokyo, who always wore dark aviator glasses on the mat. He seemed to have one technique that he was really good at, *tenchi nage,* over and over again. After class he'd crunch everybody.

So Leo continued training and I continued training. We never missed a class. Richard Moon then came into the picture. Richard Moon is now a fourth *dan,* a close associate of Nadeau, with his own school in west Marin. He came in with a group associated with Allen Meyerson of the Committee, a popular improvisational theater group of that period—they were actors and musicians. Robbie Long came in with a woman named Lola. And Lee French, who was in movies. Movie stars and actors, theater people. It was quite a mix of humanity, a strange, rich mix of humanity. I found I really liked the public class more than being alone with the teachers. I was the most advanced student, just by virtue of the fact that I had had this training for a year.

One more important thing about the church—Wendy Palmer appeared. The night that she appeared I went home and told my wife, "A homeless waif has come to our class." At that time I think she was living with her baby out of her car. And she came in and was the most humble-looking person. Her eyes were downcast; she'd look at you very humbly. Wendy is Ms. Charisma now. I mean, she is up there. We have a jazz quintet. When she sings the fire comes out of her. She has really got it, she has got it all. But at that time she was very shy and very recessive and quiet, never said a word. But she had the same experience I did. When she walked in there, she saw Nadeau—she's told me many times—and she thought, "There's my teacher and this is my art. I'll do this the rest of my life." She had that feeling. So after a while Wendy kind of became one of us. And we developed the kind of warm camaraderie that you develop in a dojo, especially when you're a student. It's really more fun being a student than a teacher. So one night Nadeau took us—there were five or six of us—to see this wonderful space on Turk Street. It had been a dance school. It had mirrors in it. Barres. A modeling school. It was a wonderful space. He said, "Do you think we should do it?" "Absolutely." At that time I think we had about twenty students. And with that hard core we started Aikido of San Francisco. Pretty soon they brought in Bob Witt and Dresen. Ed Dresen was Nadeau's partner in Mountain View. He was not an aikidoist at that time. He was a jujutsu teacher. He also was a business man and he did a lot of the business stuff. Later they had kind of a falling out.

There weren't many dojos around. Aikido of San Francisco was the mother church. I was the first student in that thing. I had the lowest number. Blue belt, that's a senior student. And then the training became more formal. One day Richard Heckler showed up from Hawaii. He'd done some aikido there. This distressingly good-looking guy comes in here, very, very graceful.

So we started regular training and I never missed a class unless I was out of town. The way we got to be brown belts was rather interesting. We went down to a *gasshku* at Mountain View, Leo and I did; this was in October '73. At the end of the *gasshku*, Frank Doran took us into the office and gave us both brown belts and *kyu* certificates. That was a much bigger thrill than getting the black belt because that again was totally out of the blue. I did not expect it. So Leo and I drove back. It was a beautiful afternoon, I can still remember it, and we went to one of those silly fern bars. We were like high school kids who had just graduated. That had come totally as a surprise. I never thought that I would reach brown belt. In fact, when I was first training, brown belt seemed so stratospheric, it was beyond my wildest hopes to ever achieve that kind of thing.

Not too long after we got our brown belts, Nadeau decided to have a basics class. So he made Richard and Wendy and me and a guy named Laurence instructors of the class. He called the class "Fundamentals" and he called us "the Fundamentalists." He'd call us all in and tell us what to do. When we started, all four of us would come to class, it was such a privilege to be able to teach aikido.

I guess it was sometime around that period we were all getting generally set for our black belt test. "Hey, maybe someday we'll take our black belt test." We couldn't believe it because, again, there were very, very few around. Within three weeks of that conversation all four of us were seriously injured. At the end of that we got together and said, "Forget it. Let's go on with practice and forget rank totally." Then the time came when our instructors started giving exams. That was another step, because way up to second *kyu*, we were so close, there were so few of us, they knew us so well, they didn't give formal exams. But then it got pretty large so they decided to start having exams. My very first exam was my first *kyu* exam. But mostly it was just "the path." We practiced. Period. We just practiced and practiced. Wendy and Richard and I became more friendly.

In early '73 I asked Nadeau permission to teach energy awareness classes. He said "sure." I think the first one I gave was at Cold Mountain Institute up at Cortez Island in British Columbia. Then I gave one at Esalen. So from early '73 to the present time I've been giving these classes. In early '83 we formalized it into L.E.T., "Leonard Energy Training." My early lineage goes directly to Nadeau. Since then I've developed lots of things on my own, lots of techniques, games and processes, but I always acknowledge Nadeau because the idea of using aikido principles with just ordinary folks who are not martial artists, I definitely got it from him. He empowered me to do so, and a lot of the techniques I first used I got from him. It's not exactly aikido, but in a sense it is because if you want to see the influence of aikido, I've introduced this work to more than 50,000 people.

Aikido definitely changed my life, radically. I mean, a lot of my work now is based directly on aikido principles, L.E.T. Sometimes when I give keynote addresses I lead the whole audience in exercises. I've gone pretty far away from it; I do things that don't seem very much like aikido. But the original impetus came from aikido.

So anyhow, there weren't many black belts around in the early days. I remember Allen Graw came once to the church. Bob Noha came once to the church. That was on a Saturday after the Esalen class had been closed. And they were actually training on the mat. I couldn't believe it. I didn't know that black belts trained with other students. This all sounds very naive, but it's the situation as it was in the early '70s in San Francisco. There just wasn't that much aikido around.

So it was not so unusual for Wendy to start a class with Nadeau's blessing when she was only a first *kyu* because there wasn't anybody else to do it. She is a natural born teacher. She's a marvelous teacher, especially with beginners. She's a genius with beginners. So she started right out here at Tam High in Mill Valley. Sometimes instead of going into the city, I'd go to Wendy's class and kind of help her out. Once she had to give a demonstration for the student body of Tam High during assembly in order to contact students. So Richard Moon and myself and maybe Steve Samuels, another one of those guys who became black belt, we helped Wendy out and she gave a very nice demonstration. It was basically a *shodan* test; she did everything on the test including sword taking, knife taking, *randori*.

Wendy then started the class for high school students, and that didn't do too well. But she started an adult class at Tam High, late in the afternoon, and that was very successful. After a while she had about twenty hard-core students which then became the core of Aikido of Tamalpais. So we continued, Wendy and I. I became kind of a regular, helping her out. I took my *shodan* test in February of '76 and Wendy and Richard took theirs in June of '76. I was actually

Wendy's *uke*. It was kind of weird, as tall as I am, attacking Wendy, 5 ft. 5 in., 112 pounds. *Hanmi handachi* was very interesting.... They gave a nice test, Richard gave an exceptional test, which you probably read my story about.

About three months after that, we decided to start a school. So if it was any body's real initiative, it was Wendy's. Richard was brought in at the very end because I was already helping Wendy. At first it was just one class a week because I really didn't have much interest in teaching. So she called Richard in and we got together. We each put in $1500, the three of us. We also called Nadeau and asked him to be our fourth partner. Nadeau said, "No thanks." I think he really thought it couldn't possibly succeed.

My understanding is that people had been trying for some time to start a dojo in Marin County. We went ahead and decided to start the damned thing. We first used a dance studio for about a month: you had to put mats down which made it very difficult. At the very beginning we had about twenty or thirty students. We had to go before the city planning commission to get the space that we have now. It was really hard to get the space. We had to present our credentials. The two previous applicants for that space had been refused by the city because the people in the neighborhood didn't want anybody there at all. We had to use all of our silver-tongued skills to get in. And we got it under circumstances where we were only supposed to use it at night and on Saturday during the day, so we're still kind of limited in how we use it; being upstairs is another difficulty. I was going back and looking at some of records, and we didn't know that Nadeau would not be our partner. We presented Nadeau's credentials, I guess he was a third *dan* at the time, because we thought he would be our partner.

So we started the school October 22, 1976. Three *shodans*. We have a picture of our first anniversary celebration, a lot of students— forty, fifty students. The truth of the matter is we have never made much money. It has just been very successful. That's the way we want it. We're doing it as a service. We've kept our dues down because we're not trying to make money.

I think the story of Aikido of Tamalpais has a very interesting aspect. The most significant part of it is that Richard and Wendy and I have made every decision by consensus. We have never had to have a vote. It has been a most wonderful, wonderful thing. Wendy and Richard have even gone through a marriage and a divorce. But we have never had a fight. The funny thing is that now we are so committed to this, so invested in it, that we would do anything to keep from breaking up or changing it. People say, "How can this be?" Think of all the exams, whether people should be passed or asked to take it again, who's ready, different problems we've had with students. We always agree. It doesn't mean we don't talk about it. If somebody really feels strongly about something, the others will tend to go along with that point of view. If two people really have a strong feeling about something, the third person will tend to give in. We'll just kind of work it out.

It has been wonderful. To work with Richard and Wendy has been one of the great pleasures of my life. We've become closer in many ways. We've done a lot of things together. This dojo has been a joy. And I think it's a great service to many people. We've successfully had around thirty *shodans* come out of our school. Starting with a very questionable beginning—the first two years were kind of strange, I think it's a good dojo and people seem to like it. What I generally hear is people say it's friendly, they like to be here. There's not much machismo, at least we try to keep it down.

We've all learned a lot more about teaching. I think the level of aikido everywhere in the U.S. has definitely risen. I think about our own training, it just wasn't at that level. The training everywhere is higher now. That's to be expected. Generally when our students go around to the various parts of the world including Hombu, they train very well as compared with people of similar rank and sometimes even higher. So I feel good about the general level of training.

We've kept training, trying to develop and trying to go to seminars and learn things. We've certainly had lots of people come through here. You know, Terry taught here for two years. That was an interesting thing. Terry left us a few techniques and much of his unique spirit. Steve Seagal has given three workshops here. Saito has been here, Saotome, Hiroshi, and many more.

I think someday somebody should really do a story on the relation between Richard and Wendy and me because we are kind of interesting characters. We do things other than aikido. People have said, "How could you have all of this harmony all this time?" You look at almost any other school, many of them have broken apart, terrible things have happened. I'd like to say we're nice people and all that, but I think probably the deeper reason is that all three of us are very, very busy with other things. Therefore when we have meetings we're always trying to give power away. "Let's see, why don't you be president, Richard?" "No, why don't you?" None of the three of us is grasping for power. In fact, to the contrary, each of us is trying to give more power to the other two. And that's not because we're enlightened people but because we're very busy. In other words, we're not primarily aikidoists in one sense. We are because it influences everything in our lives, but as far as the actual teaching, the monetary thing, the status thing and all of that, we get our money and our livelihood and our status someplace else. So aikido really is a service.

I think that there are a lot of advantages to the way we run the dojo, though there are some real disadvantages to the three of us being equal. And there's the fact that we're not always there. I teach only two days a week. Things are happening that I don't always know about. Sometimes we can get out of touch. We're very busy. In a sense it doesn't have the cohesiveness of a place with one head instructor.

Tom Gambel has a fine dojo. I've guest-instructed over there. Tom does it all. He makes his living from it. And therefore it has a cohesiveness and a continuity that we lack. Also, the joke at our school is that everybody here has to learn techniques at least three different ways. Sometimes we get together and talk about it, and sometimes I'll show Wendy's way and a little of my way and Richard's way. It makes our students much more flexible, able to open themselves to different approaches. And you know there are some aikido teachers, martial arts teachers who say, "This is the one and only way and you must do it this way and don't you dare change it one iota." I don't like that at all. We show many variations of every technique. And I'd say as far as the strengths and weaknesses of our dojo, maybe in some basics and in *ukemi,* some of the other dojo are better. I think in our flowing techniques and in our *jiyu waza,* our freestyle, I think we're pretty good because people who come from other dojo, who have advanced rank, sometimes are not quite as flowing, they're not as experienced at *jiyu waza* as our people. But we keep trying to get better in all aspects of the art.

Aikido informs and influences every other part of my life. I feel strongly that the aikido principles should be applied to the rest of your life. I know Nadeau said that from the very beginning. Look, I want to say it very clearly, none of us can do it. I mean, I blow it all the time. I'd like to blend in all situations, but I sometimes don't. But at least I know there's an option, at least there's a possibility. I feel there is something really rather terrible about one who professes to teach an art with such noble and majestic principles and regularly lives in opposition to those principles. I think that is very disappointing. When I was still at the church I felt that if you did aikido there was no way that you could do anything immoral or unethical or unkind. That was my most naive period, also one of my most enthusiastic periods—you know, that wonderful glow when you first start aikido. In my book *The Ultimate Athlete* I was still in that phase. But the more I learned about the greater world of aikido, the more I learned of discord and terrible things happening, people fighting and throwing wine in each other's face, things like that. It was truly difficult for me.

Now I think it's important to understand we all have a dark side, and there's a kind of self-pride in thinking we can be perfect or even expecting our teachers to be perfect or our exemplars to be perfect. We all have a dark side. But at least let's acknowledge the dark side. Let's not deny and continue to say we're right, that our way is right and everybody else is wrong. We're students. "Let's see if this works. What do you think about that?" I'll ask the students. I'll see a student do a variation and I'll say, "Let's try that." I always say when people come to the dojo, kind of kidding, we're a very traditional dojo. We have a very powerful tradition, and our tradition is informality. We're very informal. But I honestly don't think that we lack respect. We respect O-Sensei, we respect each other as much as anybody. But we don't do quite as much formal bowing. I have the students call me by my name: "George, would you come over here?" I'd rather not have them call me "Sensei." I know that I respect O-Sensei and my teachers and I've always tried to acknowledge my teachers. I know I have in every book I've written. In my book *Mastery* there's an acknowledgment of all my teachers because it contains more about aikido than any other book I've written. A lot of those principles are really fleshed out through this book.

So I feel aikido should inform our lives, and for God's sake let's not get bluenose and think that we're perfect or that anybody can be perfect. Let's not look down on anybody for having feet of clay or losing it, because we all do. Every one of us does. The dark side is a part of life. But boy, it's important to acknowledge it and not to deny it, not to get into this perfectionism of saying, "I'm right." I once asked Terry Dobson about this. Terry, incidentally, was a brilliant person, very eloquent, what a talker! He uses words I could never think about using in conversation, words I've seen in books but no one has ever said because they would sound pretentious. He could say them and not sound pretentious. I said, "Terry, why is there so much discord in aikido? Why do all of these terrible things happen between teachers and different schools of aikido?" He said, "Because it's based on harmony." What he meant was there's a kind of sin of pride there, that we are so perfect. "We harmonize better than anybody else and I am a *sensei* here. Therefore everything I do must be perfect and perfectly harmonious." I think what we're basically seeing is a lot of denial, denial of weaknesses, denial of the dark side. All of that is an important part of our development.

You know, Wendy says aikido is about the dark, about aggression. It's not about harmony, it's really about aggression and violence. What I often like to say to the students is this: aikido is more than a dance, these techniques are lethal. They can really hurt you badly. Look at Steve Seagal. There it is. My wife, Annie, she's a *shodan* in aikido. After the first Steve Seagal movie, she said as we walked out, "This is the first violent action thriller I've ever been to where I knew the names of the techniques by which people were maimed and killed." But to me, if aikido did not have the possibility of severe damage or even death, it wouldn't be so poignant. The poignancy of aikido is that we are at all times choosing not to hurt our partner. Every time we could be hurting our partner, and we choose not to.

Aikido is not the denial of violence, it's the refusal of violence. It gives us a chance again and again to refuse violence. Right in the middle of a storm of violence, we again and again say, "No, we'll protect the attacker." To me, anyone who purposely hurts a student . . . I am in absolute horror of hurting a student.

It was wonderful to have Terry here. I tried to take every one of his classes. It was exciting. It was kind of a special feeling, kind of a special vibration on Friday nights. There'd be a crowd. There was a great quality of the unpredictable. Nadeau has that quality too, sometimes. You don't know what he's going to do. You never knew what Terry was going to do. One time he brought his bullwhip in. Another time he brought a hammer, nails and a board and we were all doing *shomen* by hammering nails into a board. He brought a little of the edge into it. And incidentally, I think it's fine to play the edge, as long as we all know we're playing it and we do it as informed, consenting adults. He brought some of the edge in. People would get a little hurt sometimes. He wouldn't do it purposely, but . . . he made it very interesting. And I think he felt free at this dojo to try a lot of what I call *"ninjutsu* stuff."

The thing I liked about Terry was he was willing to blow it. He tried a lot of these techniques and sometimes they worked and other times they didn't work. He'd get about one out of three, and that one out of three was spectacular. The other times he didn't control the *uke* at all. But he brought this sense of the uncertain into our school. He would do another thing which every now and then was kind of crazy. He'd have someone who was not hitting properly hit him on the head. He really got hit sometimes. One time I hit him so hard . . . people later talked about it. I wanted to be a good, sincere student. So he said, "Shomen." And there was no way I was not going to make a good, clean, pure, honest strike. So I came in and somehow I had all the power, it all just clicked right there. Long pause. People said it was like when you see boxing matches and you see sweat fly out in all directions. I saw him swaying. The pupils of his eyes were going big. But he would do things like that. He'd let you hit him right on the head.

I feel very strongly that the kind of vulnerability or willingness to fail that Terry showed us is terribly, terribly important. In fact, in my book *Mastery*, I talk about the five keys to mastery. I devote a chapter to each one, and one of them is "Surrender," even surrendering competence to gain a higher competence. If you're shooting in the 90s in golf and you want to shoot in the 80s, you'll probably have to give up the 90s for a while and shoot 100. I went through something in my music. When we got our group together, I had to relearn everything because I was playing new chords. I had to play a new key so Wendy could sing. I had to get worse for a while. You have to be willing to surrender. I just love the idea. If you're boxing, you cover up your face, you turn the side of your body, but in aikido you open up fully. Aikidoists choose to be open, "Come on, come on, come in." Like in *randori*, I learned it's the best thing in the world to smile and get them to come faster. "Don't go away, come faster, harder. Give it your best shot."

So aikido, probably more than any other martial art, allows for surrender. I think that people who armor themselves in aikido and try to always be invulnerable, well, it creates a certain disharmony. Then eventually you might get clouted 'cause there's always some bigger bull.

In *Mastery* I also talk about thirteen pitfalls along the path. And this is not necessarily the aikido path; these are very practical things, like injuries, perfectionism, little things like drugs, I just say all of the things that can knock you off the path. But I think there are pitfalls that are specific to aikido. There are things that can go wrong after you stay on the path for a while.

One pitfall, one of the things that takes people off the path, is vanity, wanting to look good, being unwilling to look like a klutz. The epilogue in my book is on "the Willingness to be a Fool," which is the very essence of learning. If you're not willing to be a fool and take pratfalls, then you're not learning anything. My daughters when they were teenagers learned the new dances before I could; they were more willing to get up and be a fool than I was. I always tell new students when they come in, especially when I see it's a fairly young man who's an athlete, "Don't try to get it! Don't try to make any progress. Be willing to be klutzy. You will be. Everybody is." We had a gold medalist, an Olympic gold medalist who came. He dropped out after three classes. He said, "I'll get this thing right now." But you're not going to get it. You can't get it. Don't try to get it. Just stay on the path.

I think this business of thinking that my way of doing it is the only way of doing it, therefore your way is not good, leads to the possibility of cult formation in aikido, which is another potential pitfall, where either you do these things or else you're not in, not one of the in-group. If you can't feel a certain kind of energy, it shows you're not sensitive. Therefore, who wants to be left out and called "insensitive?" One of the things a cult has to do is get the devotees to do something that's quite disgraceful—you know, the initiation rites of the Mau-Mau, drink urine and things like that. It's very important. Because you've done something demeaning and humiliating for this greater cause, the cause has got to be really great or else you wouldn't have done it. And not only that, if you can't feel this, you'll get sick. Have you heard that one? Somebody told me that.

You see, aikido's so profound, it's so huge, it's so endless, infinite and so forth, that it has room in it for the devil as well as for God, for the bad as well as the good—for the dark side. Some things are so small, you know. Not much room for the devil. But aikido is really big. This could be something that would be the cause of cliques. You've seen cliques evolve, you've seen some things that might be

called "cults." The "in" and the "out," the people who feel and the
ones who don't feel, or the ones who refuse to lose their integrity.
It's aikido's largeness, its profundity that allows room for the dark
side. All sorts of things can happen. I've seen ugly things, people
being demeaned, people mopping up the mat with their partners.

Let me say this: If aikido is big enough to have the dark side in
it, it's also big enough to be non-Japanese. My own particular prej-
udice is that if aikido can only be truly understood by the Japanese
sensibility, then aikido is not really big, it's not really profound. I
think there can definitely be a Western aikido, and that Western
aikido will include within it a huge respect for the Japanese and
their contribution, a huge respect for O-Sensei. Going back and
acknowledging your lineage is very important; I really believe in it.
But having acknowledged it, I feel we have to say that there can be
an American aikido just as good as Japanese aikido; maybe it'll go
beyond Japanese aikido. Even some Japanese teachers have said
that—Saito Sensei, for example. I think with our spirit of innovation, eclecticism, the kind of thing you see right around San Francisco with so many different things all coming together, it's like the
Renaissance: different strains of culture come together and then
there's an explosion. I see wonderful techniques coming out here,
new things developing all the time; it's a carnival, it's wonderful! But
we can't lose our center, we can't lose our grounding or our respect
for our roots. But within those constraints, let the sky be the limit.

Again, if it can only be done one way, then it's not as big as we
think, not as profound, not as deep. O-Sensei had the right idea. He
allowed his students to go many different directions. These disciples who are so different, Hikitsuchi and Saito, it's wonderful. It
would be horrible if aikido had to be systematized, broken down to
one correct way of doing things. If a teacher says, "This is the one
way, the only way," it bothers me. If you look throughout human
history, where people say "I am the one and the only," somewhere
down the line you might be smelling burned human flesh.

I was invited to Portland to give an L.E.T. workshop, and they
said they'd like to see an aikido demonstration. I said, "Great. See

if you can get me at least a first *kyu*, second degree brown belt or a black belt at least six feet tall." Of course, being tall is kind of a disadvantage in aikido. So they say, "Okay, no problem." About two weeks later they called back, sounding kind of embarrassed. "You know, there are four aikido schools here and unfortunately, none of them can work with you." They were all Ki Society. I said, "That's ridiculous. Let's forget it. Forget it. I don't want to cause any trouble or get anyone in trouble." To me, what is that? That is limitation. It's important to preserve the openness and the endlessness of this art. Another thing I think is very significant: as far as I know, aikido is an open art. We have visitors any time. If you go to certain karate schools, they say, "Come no further. You cannot get in the back room and see our secrets." We say, "Please come to our dojo. It's an open art." We love to have visitors. Of course, the other thing is that people could watch aikido for ten years and unless they actually practiced it, got on the mat, they would never be able to do it. You can't get it by watching it.

In my workshops I always talk about resources in the last section: "If you want to do this ... If you want to do that...." I say, "If you want to take aikido, look in the Yellow Pages. First, it should just say aikido. Probably shouldn't say "aikido, hapkido, tae kwan do" and everything else, that's probably not a good school, probably not. It's all mixed together. Then call them and ask if you can come visit. If they say "no," it's not an aikido school, not the kind I know. To me that openness, that's another big part of aikido. Philosophically, aikido has so much to offer. In the Bay Area, we have about forty dojo in our Aikido of Northern California, and just around Marin County there are probably ten or fifteen fairly good-sized dojo. And the dojo-hopping that goes on: People going back and forth and training in different places. Certain nights they'll all go to one school and then another school.... I mean, we may be open and eclectic to a fault, but it's still exciting. It's much better this way than "You must not go and train with so-and-so."

There is another big question going through my mind—why doesn't aikido grow more? I think it's because it's so difficult. I feel it's the most difficult of the martial arts. There's an article in *Scientific American* from '79 written by a *karateka* and *judoka*. It's a study of the physics of aikido and judo. The author makes a statement unequivocally that aikido is the most difficult of the martial arts. Every attack is different, every person is different, you're not just striking out at something or making a power move, you're having to blend in with some other motion, some other energy, whatever it is or whichever way it's coming. It's very hard and it takes so long: you don't look good at the beginning, you don't have quick results, you don't get a quick fix, no self-defense fix, none of that. This is the theme of *Mastery,* that we have fallen prey to something really quite insidious, this quick-fix mentality. My book is basically an essay against the quick fix. I'm hoping the book will have some influence. I hope it will also bring some more people to aikido.

A lot of people have come to aikido because of my writing; I'm very happy for that. Frank Doran said he once did a survey: where did you hear of aikido, why did you decide to come here? And the most frequent answer was my books and articles. So maybe *Mastery* will bring more people to the art. On the other hand, maybe it's all right if it's never really popular. Karate is so much bigger. Richard and Wendy and I don't particularly try to get it to grow because in a way it's kind of hard. It's okay the way it is. We don't advertise at all. We have a very small notice in the Yellow Pages, very small. And yet, if we were really going to be altruistic, if we believed that this is good and wholesome, just like it is, we might hope that it would grow. Maybe some of its influence will be through things like Tom Crum's book and through L.E.T. and Dobson and his book, taking it out to the people in other forms. I think that's fine. But I think you've always got to keep the purity of aikido.

The best thing of all for me is that aikido keeps getting richer and more mysterious. After I had been in the art for a year or two, I really knew a lot about it. I wrote about it. I was on the cover of a national magazine in my *gi* with an article called "Aikido and the Mind of the West." After more than twenty years, I seem to know much less. In December of 1992, Wendy and I had the privilege of doing our fourth *dan* demonstrations for Sensei Frank Doran, and for many students, friends, and peers. We only had about three weeks to get prepared, and I decided to really push myself, creating a rather long and quite complex demo. The push was wonderfully strenuous and the evening was sweet, but at the end I had a powerful realization of how little I knew or could ever know about this marvelous art....

Now I hesitate to write anything at all about aikido, preferring rather to glory in the endless journey it offers for whoever is willing to stay on the path. As the swordmaster Tesshu wrote: "Do not think/ This is all there is./ More and more/ Wonderful teachings exist./ The sword is unfathomable."

10

RICHARD HECKLER

Along with George Leonard and Wendy Palmer, Richard Heckler is one of the co-founders and co-teachers of Aikido of Tamalpais. Heckler's place in aikido history was made when George Leonard, in one of his books, described Heckler's black belt test in semi-mystical terms.

Like a number of other people who have been drawn to aikido, Heckler recalls what might be termed a personality split. On the one hand, there is a desire to do physical and aggressive things, like football, and on the other hand there is an attraction to intellectual and spiritual matters. In American culture, there are two different social groups, two different languages, and two different places to be. Heckler points out that aikido bridges these two worlds.

Heckler has taken aikido off the mat in two rather remarkable and different ways. First, he has been involved in creating and teaching a kind of bodyworks called Lomi School. Over a long period of time he had incorporated aikido training and principles into Lomi School. In this way, he has forged a close relationship among psychology, bodywork, and aikido.

In a more dramatic move, he accomplished the challenge of teaching aikido to units of military elite Special Forces. The result of this controversial experiment in "aikido off the mat" has been described in the book In Search of the Warrior Spirit.

In this interview, Heckler makes an interesting argument about aikido's place in the search to find one's true nature. He says that aikido's thrust is not up, not to transcendence; it does not take you up

239

to heaven but is a descent into the ordinary world, down into the dark places of life, where we find the existential contradiction of our death. Aikido becomes a way to live the pain and terror of the ultimate contradiction.

I come from a military family, so for about the first thirteen years of my life, we traveled all over. I can remember one year when I went to three different schools. My martial arts background started on a Navy base. I saw soldiers and sailors going overseas and coming back as judo black belts and karate black belts. My father was an enlisted man, so the streets were kind of tough. I was afraid a lot. I wanted self-defense; I studied martial arts for real practical reasons. I went to high school in San Diego and kind of roamed with a little gang. Also, I was the first person in my family to go to college. I went on a track scholarship. I ran in the Central American games, the pre-Olympics.

I won NCAA track titles both years I was at San Diego State College. I was an All-American in Track and Field. After college I spent some time in the Marine Corps and got a little bit into their hand-to-hand combat. I did one tour of duty and then went on to get my Ph.D. in psychology.

I studied clinical psychology but with the help of my chairperson I was also able to emphasize the mind-body relationship. I got a fellowship at the University of Washington, and after I studied there for a while, I finished at the Saybrook Institute in San Francisco.

As for my martial arts training, I started with judo, then did some jujutsu and karate. For a couple of years I also studied t'ai chi with a Chinese man who had come from Hong Kong. He was a fighter and he was all broken up. Later I went to Hawaii and eventually saw aikido in '72. In many ways that was connected with the founding of the Lomi School, which I started in Mill Valley with my partner Robert Hall. That was in 1970. Then I ended up in Hawaii, and because I was in Hawaii, I wound up starting aikido.

That was in 1972, early '72. Aikido had been recommended to me for a long, long time. As I said, I had been doing t'ai chi, but t'ai chi wasn't fulfilling a need I felt, and yoga wasn't fulfilling it. I ran in college and I didn't really want to do that any more. So I think on that level I was looking for something. Because I had started so early in martial arts, that idea was always strong. A friend told me, "You'll like aikido." So I called three dojo and they all said they didn't have room. They asked me for my name and when I told them, they said they didn't have room. Later on I realized that was because I was white. Finally I found a place on the other side of the island; it took 45 minutes to drive there. I went and checked it out and it was instant love. I stepped into the dojo, and as I said in my book, the thing that went through my mind was "they're doing the Tao." It was incredible because everybody can talk about all that but I saw that they were doing it. Even though I had done these other arts, like t'ai chi and judo, aikido seemed still more profound. It just pulled me. It was beautiful, I mean "beauty" in the real sense of the word, "beauty as truth." It wasn't beauty as something that was flaw-less, necessarily, it was much more the feeling that it was something real archetypal: there was something very old, there was something very wise there. It was true, it was just simply true. I saw these peo-ple doing aikido and I was magnetized instantly to do it.

There was one man in particular who inspired me. He was named Tokei Sensei and he was at that point really going through his changes because of Tohei's split. He was connected to Tohei because Tohei had started aikido in Hawaii. But Tokei Sensei, who was a sixth *dan* at that time, had a lot of influence on me because he essen-tially really modeled what he was talking about. He was a man who had a deep center of gravity, physically and emotionally. He was a man I saw as being basically balanced within himself, and he was also the kingpin there on Kauai. But I was that age already that I was looking for more than just beating somebody up. I had already competed a lot. I had been in a gang, I had fought, I'd been in the Marine Corps, I'd done all that stuff. So really I wasn't necessarily looking to be real strong and real tough at that point. So I watched him with other people. I watched him walk in the dojo and what he did. I could see that he was at that time really struggling with the notion of aikido and his role in it in terms of Tohei's split and all the power struggles that were happening in the area. While he was balanced, he was also struggling with something, so it was creative that way, to be a part of it at that time. I was also white, and he was very non-racist about it.

When I look back now, I can see that the practice was by the numbers and the dojo was mostly Hawaiian. I was the only white person in the dojo, the only Caucasian. It was stiff, it was basically real stiff. It was one, two, three. But it really struck me and helped me. I went three, four times a week. I was tolerated and I was taught well, but I knew I would have to be there a couple of years before they would accept me fully, I could just feel it. I had already been in Kauai for almost a year and was in the surfing community. I was surfing a lot but still no one out there would talk to me. It was the same people and the same waves every day. But it was always their wave, too: if there was a choice between them or me going off on a wave, it would be their wave. It was the same deal in the dojo. So I thought, "Well I'm just going to get what I can get here."

In many ways it was really very isolating for me because the people I was with who were my community and who were very much in touch with each other really couldn't understand my love for aikido at all. They thought I was actually crazy to drive across the island around sunset; while you were in Hawaii you were supposed to be mellow and all that. I was just in love, basically, I couldn't not do it, it was one of those kind of things.

We had a falling-out among my bodyworks community in Kauai, we kind of split up. So about six months after I started aikido I ended up going back to the mainland. And one of the first things I did was look up Aikido of San Francisco, which had just opened. That was a time in the Bay Area when brown belts were goddesses and gods. I mean, they were just up there. And then there was Bob Nadeau, Bill Witt and Frank Doran. They were like this other class of people. Bob Nadeau and Frank Doran became my primary teachers.

It was a real classic city dojo where a lot of disparate elements came in. There were three different teachers; it was really at that

point taught by committee. It became the model for Aikido of Tamalpais, where Wendy Palmer, George Leonard and I teach, which we
continue to teach by committee, the same way. We saw these guys
running it, and we saw that they had different styles. There were no
apparent surface differences that were very explicit. I mean, people
weren't saying "you should do this" or "stay here." There were six
days of aikido plus weapons. A full meal.

Every once in a while you would see somebody come by with a
skirt, a man would come by with a skirt. That was always very
impressive. The skirt just adds to the whole beauty of it, the mythology of it.

I went to Japan in '76. I spent over four months there, just at
Hombu Dojo. I disliked Tokyo immensely. I connected with some
teachers there; Yamaguchi Sensei was one. When I say "connected,"
I mean "in my heart." I don't think they really knew who I was. And
I studied with the Doshu and Osawa Sensei. But Yamaguchi and
the Doshu I really watched. I studied six to eight hours a day and it
clearly told me that I really didn't want to have a dojo, because it
was very hard training. Then I talked to part of the European community about how in Japan they have these "dojo busters." If you
got a dojo, a guy would come in and just challenge you. Steve Seagal, by the way, has some interesting stories about that. But I was
in a non-fighting art. How would you deal with dojo busters? I'd
been in fighting arts. I wasn't interested. I was working on my own
levels of aggression. I also was a professional in my own field. So I
really wasn't looking at aikido as a job. I would want to share it
where I could and I was already starting to express it through the
Lomi School and my psychotherapeutic practice, things like that.
But I really didn't want it as a job necessarily. I liked it that way. And
then we started Tamalpais Aikido after we all got our black belts.
When I look back now it just seems at some level really presump-
tuous almost that Wendy and George and I would open up this dojo.

We were all basically at the same level. We were all brown belts,
ikkyu. Some people asked Wendy to teach at a small adult education class in Mill Valley. So she'd go there and have maybe six to ten

students, people dropping in. She'd ask me or George to come by and help her, be *uke*. I think she did it two or three times a week, something like that. So we helped her and it was really great, it was fun. Then the notion came up that we should start a dojo, so we brought it to Bob Nadeau and Frank, we were mostly connected with them, and asked Bob if he wanted to do this dojo. The four of us would do it and he would be the main teacher because he had all these other dojos and we would support him. He said he wasn't interested but he basically gave us a blessing to go ahead and do it. And I thought "What is this? What does this mean in terms of my commitment?" It had already broken up one marriage, this love of aikido. Well, then we did a summer at Anna Halpern's Dancers' Workshop and people started coming from all over. Then we rented this big space in 1976, the same place we have now. All that time we've run it by committee, which I think is very interesting.

We do everything by committee and consensus. We all agree on everything. It's gone through a lot of permutations in terms of our changes, our personal changes, professional changes. None of us has really a big investment in being the head *sensei,* for example, or "We're going to run it my way ... or it's going to be like this ..." Naturally some people will gravitate towards Wendy, some towards George, some people towards me. We spread all that out. We make every effort to give the same *kyu* test. And it grows and continues. I think there's not too much of that around, clearly not on the East Coast, by which I mean dojo by committee. Bob and Bill and Frank did it for a while and then clearly it became too difficult for them: when they lost the space they clearly made choices not to come back together again. I feel in my lifetime real good about the way we run things, I feel real good about it, because I think that people have been served by it. And it's clearly not because we haven't had disagreements, it's much more because we've tried to put those aside, tried to integrate those into other things.

Of course, there were always a lot of jokes about "Marin Aikido." You know Marin, it has a certain reputation. But our aikido is real strong, real lasting. We have a number of other *nidan* who are really good, and we have advanced weapons classes. Because of all our different connections, we have an incredible amount of people come through there. All of the Soviets have come through Michael Murphy's Esalen-Soviet program. We've had a lot of Olympic athletes come through, a lot of professional athletes come through.

George and Wendy and I, we don't make our living primarily from aikido. In fact, often we'll put the money back into it. And still basically we're doing aikido maybe four or five days a week. I think at some level, and I consider myself a professional, at some level that has been real healthy for our dojo. I don't think it's necessary to be a full-time aikido practitioner to fully express aikido in your life. Also, I think that it's easy to get into a romantic notion about the poor martial artist—there's an image, an archetype about that.

Terry Dobson was connected with our school for a while too. I met Terry at the St. John's summer camp, I think that was in '78. I enjoyed him. He was still connected with Bond Street Dojo then, but in a shift we asked him to come out to California. He taught classes at Mt. Tam for well over a year, became a resident there. When Steve Seagal came to America, he came to our dojo. He stayed with me, actually, and taught at our dojo. When Barrish started to make his inroads, the first place he taught was at Tam. One of my students went to Washington and said, "I trained with this guy. He's really interesting and I took a video. Why don't you look at it?" And since we were always pretty much open to people coming in with all kinds of different styles and expressing them if they wanted to, I really trusted this guy so we invited Barrish down to teach. My whole thing always was I want to see the guy first and train with him first. You know what it's like in the martial arts world, it's full of megalomaniacs.

In a more personal vein, I have made aikido an important part of the Lomi School. It wasn't part of the school in the beginning, but of course, I integrated it. I would, as a brown belt, just start teaching a lot of centering and grounding. I was actually doing a little of that before from my judo background. Then of course, it's outlined so clearly in aikido that it can be presented like that. And now it's a big part of Lomi School; in fact, people who go through the three-month training all take their fifth *kyu* test. There are a lot of people who start their aikido at Lomi School and who go on to get their *shodan* and end up teaching. For other people that's the only thing that ever happens for them. But aikido is really an essential part of the school now, not only the movements, but the whole philosophy, which I think at essential levels grew out of the same philosophy as Lomi School, which is "there's an *aiki* way of doing things."

In the Lomi School, we teach people how to work with other people bodily—that means through touch, breath and movement. And because of my background in clinical psychology and my partner being a psychiatrist, we also do verbal, psychological work. Essentially, we try to integrate Western psychological practices and Eastern spiritual disciplines, all within the context of embodiment, the body as a path. The Lomi School teaches a way of being with somebody. I'd like to see the students come away from Lomi School knowing how to touch people deeply, clearly, how to touch people softly, energetically, how to work with their breath and how to show them some real basic movement skills and principles. Wasn't it Xenophone who said, "Anything that is forced or misunderstood cannot be beautiful?" By that I think he meant "cannot be truthful." And I think that basically that's the same approach that we have in Lomi School, it's an *aiki* approach.

I think that there is something so intrinsically natural or universal about aikido that we see it in other things. In other words, I think that there was something *aiki* about what we started to do in the beginning. At least we were reaching for it. And then when I saw aikido, it was like "Oh, my god. There's actually a form." In my first words, I saw that people were actually doing the Tao. This is what it is. And we can learn from it.

The Lomi School has always been and continues to be a growing organism. It's not like "Oh, this is what it is; we're still doing that same thing." It has changed a lot. I think in the beginning we were a little younger in the sense of trying to push people through, we

were a little more pushy. And I think over time and under the influence of aikido we've realized that our path really is one of going with
things.

In '84 we put the Lomi School down to redesign the program. It
was successful and it was filling and people were getting a lot out of
it, but all the teachers were saying, "We really need to do something
else after fourteen years. We really need to look at it." As the programs were going on it felt almost impossible to redesign it, so we
really needed to put it down for a while and look at it. That coincided with the project I did with the Army Special Forces back East,
which took me out of that network for about eight months. So it was
a perfect time to do that. When I got back in '86 I established myself
back in the Bay Area—actually moved up north to Petaluma, I own
a small ranch up there—then started doing the training again with
a new design. So we took a couple years' break and started up again.

All totaled, with all the different programs, probably about 2,500
people have gone through the Lomi School program. It's a lot but
for more than twenty years it's pretty small. There are programs
now being run in Europe. And we've done programs in Latin America and South America, Canada. I think overall, if we figure all those
in, the total is probably more like 5,000.

One of the reasons we teach aikido in the Lomi School is that
aikido can be used as a metaphor in many different ways. The notion
of aikido being a metaphor is powerful, it's built into the art: people grabbing might represent pressure, people striking at you might
represent people yelling at you. And then how do you work with
these principles of centering and grounding and energy within that
context, how do you lead their energy? But it really is based on a
martial art, a notion that training with Saotome Sensei has really
sharpened for me. We do these things for certain reasons. Why do
you grab a wrist or why do you strike this way? Or if you grab, what
are you really grabbing for—so you can punch? So if somebody
grabs me, I also have to pay attention to this and this.

Teaching Special Operations people and police people has also
influenced me here because it's a very pragmatic thing for them.

"Does this work? If it doesn't work, I'm really not interested. You have a nice thing, but if it doesn't work, I'm not interested because I'm out here in the trenches," for example. That has really made me re-evaluate a lot of things. I think the strength of aikido lies in maintaining it as a martial art in that context or in the sense that what you really learn here is a martial training, martial wisdom.

The main context there is a somatic context, that if we can learn these principles bodily, they can be translated into other dimensions—a mental dimension, an emotional dimension, or a spiritual dimension. We say that we do a lot of wrist, arm and shoulder grabs in aikido; well, this will represent any kind of grab in your life. People don't know what that really means until you grab them. And most people who aren't accustomed to it will basically go into what I call "a conditioned pattern." They want to fight back, they want to leave, they want to study it, they want to disappear, go into denial. And then they realize, "Oh, this is the same thing that I do when my boss shows up or I'm caught in traffic." And if you get an audience that comes to the dojo because they want to work with themselves, they accept the metaphor very readily because they actually experience it within themselves.

My sense is that if you do train and if you do a lot of vigorous physical training without talking about aikido as a metaphor or anything, it will work. But I think if you explain it and if you set it into a real frame of reference point, it will speed all that up. It will speed it up an incredible amount. I think that if you do it over time, it will go in your body and it will become more like a reflex. If you're talking about it and framing it, I think that people will step out right away and they'll find their life changed. I really do. I find that over and over again. At the Tam dojo people have been training there for a long time and they really are in touch with the metaphor. So in a regular beginning, intermediate or advanced class, there can be redundancy about that. So if I scan the class and I see we're speaking the same language, then I don't need to mouth off about this stuff because it's integrated and it's happening. People come in to our basics class and I feel at that point I'm starting to create this language, which is a language of the body, which is a language of aikido, one you feel muscular with. But after a while not only is it not necessary to talk about the metaphor, but people don't want to have it hammered in all the time.

I think that there's another piece, too. It's really clear that what happens in the dojo is relevant to your life, but life isn't necessarily just at the dojo. There's a small distinction that I'm trying to make here. I mean, the first one of course is that you take what you learn in the dojo out. But the other part of it is that you don't make the dojo your life.

Aikido is about being present, being with what is. And the tools are being centered, grounded, knowing how to mobilize your energy, how to expand it, and how to use it as a magnetic field to draw things in. One of the essential pieces about it for me is that it has a real potential of teaching us how to live in the contradiction, how to live in the paradox. And no one really wants to do that much. What they really want to know is the answer. They want an answer about how to do it. You see, the books that sell the most give you simple answers. I'll go on the record and say that the aikido books that sell the most are the books that tell you when you get in the dojo what you should do, how you should walk and when you should bow. Those books are needed, but I think it reflects this need to have someone tell us how to do it and what the answer is. And once we have the answer we try to manipulate the situation to have the right question to fit our answer.

I don't think that aikido builds an ascending structure. An ascending structure is usually what religions do—people get faced with their dilemma, their existential dilemma, and they build an ascending structure, Christianity or Buddhism, so they can climb out of this hole, this dilemma, but it's built on a false bottom. That's what I mean by an ascending structure. But I think that what is needed is more of a descending structure where we'll be able to allow ourselves to settle into that hole, to drop into it and to be with it. I think it's the most difficult thing because it's the most terrifying, it's clearly the most terrifying. And yet at the same time, in settling into it, I think we are more accountable for our aggression because we're dropping into it and not saying, "That's pretty terrible and that's going to get us in trouble and I want to stay away from that." It's an *irimi* movement, a movement into it and dropping into it. If we don't do that, all the energy is always to move away from it or to transcend it. And yet it never goes away.

A simple way to look at the hole is to say that it's just the dilemma we face as human beings. We know that we know, and what that means is we know we're going to die. That knowledge shapes our thinking and our way of living. Most people really don't want to look at that. In other words, we really have to look at the notion of impermanence in a really clear way. How is it that we are here and why are we here? We know that we're going to die. Everyone knows that and everyone reacts to it in different ways, from Donald Trump to people who retreat into their cells. Aikido asks us both to develop something inside ourselves and at the same time express it to the world. This is to me what's really exciting about aikido.

You know, I worked myself up from kind of a lower-class background, got a Ph.D., bought a car on time payments, I've got an answering machine and all that kind of stuff, I did that and also followed a meditation path. Basically they seem in separate camps, just like when I was in college: I could go out with the jocks and run, feel alive, feel the inspiration of being outside and the sky and the grass, and then I'd have to go to academia to talk to Wittgenstein or somebody like that. And in aikido I can go out there and somebody's going to jump at me or grab my throat or punch my eyes and I can deal with that, but that's not what I'm really trying to perfect. I'm really trying to perfect where I'm rooted inside of myself while I'm dealing with the world. I really think that is one of the profound things about aikido. And I think that those of us in aikido who get more and more involved in refining wrist-twisting, refining technique, basically lose that. I think that people who do that are really running from that profound aspect. I really do. And I think that it demeans the art in the sense that it really doesn't allow the profundity of it to blossom. It's a deeply profound art. You only need to see some of the masters of the art, which I feel personally that I've had the opportunity to study with, express that. There's something very deeply connected in them in the way that they can handle both internal and external aggression.

For me the hole is not just an existential thought. It's really a somatic experience, the kind of experience that one can directly experience in the body. It's down that line, it's down that central line. So we have the existential thought that we're going to die and there's some kind of fear. But the hole actually represents, actually is, in my experience, a place in which we haven't been fully authorized into who we are. We haven't fully received the notion that we are lovable and okay as we are. In pre-industrial times, the father would look at his son and see how his feet are on the ground, the sparkle in his eye, acknowledge what he's gone through and say, "You're a man. You've made it. You've done these things. And part of that is because I've transmitted that to you. And now I'm telling you directly that you have made it. There's not a question about that. You are unconditionally a man and you are unconditionally lovable for who you are. We may have separate politics in the community, in the tribe, but that has nothing to do with this, and here's your toma-hawk, here's your spear, here's your basket."

I feel that if that's not done, if that's not communicated to an individual, it leaves a hole. My experience is that it's a felt hole, that if you start to drop your attention down into your body or you start to seat yourself, if that hole hasn't been filled in, one of three things happens. You jump over it. Somebody feels their heart and then they go to their genitals. "I'm in love with somebody, let's have sex."

The second thing that happens is that if we go down and hit that hole, we go back up: we can't tolerate that. It's too painful because basically what it's saying is that there's something missing inside of us. And everything that is built on top of that is essentially built on a false bottom and so we question who we are: Am I really genuine? What do I really trust? Is this authentic? These are the kinds of questions we all face.

The third thing that happens in my experience is that people will take a part of their attention, I call it "satellite knowing," and actually separate it from the body. So people will say: "I feel my stomach," but they're not experiencing it; they're actually kind of bouncing around themselves to feel it. You know, "The book says I have a stomach. I know it intellectually." The other way of feeling your stomach is to drop into yourself, actually feel your stomach. And I think that aikido has an opportunity, if it's used and focused this way, to fill in that hole. This has to be done consciously.

I don't think that becoming whole can all be done in aikido: you know, there's an attitude that says this is my path, if I do enough *ikkyos* or even if I do enough *ikkyos* and pay attention to what I'm doing, if I'm aware of it, then that's enough. I think there are places, and this is one of them, where maybe aikido isn't a complete "way," i.e., aikido as the form that we know, the dojo form. So one may say, "I need to do some therapy and talk about this without a *gi* on, without my credentials of whatever *kyu* or *dan* that I am." And if they're really integrated, they will do their aikido there, it will still happen. But I don't know if it will just happen in the dojo. And when I say "that," I'm talking about the sense of our own individuation. I've actually seen people, and I know that it's true, that we can use aikido actually as a cover for these other things. If I'm strong enough, if I'm fast enough, if I speak well enough, I'll get away with this.

My current definition of aikido, something which changes all the time as I change, is that aikido is being in harmony with what is. And if we're really asking ourselves to do that, it starts with who we are, what's happening in ourselves. And eventually we will feel where our limitations are, where that hole is. In doing *ikkyo*, in trying to do it the right way, I can miss that. But if the search is really genuine and honest, one will run into that hole.

In my experience, that search is really in the air in most dojos that I go to. It's much more in the air in some dojos and less in others; sometimes it's so much in the air it's a little stinky and there's a kind of spiritual stink about it. Some places it's not much in the air but it's there, it has some kind of composition to it. I think that it's a fine line how we explore that within the aikido structure because

I think that it's important that we keep it as a martial art, that that's what makes it powerful, as opposed to a dance form. We need to be continually reminded of that.

I think that there are a couple of things about aikido that make it work for me as a means to conduct that search. One is that there is no competition. There is no external competition so we have to deal with our internal competition: there is as much emphasis on *ukemi* as there is on the person throwing. In fact, I've always felt that the first two years are about *ukemi*. I think that the attack is one in which we're not trying to fake out the other person, that it's just one straight-line attack: what you're trying to train into your body is that there's going to be one clear message here, that I'm not going to try to fake you out so I can get you some other way. I think that that's a piece of it.

Another part of that search has to be about aggression. I did this art called capoeira for about six years while I was doing aikido. Capoeira is a Brazilian martial art, and unlike aikido it comes from a peasant, oppressed class of people, people who were really fighting for their freedom as black slaves in Brazil. My teacher was three times heavyweight champion of Brazil and basically one of the best fighters I've ever seen, a very, very powerful man. He came to the Bay Area to start teaching capoeira, and people from all these other arts came in—judo, kung fu, karate, wing chun, t'ai chi, all these different people and aikidoists. He told me that aikido students are by far the most aggressive. I explain that in two ways. One way is the *irimi* aspect of aikido, that we're really taught to enter. And if you go to another art, you'll see that come up. I mean, if you're really learning your lesson, you will let yourself enter into an attack while you're off the line. I think the second thing is that aikidoists are full of aggression and we come to the art to learn how to deal with it. And when we get into a new art we have to reorganize ourselves because that aggression comes back up, and I think that that's what he saw.

I think that even while people talk about *aiki*—that it appeals to them because of the harmony or the truth of it or the beauty of it

or its connection with nature—there's still some underlying unconscious impulse to deal with the dark side of aggression. I feel real
clearly that that's true for me. A great thing happened to me working with these Special Operations soldiers. These were young guys,
late twenties, the ass-kicking types. One time we were in this car,
driving to do some operation, and I asked them, "What about
aikido?" One guy said, "It's good, but I don't know if it would work
in a fight," and another guy says, "Yeah, it's fun, but I don't know if
I'll do it again," and this other guy says, "I love it. It's the greatest
thing and I'm going to do it as soon as I get out of this program."
"What do you like about it?" "Well, in a fight I think I'd still use a
baseball bat, but you know, it has helped my skiing, it has helped
my shooting." Then he said, "You know what, I don't beat my kids
anymore." And I thought in that moment, "It's a success, this stuff
really does work." I think that what he found was a way to deal with
his aggression on his kids. And he was the son of a father who beat
him, too. And his father got beat. What he did was he broke that
karmic chain. Basically that was what he was learning in aikido.
For me it was extremely moving because I had a lot of questions
about why I was even there and was I successful or was I just one
end of a double-bind for these guys.

Sometimes aikido doesn't allow an outlet for aggression. I've seen
that happen. And I think that's unhealthy. I'll see that there will be
a lot of people in aikido, especially younger men, and they'll take
up another art, go away for a while and come back. I think in the
view of martial arts people, aikido is the best art. A karate guy in
my home town told me that. But he also had guys who were twenty-
three years old and wanted to fight. He said, "I know they'll get there
but that's what they're doing now." That's true for me. An aikido dojo
could get somebody to go in there and just really teach the students
how to punch if the *sensei* doesn't know how to do it or how to kick.
I bring that in a lot. I bring in kicks and punches. The guys that I
taught, Navy Seals, they were very educational for me. They would
never do a *shomen*. They wouldn't ever do a *shomen*. I'd go over
shomens again and again. And a *shomen* was always a pluck at the

eyes or a throat grab or a punch to the nose. So basically, that's what I did. It was like they just couldn't relate.

I clearly can feel my aggression. I can feel my aggression if all of a sudden I just get anxious and I need to leave the room. To me there's aggression in that, self-aggression. My awareness of it gets finer and finer. I don't feel that I need a lot of reminders or that I have to try to make up reminders that I'm aggressive. If it's a bad day and somebody cuts in front of me, I'm Son of Sam. I'd just as soon drop a grenade down their gas tank, shoot their kneecaps out. I think it's important that we surface that stuff, look at it and say, "Yeah, this is here, this aggression is here." But I don't know that we have to go into it. This is slightly different but in *tanto*-techniques, I'll say to people, "Okay. Grab this knife, it's razor-sharp. Now try to cut the other person. Don't do an aikido thrust. Really try to cut them." Well, you know, in five seconds you've done four or five cuts. So if you have a knife fighter, you give him your money. You give him your change and you walk away. That's true even with somebody who's not a knife fighter with a knife.

One thing that's really important for me is that when I see people individually, in my therapy practice or if I'm teaching aikido, I'll ask them, "What do you want? What are you looking for?" Somebody might say, "I'm in a tough spot. My neighbor is constantly hassling me. I'm a woman. I can't use any kind of a weapon or a firearm. I want to use self-defense." So I'll say, "Go take boxing if you have just three months. I mean, if you want to start now, aikido is not necessarily going to do it for you. You might learn about centering and all that's good, but if it's really physical stuff you want, take boxing." But somebody could say, "I got a *nidan* in judo when I was nineteen and I've gone through all of these things and I'm thirty-five and I see I'm beating my kids. There's something wrong here." "Well, this might be the perfect arena. I'll teach you to work with your aggression." So I think that's important. What do people want?

When new people come in, I ask them, "What do you want?" I try to get real clear about that, because it also helps me become a better teacher. I can really see if I can give them what they're looking for. I had a young guy come in the other day who was a little Thai man, a Thai boxer. He was like twenty-three, had done a lot of things, and I said, "What do you want?" He said, "I've been beat up enough and I'm looking for a more spiritual thing." I said, "Maybe this will work. Let's see." Guys like that can get into thinking: "I can beat the shit out of everybody in this dojo. What am I doing here?" I'll say, "Yeah, you probably could. But we're here for something else." I can remind them "You're here for something else. You can do that in another dojo if you want. You're here not to beat everybody up."

One way of looking at aggression is to see it as connected with the shadow, the parts of ourselves we don't want to look at. I think that in many ways aikido brings up the shadow because the whole thrust of it is towards this notion of harmony or blending or some ethic of eros or love. And of course any time you go down that one direction, the other part is going to surface. I think that if we really pay attention we'll see that shadow side come up because aikido has this one intent, this one direction. If I have a problem with aggression, what I'll do is I'll put that back in the shadow. I don't want to look at that so I'll put that back in the shadow. I'll do aikido, but gee, this guy's messing with me, so I broke his arm. Where did that come from?

But there's more in the shadow than aggression. I mean, as teachers and *senseis* we really have to look at this in terms of being in positions of authority, because we're out there, we put on this costume. We get out there, everybody is sitting down, we're standing. They come up, we throw them. There's an agreement there. We throw them, they go down, little people throw big guys, blah, blah, blah. We're a perfect projection screen. I think it's real easy to start to believe our own bullshit that way. And I've seen within aikido teachers that we have a certain vigilance about that shadow coming out in that position of authority, in terms of power, of sexuality. People are starting to address that more and more.

Sometimes the shadow comes out like this: I think people will get what I mentioned earlier, a kind of "spiritual stink" about what they do, a real kind of high-falutin' morality. And I think that part of that comes about because we're not competing with each other. I can't say, "Well, I'm better than you are. I can just beat you up." And so the whole nature of it becomes very inner. In defense of that people will start to create a moral structure around it. "We don't do this in aikido." Or "We should do this." Or "This doesn't happen." Or "The best way to do it is. . . ." Or sometimes you hear about "The real aikido," or "The aikido that can't be seen." Or the soft stylists complain about the hard stylists and vice versa. I think that this moral structure begins to happen as opposed to "Okay, let's get in the ring and throw it all in there." "Let's shoot hoops" or "let's run" and then it's real clear. It's just not that clear in aikido. And I think as a defense for our own inadequacies, our own limitations, we build up this moral structure.

Since aikido is a martial art, it deals with power. I think that true power is being genuine in every moment. But we're also in a physical art and there are many levels of power too, and you can be seduced into them; the shadow can come out there, too. I think that it's essential there's a "heart element" in it. I don't want to make that sound soft-minded or mushy, but there needs to be a compassion element. I've seen and continue to see power without compassion turn back in on itself. That has been a great teaching for me in my life.

I've seen people in aikido get real blown up about the kind of energy that starts to move through them. I've seen people become very powerful and charismatic and start to go into areas that you define as "cult," the classical definition of "cult." Their power starts off as something brilliant and bright but over time it starts to turn against them. I think the only way that will happen is if we cut ourselves off from the feedback loop, if we're not listening to our community, our training partners. If I'm out training with partners and they're saying, "You're too far to the right. You're too far to the left. You're getting weird, man. I do like your power, but there's something missing"—I have to listen to them. I think if we do cut ourselves off from that, it returns and embraces.

There are probably identifiable stages in aikido training. I think there's an initial magnetism. You see this thing and it rings that bell inside of you, it's true inside of you. So you jump on it. And you find out it's difficult, it's a steep climb for the first six months. But it's so enthralling it doesn't matter. At some point somebody gets their finger tweaked or their toenail out or something like that and they think, "I don't know if I want to stay in this." The other thing I've found is that when people learn their forward rolls, it's a major turning point: there's a whole bunch of people who get lost at that point, which is interesting because you'd think a lot of them would go on. But I think what they feel is their level of responsibility has really expanded. "People will be able to throw me now. I don't want that responsibility." And then I think that there's an integration level into the dojo where you actually start to meet people there and you find them interesting and that they have different professions and jobs. People have relationships and love affairs. And then these people start to become resources for you. We have a woman who's a physician in a prison. Well, now she's bringing some aikido people and they're becoming resources for each other. "Well gee, I have this earache." It starts to become *Sangha*, our community base.

Then there's a stage where you think, "I'm just not getting any better. And I'm not even sure what it means to get better. But it just feels like I'm not getting any better. I've just spent six years going to this dojo and it's a little bit harder to get up in the morning." A whole bunch of people get lost then. And then I see that especially in America now there's a phase where people will maybe start to get input from another teacher. It wasn't happening so much when I started. But there are so many people around, and people traveling, and sometimes when people experience a new teacher, they think, "Oh, that's real aikido. That's fantastic" or "I like it. That feels like it" and there may be a real connection to that teacher and they may start to think, "Oh, this is a real student-teacher relationship." And then there's another whole plateau that begins at that point.

I also think there's a stage where you wonder, "Does it work in the sense of what would happen 'out there,' in the world? Does it work out there?" When I was *ikkyu,* brown belt, I lived in San Francisco near Golden Gate Park. Sometimes after a real juicy training, I'd walk in the park, with a *bokken.* And it was like that feeling of "Oh boy, a mugger!" Fortunately, probably for everybody, that never happened to me. But you know, I went through that phase.

Eventually, you reach the place where technique loses its fascination and you start wondering about the deeper issues. I often call that the place where form is endless. In other words, you can learn variation upon variation and always do different things and then you start asking a question like, "What does he mean 'drain the aggression out of your body'?" Some people start to look at their own lives and they see that they're still angry and they're still getting pissed off and fall into some pit then. "Gee, I've done this for seven, nine, ten, twelve years and look at me now. What good is it?"

And then I think there's actually a place where the real profound notion of a discipline comes in where I'm creating an environment that supports wakefulness. And I'm coming here not to get better and not because I'm escaping, but I'm coming here because I'm choosing to come here and wake up a little bit.

In aikido it's necessary to constantly question the art, to pose a kind of an ongoing question. I think it plugs into every domain, all the way from simple technique—where the finger goes, should it always be that way, which has its own level—to the basic setup of aikido as a martial art, attack and defense, to the question of what happens if I bring in this other stuff, what if I do this other kind of kick, for example, to the domain of wisdom about it. But I also feel I have to remind myself all the time, "Gee, I'm just happy to be moving, that's all. I'm just simply happy to be moving on this mat. I can sweat, I can be muscular." And in thinking that too I have to remind myself that I always want more than that. It's true, I do want that. But I want more than that and I have to let myself keep opening to that.

One of the things that I've been looking at lately is something I call "finding yourself lost." This is probably more in-house aikido stuff, but for me what has become the most interesting thing is this:

once everything is established, once you become present and you know all these techniques, how then do you let go of them? You know, that whole idea that we're really learning about the self, becoming aware of the self, but in order to do that you have to forget about the self. At least at the stage that I'm training now, that feels really up front for me. You know, *shomen uchi irimi nage,* I can do that, I can translate the words, I can do that business. But where do you start to allow something else to come through? It clearly has to do with this notion of being relaxed, more in the feeling self than the thinking self. But I feel that aikido is a great place to look at that.

II

WENDY PALMER

Wendy Palmer is a spare athletic woman with short, thick dark hair sprinkled with grey. She laughs easily and speaks with great anima-tion, enthusiasm and self-confidence. She began her aikido training under Bob Nadeau. About the time she got her black belt she and fel-low students George Leonard and Richard Heckler founded Aikido of Tamalpais in Mill Valley, California. Many well-known aikido instruc-tors have taught at that dojo, and Palmer describes her experiences with several of them, notably Terry Dobson, Steven Seagal, Mitsugi Saotome and Hiroshi Ikeda. In one fascinating story, she tells of a "visit" she had from Dobson shortly after his death. Palmer also explains why she views O-Sensei as her "spiritual father" and why she now con-siders herself primarily to be a student of Saotome and Ikeda.

Palmer has long been well-known in the San Francisco aikido com-munity for her focus on aikido as a vehicle for self-understanding. In her attempt to bring aikido principles and the insights she has gained from her more than twenty years of training to people in little or no interest in the martial applications of the art, and to explore more explicitly the emotional interactions that happen on the mat, she has developed her own system of mind and body training called "Con-scious Embodiment." Central to that system are two "attention states": "dropped attention" and "open attention." In "dropped attention," the focus is on the individual, on becoming centered and grounded. In "open attention," students learn to stay centered and grounded while allowing another person into their "space," regardless of the state of the other person. She has recently published a book and video, both called The Intuitive Body, *published by North Atlantic Books, explaining and demonstrating her system. She also directs a holistic health program at a federal women's prison.*

started aikido in 1971, I believe. It's hard to know. Those days were pretty wild. I was living pretty loosely, working at a health food restaurant owned by Richard Moon and four other people in Larkspur. I was a waitress there. Some friends of mine were working there too and one day they said, "Oh, you should come to aikido class." They were about to leave in a van so I piled in and went to aikido class.

The class was held at the Unitarian Church in San Francisco and Nadeau was teaching. I remember just looking at the movements and I had an eerie feeling that it was very familiar, even though I had never seen aikido before. I couldn't put logic to it, except it felt familiar. If you believe in past lives then you can think, "Well, maybe it was something like that." But it definitely had a familiar feeling. I cannot explain rationally why that is so. And of course I loved the movements. The aesthetic always charmed me. But it was deeper than just the charming aesthetic. There was more to it than that. It was something that rationally I cannot explain. And not only was it familiar, I also had the feeling that I would do this for the rest of my life. I told that to one of my friends and their reaction was, "Oh, sure!" because we were pretty stoned-out hippies, you know. Everything was sort of "go with the flow," "wow" and "far out!" in those days. But that was genuinely my feeling.

As for Nadeau, he appealed to me because he reminded me of my riding experiences when I was a young girl. It's very interesting. I was a fanatic horseback rider and I was good. I had ridden from the time I was five. I wanted to be on the Olympic team. And when I used to train horses it was English style, so you'd ride the horses in these circles and as the horse circled I would go "E-asy, E-asy" to myself. And Nadeau would always do this thing when he set up for a throw, he'd go "E-asy, E-asy" so he wouldn't rush the timing. It was his way of teaching us about his own process, which is a very good way of teaching—it's one I use, I think. Anyway, it was so familiar. And Nadeau himself reminded me of one riding teacher I used to have. So Nadeau definitely triggered something in me that was from those days.

After that, for years I never missed a class. I would hitchhike into the city. And then some time later Doran Sensei started teaching there on Saturday mornings. The first time Frank came was also the first time I ever saw a picture of O-Sensei: Frank brought a picture with him and set it on the stacked chairs next to where we practiced. This was six months or more after I had started to practice. I had no idea who O-Sensei was, of course as you know, Nadeau can be really off the wall sometimes. Those were some wild times. George Leonard was there as well, though Richard Heckler didn't appear on the scene until after we opened Aikido of San Francisco on Turk Street.

Opening the Turk Street dojo was a thrill, by the way, because Bob had meditated in that same building twenty years before. He'd had his first meditation experience in the same place. There was a lot of synchronicity in those days. Those were fun days, the '70s.

Some time after I got my brown belt I started teaching. Now I can see I was way too young in the art, but back then, who knew? We were training at Turk Street and there was a man in the class who was a teacher at Tamalpais High School. One time he turned to me and said, "Would you be interested in teaching at the high school?" And I said, "Why me? I'm not the most advanced student." He said, "You're a teacher." George had always said that about me. Basically, to be honest with you, I was a stoned-out hippie. We were stoned all the time. But George would say, "Wendy, you are really a teacher." And this guy said that, too. I mean, it was not my goal. I wanted to be a jazz singer. I never wanted to be a teacher. So this guy set me up with a class at Tam High. I taught high school kids for a while and then they set me up with an adult education class. At one point I had forty students, it was totally bizarre. I couldn't figure out why I had so many students, to be honest with you.

So I taught there for a couple of years and then Proposition 13 came along and they shut down all the funding for martial arts, yoga and meditation in adult education. I said to the students, "Now, you go study with Nadeau." He had come a couple of times and taught but the students said, "We don't want to study with him. He scares us. We want to study with you." I was in shock, let me tell you. I went to Nadeau and I said, "They say they want to study with me and I'm embarrassed about it. But that's what these people say." And he said, "Well, I'll tell you what. You find a space and we'll set you up with a dojo, a sister dojo." I was not ready to take on the responsibility, so I asked George and Richard who were friends of mine if they wanted to start a dojo with me. And interestingly enough, they were both a little reluctant. I mean, both of them were busy and had full lives. It wasn't like that was what they had in mind. So we started Tam Aikido. We started off with thirty students, from the get-go. Some of them had already been practicing two years with me. It was really nice.

When Tam Aikido opened, I was deeply involved in aikido. It was my whole life besides raising my daughter. I wasn't in my grownup space. I was in my hippie space. I feel that Richard really pulled me out of my hippie space into a grownup space. I'm really appreciative of that. We got married after the dojo opened and had a son together, Django. After we were together I started teaching at the Lomi School. Eventually we got divorced but we're still good friends. I think Richard is wonderful. Actually, we're probably the best of friends we've ever been except for the brief romantic period in the beginning. I love him. I think he's a wonderful person. I have great respect for him. He's a good father. He comes by and sees Django a lot and they hang out a lot. Our son is a track star and Richard was a track star. And it's just a wonderful place they share together. It's so touching to see him at Django's meets: he gets as nervous as Django does. He feels like he's going to throw up too. It's really wonderful.

The dojo has worked out real well over the years. As George says, it works because none of us has ever wanted to run the whole thing.

I don't think that any of us felt that we should. We always felt pretty much that we were very young to be in this situation, in terms of our experience. Our dojo has always collected a very interesting group called *ronins* because there's not one *sensei,* there's not one set way to do it so we're very liberal. So people from other dojo, people from other styles, fourth *dans,* third *dans,* come and train there because we don't have any set way of doing things. All we ask is that they don't hurt anyone. So our dojo is kind of wild. It's almost like coming to a seminar when you train there 'cause you'll have five or six completely different styles on the mat at the same time.

It has also been interesting because of all the different teachers who have come and taught here over the years. Terry Dobson taught here regularly for a while. I met him for the first time at a Saotome retreat in the late '70s. I was so impressed with him that I invited him to come and teach my classes, and he took me up on it. He came out and I gave him half my classes for three years.

Let me tell you, what a combination of a guy he was. He had this veneer that he would put on that he was this street person, but in truth he came from a very rich family. Terry didn't really want people to know about that side of him, but I found out about it. *The Lomi Papers,* the Lomi school newsletter had just published Terry's story, "A Kind Word Turneth Away Wrath," which subsequently became very famous. A short while after it came out, I was up in Canada at a summer place my family had. I had the magazine with me, and a man who was my father's general business partner in a law firm was staying at our lodge, and he happened to look at it and saw Terry's name. Well, it turned out Terry had been his roommate at Deerfield, an exclusive Eastern prep school. So when I came back that summer I said, "Yo, Terry? Hank says hello." And he says, "Don't you ever tell anybody!" That actually created a special connection between us.

You see, like Terry, I grew up with a lot of money. So there's a lot that I understood about Terry because we shared the same background. I grew up in a rich suburb of Chicago, Lake Forest. I went to boarding schools, too. I went to boarding school in Europe, and unless you've done that you can't understand it. And the coldness of that WASP angst—I only remember my father hugging me twice in my life. And my mother was an invalid so I don't remember any physical touching or connection in my whole life. I never remember seeing any of my friends ever hugged or touched by their parents. I was brought in to my parents each night and told to say good night to them, and then I was taken to my room by the nurse. I understood a lot about Terry that a lot of other people never did. Both of us were so embarrassed about this, especially during that era. Even now I'm embarrassed about it. We also both knew what it does to you as a person, not to have had that kind of warmth and affection. We'd look at each other sometimes and a silent understanding would pass between us.

My joke about aikido is that "I like my intimacy abstract. That's why I like aikido." During practice you get as intimate with your partner as with any lover that you've ever had, maybe even more intimate. And then when it's over you bow to each other and the intimacy is gone. Sometimes I don't even know the names of my training partners. I have no idea what they do. I don't know what they wear outside of their uniform, but I've had the most intimate connection that I know with them. And I think there was a way that Terry and I liked that. I mean, I think that was something that we understood. It's a real interesting thing. Very few people, I think, come from that place that we came from. And we were both disinherited. Terry turned bitter about it. For me it was something that I did consciously. And I'm still grateful that I did it because my life would have been very different had I had that.

Since Terry's death, I've read some extraordinary letters that were exchanged between Terry and that friend of his from Deerfield. The level of their communication was really amazing. I mean, he had all of these lives. For me, whatever my karma was with him, I was able to recognize this certain kind of life that very few other people knew about, this very sophisticated, intellectual life with these men who were very wealthy, who came from that whole echelon.

After he had been here about three years, Terry left. In fact, I asked him to leave. And I'll tell you, I felt like I earned my *sandan* when I did that. That was really a lot for me. I used aikido, in fact, Terry's own "verbal aikido." The tension had been building for a while. When Terry first came he had fifty or sixty people in his class and I would have, you know, a normal amount, eighteen or twenty. Over the years Terry made so many enemies and hurt so many people physically and emotionally that fewer and fewer people came to his class. At the end only six or seven people were coming to his class. And I still had twenty or thirty. I had stopped coming to his class. I would teach basics and then I would leave because I couldn't stand it. He would do these things with your fingers and toes, and I was afraid, you know, I would say, "Terry, I'm afraid you're going to break my finger," and he would say, "It's only a finger," and I'd say, "You know I play guitar and if you break a finger I won't be able to play guitar anymore." He kind of understood it, but his whole thing was, "Well, I broke fingers in Japan. It doesn't mean anything. It doesn't matter." He had it at that level.

So anyway, at some point I had to say to him, "Terry, this is not working." And because of his personality and who he was, I had to say it in such a way that he was not wrong. So what I finally said was, "The reason that I can't come to your class is I can't take *ukemi* from you. And the reason I can't take *ukemi* from you is because I keep getting injured. You always talk about giving yourself, but every time I give myself I get injured. So I can't give myself anymore. I'm unable to handle it. I can't do it and I can't take responsibility anymore. It's my lack of development that has created this situation. But because I'm not developed enough, and because I can't do it, this isn't going to work." And he understood that.

But you know, on one level I agree with what Terry was saying. He had this thing which I'm to date very interested in, this whole idea of enduring pain and learning how to work skillfully with it. There's a part that's very fascinated by that idea. As one martial arts teacher told us in a seminar I was at, "You really have to develop your capacity for enduring pain, not in a sick way, but in a way where you can relax and understand what's happening." I can see, for example, that the training in Ikeda Sensei's dojo is very strong and the people who are able to absorb the most from him are the strong guys who can endure his intensity so that they can stay awake and see what he is doing inside of it. And the people who freak out when he throws hard don't know what's happening and therefore can't learn. So in a lot of ways I agree with Terry.

Anyway, Terry left. Then he gradually became quite ill and in fact he died when he was out here in the Bay Area later doing a seminar. In my opinion, Terry fought his way through his death as he fought his way through life. I happened to have some personal experiences of him after he died and he was still fighting. And that's okay. I always loved him for that.

What happened was this. Shortly after Terry died, I was living with a man, a musician, who had never met Terry but was kind of an intuitive guy. We were sleeping one night and all of sudden I woke up to these papers rustling. And I mean loudly. Now mind you, there are a couple of books in the room, but they're closed and even a couple of books could not have made that level of noise. It went on and on. So I sat up and I said to this man, "Do you hear that?" And he said, "You mean all of that paper rustling?" "Yes." "It's that guy looking for his map." I said, "What are you talking about?" He said, "Oh, never mind." All this time we're half asleep, half dreaming. Finally the rustling stopped and as we were going back to sleep, he said, "I hope he finds his map." "What map?" "I'll tell you in the morning." In the morning I got up real early: I had to be at work at 4:30 and I didn't get a chance to talk to him until after I came home. He said, "That friend of yours who died, is his name Terry?" I said, "Yeah." He said, "Well, let me tell you, he was in the room last night. And he was trying to find his map. He said 'I can't find my way home until I find this map.' He was looking around and he was very freaked out. And then this figure in white," and of course I'm projecting O-Sensei, because this man wasn't all that tuned into the whole aikido trip, "This figure in white came and said, 'Okay, Terry, here's your map. You can go home now.'"

Terry and I had a personal connection. But the main reason I think Terry's spirit came there was because he felt O-Sensei's presence in my house really strongly. And I think he was lost like he was in his life and still looking and still searching. I'm sort of a Tibetan Buddhist and I really believe that we continue on, that death's not the end.

And there were a couple of other small things that happened, too. I actually had to do a ritual with myself and just ask Terry to go on, that I really wasn't willing to house him. It's interesting. I did it in life when I told him to go, and in death I had to tell him to go, too. That was my feeling. The same sort of thing has happened to me before. Even though I can work very intensely with people who are going through a lot of problems, their energies don't go into me. You know how people who do body work will sometimes say "I've absorbed someone's energy, it transferred into me"? Well, that doesn't happen to me with people who are alive— it only happens with people who have just died. I've got to watch that one. So now I'm trying to be a little bit more skillful about differentiating. It's like "That's you and this is me. And no, you can't come hang out in my energetic space."

I loved Terry. His struggle with himself was part of his richness. He manifested all of our complex darkness, only he manifested it so radically that I never thought that Terry was wrong. I just saw myself in his struggles but in the most extreme context. There was something in the level of conflict and struggle that resonated in me, too. He just put it right out there.

Perhaps I should explain what I said about O-Sensei—that I thought Terry came to my house because O-Sensei was there. I had an experience a few years ago with O-Sensei and he has really been very alive to me ever since. I have pictures of him in every room in my house. I talk to him every day.

Let me tell you about it. I can't remember now exactly how many years ago it was. I was in New Mexico doing a workshop. There was a man there who wanted to take the workshop but didn't have the money so he offered a trade, which was that he could lead me on a shamanic journey. Usually I don't do those kinds of things, but I talked to a friend about him and she said that he had put in some years with some real shamans. So I decided to give it a try.

He didn't use drugs. He put on a tape of some drums, led me through a little ritual beginning, cleaning, purification, that sort of thing, and then after I had entered a light trance he began to lead me on my journey. I can really affect myself through visualization. I can really change my states. I'm very good at that. So we went through a number of stages which were very interesting. I saw myself going down into other worlds through these tunnels, and as I went I found different spirit guides. He would say, "Ask this guide whether it's something that wants to help you on your way or not." And I would ask, and if it wasn't going to help me its eyes would turn red. This one being came to me who looked like a gorgeous young Indian man. And I thought, "This must be my guide." But when I asked it if it would be helpful for my spiritual life its eyes turned red and it turned into this ghoulish thing and left.

It was an interesting process to find my teachers, my real guardians. Classically, some looked good and weren't, and some looked funky and turned out to be really helpful. Anyway, I went through a whole number of stages with that. At first I had to deal with a lot of shit and the guy was very skillful in helping me with that. But after going through a lot of dark stuff and meeting these dark parts of myself over and over again and having the aid of this one energy I found to support me, we got to the second part where the teachers were. And there were two teachers there. The first one was great, he was a Zen teacher. He was like a regular *roshi*. We were sitting at this table. He was wearing the symbol of his office on his chest and he was bald. He took a cup of tea and he said, "I'll show you how to hold the truth." And he handed me the cup of tea with great care and deliberation and the message was "very, very carefully." I took the cup of tea and held it and then he gestured for me to hand it back to him. I handed it back to him and he said, "And then you have to throw it away." He threw the cup up in the air and laughed and laughed. And I thought, "What a teaching. Hold the truth carefully and then throw it away." It was great. Then the guide said, "Is there anyone else there for you?" And suddenly I had this experience that O-Sensei came, and it was really a powerful experience. He was in his white *hakama* and he had a kind of luminescent quality to him. And the guide asked me, "What does he say to you?" As clear as daylight O-Sensei said, "Wendy, you're between heaven and earth." For me that meant something very specific. All those years training with Bob my study had been about "deep" and "base" and "ground." I had spent years trying to get down, and the thought of going up was heresy to me. It was scary. I was afraid that I was going to lose all of that. But I felt that what O-Sensei was saying was, "It's really time now to go up." I knew that's what he meant. And it was real powerful.

After the trip was over I was kind of lying there and I felt O-Sensei's presence. And from that time onward, especially for the first six months, it was like he was with me every day. It was eerie. And he was always reminding me, "Wendy, heaven and earth." That went on for about six months. I would try to ask him questions and I would try to connect with him and he would always just say "You're between heaven and earth," always emphasizing the "heaven." And then it switched about six months later to where I'd be sitting and I'd feel him up above me and he'd say, "Come. Come up. Come up." And I was really freaked out at the idea of going that direction. But steadily of course, I began to develop this intention to expand upward. Now this happened daily. I would be driving or walking around and I'd hear his voice, I'd feel his presence. And usually he was above me. But after another six months he started coming down and being around me. That was a wonderful period. I actually felt him surround me, instead of being up there going "come on! come on!" And at that point, after months of saying the same thing over and over again, no matter what I asked, he started saying, "Don't give up."

That sort of thing is still going on and it's been years since it started. The first months were the most intense. One time, some weeks or months after I came back from New Mexico, I was doing this breathing practice while I was walking in the wetlands that are about a mile and a quarter from my house. Whenever I put my foot down I would say "The mother holds me," and I would inhale as if the inhale was coming up from the earth, the mother. And when I exhaled it would come down from the father, which turned out to be O-Sensei. And as I was walking, I found myself all of sudden walking on a little bridge over this little waterway, and I stopped and realized I was crying. Tears were streaming down my face and I felt for the first time in my life that I really had a father. I really did. I felt completely loved. I'd never felt so loved in my life. And I realized I had a father after all this time and he was there and he cared for me and he loved me. And I remember Terry talking about O-Sensei like he was his father. One time we were going to do something really off-the-wall. And as off-the-wall as Terry got, he said "No, I will not do that in my father's house." I looked at him, it was so reverent. But I understood what he meant, I really did. O-Sensei was there. There was just this unbelievable feeling of love. And since that time all I have to do is remember. I can get amnesia, I get into my wanty-needy thing, but as soon as I remember I just go, "Oh, it's okay." That was such a beautiful moment. So through that period of time little by little, without even planning it, I started putting pictures of O-Sensei in every room in important places. He's definitely my strongest guide. I have many, but he's the one who's really the father. He is my father, you know, in the most visceral kind of sense.

And I really do believe it's O-Sensei. I've had other spirits come into my body and I've asked them to leave. I've been through that. But this is totally different. Now interestingly enough, I can't run his energy when I do aikido. I tried twice. When I do, weird things happen and I get completely freaked out. I don't have the capacity to do that. I can call Saotome Sensei through my body, I can call Doshu through my body; but I don't call O-Sensei into my body. I don't ask him to come do my aikido for me because the couple times I have I really got the message "No way, honey. You can't begin to run this energy." I can call certain people through my body and try to run their energy when I'm doing aikido. It's a really interesting thing to do. And I get different responses. But he's not somebody that I can do that with. There's way too much voltage, way too much voltage. It feels more like he's encouraging me spiritually in a fatherly sort of way. And sometimes he'll hold me. I can't ask him to come hold me but sometimes I find him there. Usually I feel him above me, saying "come on, come on" in the sense of a guide. I don't necessarily feel him more, maybe even less, doing aikido. My aikido's my aikido. He doesn't interfere with that. In terms of my meditation and in my daily life, that's where I feel him most strongly. I feel that he is encouraging me to increase my capacity for "sword-compassion," a strong, fatherly compassion.

I already have an entity that's a mother, a female part of me. If I just did his energy, it would be totally out of whack. O-Sensei is the doing part; he wants me to do it, absolutely. But there's another energy that I work with that balances O-Sensei; it's a part of me that says, "Be, don't do anything." I feel that his thing is always, "Go for it! Reach up. Don't give up. You're between heaven and earth." It's very *yang;* it doesn't have a *yin* in it. But there is an energy I work with on the *yin* side. There has to be a balance.

That took us a bit far afield, but I just wanted you to understand why I said that about Terry. Let me get back to the teachers who have visited our dojo in the past. Bruce Klickstein used to come over and teach. There's a guy named Obata Sensei in L.A. who teaches aikido and *shinkendo,* a sword style. He holds the world's record for cutting the most bodies-worth in one swipe, and he's in all the Ninja Turtle movies. He has done some seminars with us. Barrish has been here. And Steve Seagal was here, too. That was interesting, particularly in light of the fact that he became so famous later on. That was sometime in the early '80s. Actually, during the time that Terry was here. When Steve first came, Richard and George were both out of town. One day he came to the dojo and we had this talk where I told him that he had a reputation for being aggressive and sometimes hurting his *ukes.* I said, "I want you to know that if any of the students behave in a way that feels inappropriate, please come to me and take it out on me. It's my fault, it's my responsibility. I'm their teacher. I understand you come from a more traditional trip."

So he said, "Oh, I never hurt anyone." I said, "Well, your reputation precedes you. So I want to go down on record for saying please don't take it out on the students. Please see me; take it out on me." He repeated, "I never hurt anyone." So I said, "I just want you to know . . ." We went over this three or four times together. It was real funny.

So I arranged for him to give a workshop. As I say, Richard and George were out of town so I was the only teacher there. During the seminar he'd go around throwing people. He has great throws. Very energetic, very fast, very powerful. He would throw me—bam!—I'd hit the mat; the spit would fly out of my mouth, that kind of thing, just really powerful. And he'd say, "See? You're okay." I'd go, "Uh huh, my teeth are still in my mouth. I'm okay." I'd get up, he'd throw me again. Every time he came around and threw, we'd go through that. It got to be sort of a joke between us. And in fact he didn't really hurt anyone.

Steve brought a couple of guys with him who ended up staying in our dojo and teaching on a regular basis when he left. Anyway, Steve taught the workshop and then he kind of hung around, and sometimes he would come in to my Tuesday class. And Terry would come in and Bruce Klickstein would come in. I never knew who to ask to teach, and sometimes I would teach and sometimes I would ask the first person who came in. It was an interesting little scenario that would come down. I think they were all like dogs who were sniffing each other's butts to see who was top dog. Steve wanted the dojo. I think that he felt that since he'd had a dojo of his own in Japan he should have the dojo. And of course, Terry wanted the dojo, too. And Bruce was there kind of sniffing around to be sure he was defending his territory, that these guys weren't coming in. They would sometimes train together, but in an *aiki* way, politely. At their level you can't do anything but train that way. So everybody just kind of went through the motions. Mostly they would just hang out or talk or kind of be on the mat. And that was interesting.

As I said, Steve had a dojo in Japan. And I think that that's why he had to develop that tough attitude and that tough front. It would

almost be like a Japanese trying to teach baseball in this country—
you had to be good and you had to be tough, although to be honest
with you I never thought Steve was a particularly tough guy. I thought
he was very arrogant, but you know, he had very good aikido. He
really did. He threw me very energetically. At that time he was not
particularly muscled. He was strong, *aiki*-strong, but he didn't have
a kind of gym-muscle body at all. His throws were very fast, very
energetic. You never knew what happened. He could do the art. His
irimi nages were *atemi irimi-nages,* but I never felt like he was particularly physically aggressive. He just did it the way he did it. If
somebody didn't do it that way, like many aikido teachers, he'd just
go throw him.

Steve had two visions—one was to go to New Mexico and establish this center for traditional arts and the other was to make movies
and be like Clint Eastwood and make aikido famous. When he told
me all this, I was pretty dubious. But when his first movie came out,
all I could say was, "All right, Steve!" But his center for traditional
arts did not develop and that's understandable, too. There's a lot of
him that's very young and still very reactive. To do something like
that you need to be a true master, like the man who had run the dojo
there before Steve came, Nakazono Sensei. Nakazono was incredible. He had all those things that a master has. Steve was a good
aikidoka but I didn't think he was a true master the way Nakazono
Sensei was.

But my feeling about him is that he could turn the corner at any
time. Something really intense could happen in his life and he could
make that corner turn. His body knows some principles. He threw
me nice and strong, real powerful and did not hurt me. He didn't
damage me, put it that way. I've been thrown that way, strongly, by
Hiroshi, Saotome Sensei, Bob Nadeau. I've been hammered by those
guys. Steven hammered me real fast, real clean, real good, and didn't
torque my elbow. I didn't get any strains or anything, it was more
like seeing stars. I'll take that any day over tendonitis, which you
can get from some of these other guys that look so nice.

One time Steve and his teacher did a really neat seminar called

"The Sword and the Pen." It was very cool. One day he said, "I want to bring my calligraphy and aikido teacher here." That was Abe Sensei, who actually taught O-Sensei calligraphy too. He was this tiny, luminous eighty-some-year-old Japanese being, not a grey hair on his head. All weekend Steve taught *bokken*, and Abe Sensei taught calligraphy. It was awesome.

And then there was a great moment when Takahashi Sensei arrived. He's an *iaido* master who lives in Palo Alto. There's a lot of mystery around him. Some people say he's here because he assassinated somebody in Japan. Anyway, he's a trip. He's really seriously amazing. He's from another dimension, like fifteenth-century Japan. So here we are in the middle of this workshop and suddenly the door becomes darkened with his presence. Everybody stops and turns around and Takahashi Sensei is standing in the door with his kimono and his *gi* and his topknot. And everybody just stops, turns and bows. That's the level of presence this dude has. When Takahashi Sensei arrives, Steve Seagal is standing next to me and he goes "O-h n-o!" I go "What?" "Oh, now I'm really nervous." "Great, Steve. You're nervous? What am I supposed to do? I don't want anybody weird here who's going to hurt our people." "He won't hurt anybody but me." "Well, that's okay!" Then Steve went over and talked to him and invited him in.

Later, whenever Steve would be teaching *bokken*, Takahashi Sensei would just walk around the mat going "O-h-h!" [throaty growl, inhale through nose] and then patting his *hara*. It was very disconcerting, very interesting. And when Abe Sensei would teach calligraphy, Takahashi Sensei would take the calligraphy part. At the very end of the seminar, we all had to take turns sitting in Abe Sensei's seat. We'd been studying the character *"ki"* all weekend long, and we all had to take his brush and this big piece of rice paper and do the character *"ki."* When it's Takahashi Sensei's turn, he sits down and pulls open his *gi* and starts saying this stuff in Japanese, which Steve translated for us. He wanted everybody to watch his breath. When you do the calligraphy, you have to take a breath, hold it, pick up the brush, do the character, put the brush down, let the breath out. When Takahashi Sensei goes to do the character *"ki"* he takes this big breath and the rice paper just crumples into this little ball. I had this moment where I thought, "Oh my god, what's going to happen?" But he put the brush down, let his breath out and started smoothing the rice paper out. And he started kind of going "ho ho ho ho." He seemed to like it. Then he picks the paper up, takes it over in front of the *shomen,* bows, and puts it on the *shomen* to O-Sensei. It was one of those great moments that I was so appreciative to be part of.

Koichi Barrish came through a couple of times. The first time I just loved him. I loved his aikido. He felt a lot like Terry except softer, and he could be a little bit slower, not as frantic as Terry got sometimes. With Terry when the *ki* came through it was like grenades going off or plowing through a mine field. Barrish could slow it down a little bit and there was a tremendous kind of softness to his art. It was just wonderful. Unfortunately we had a falling out when he visited the second time so we've never invited him back.

Of course, many teachers visit the Bay Area and not just our dojo. Probably the most important such visit for me was when Saotome Sensei came here in '75 or '76. He taught a workshop to which Bob had invited him. Actually, Bob even introduced him, which is rare for Bob. He said that when he was at Hombu Dojo, Saotome Sensei was one of his favorite teachers. I was very impressed with Saotome Sensei. He seemed to be more empty and more androgynous than anyone I'd ever seen except Doshu.

Doshu had already been to the Bay Area some time earlier. Doshu for me represents the most androgynous of all the teachers I've seen. He's so generous and so beautiful, just the way he stands. It's kind of embarrassing, but he always reminds me of those statues of the Virgin Mary, with her arms pointing out and down, a modest expression on her face. When I saw him I thought that Doshu represented something I could really want to embody. I loved Bob and Frank, but if I embodied them, I was going to become a guy because they're both very *yang* teachers. I could train the principles, but I'm the kind of person who tends to take on or virtually embody the kind of style of my teacher. At a certain point after a number of years of training it was really great to start seeing aikido teachers who had more androgyny and had an emptiness to them. Doshu has a great emptiness, and by "emptiness" I mean not much personality, not much ego, not much personal flamboyance in the quality of energy.

Ikeda Sensei has an emptiness to him as well. I mean, the thing about Ikeda Sensei, he has thrown me harder than anyone has in my life. He has thrown me so hard that spit flew out of my mouth, and snot flew out of my nose. I've been covered with bruises but he has never hurt me. And I feel it's because of the emptiness. There's no content in his throws. I've been thrown a quarter as hard by people and felt really brutalized because of that quality of content. And Doshu has that kind of emptiness, too. There's nothing he's trying to prove. No statement trying to be made, just "this." Very Zen. Just "this." And that was very important and appealing to me because I was coming to a point where I really had to go deeper into the art or I was just going to "plateau it" as George would say.

Anyway, that's why Saotome Sensei was so appealing to me. There's a way he would just stand very still in the space and hold the space. And I remember his saying, "It's always deeper, wider and finer." That was really great. And even though his English wasn't very good then—which meant he didn't talk so much, which was neat, too—he really talked about "the space," what I call "the field," the dimension of it. He didn't talk about how you twist your wrist or how you do the technique, he talked about the field, he talked about the space and the depth of it and the quality of it and the movement of energy in it. And that was music to my soul. I love that stuff.

But the most significant thing happened when he was walking around helping people. I was training and Saotome Sensei came along and threw me, and when I got up he said to me, "You're stiff." And because I was so stupid and blatant in those days, I said, "Oh no, that's my extension." He looks at me for a minute and he says, "You're stiff," and walks off. He didn't even bow. And I stood there with this look on my face. It was one of those horrendous moments in life where you realize "the guy's right." I had trained tremendous amounts of hours and time and energy and psychic and emotional focus to become stiff. And all of my being wanted to make that not true, make him wrong, make me not really stiff, make it okay. But at some deep level I knew he was right. I kept training, as you do, but something really deep had changed in me in that moment. And it was a very, very painful next couple of years while my ego struggled with it. I could no longer go back and keep going the way that I was going. But I couldn't make the transition. I couldn't become Saotome Sensei, as much as I tried. And I couldn't go back and do Bob any more. I was really between a rock and a hard place. At the time I was teaching and everybody would say, "You're such a good teacher; your art is so great," but I felt my art was horrible, and I thought, "If they only knew who I really was they wouldn't want to stay with me!" So it was a very painful period of my aikido life. But I couldn't stop because I guess it's my destiny to do this stuff; I really wanted the stuff but I wanted to quit.

I was really stuck for a couple of years. And then slowly I started finding myself. You know, I had kind of copied Bob and taken a little bit of Frank, but the thing about Saotome Sensei is he doesn't let you copy him. People can't copy him. You can copy Ikeda Sensei some; I really let him come into my body. But Saotome Sensei is a little more like O-Sensei that way—his students all look different. And O-Sensei's people all look different, which means something very interesting is happening. When a teacher teaches and everybody doesn't look like him, that's far out, because the general thing is everybody will start to look like their teacher. So anyway, meeting Saotome Sensei was great for me because it made me start to find myself in the art. Who am I? What am I going to do and what does it mean to be a woman in the art, a woman teacher in the art? I went around and asked the other black belts, "Do you throw me the same way you throw the men? Well, why not? What's the difference?" And for two years I was on this big quest to understand what it meant to be a woman in the art. I never solved it, never found the answer. I learned a lot by asking the questions, but I didn't solve the mystery of it.

I've been in the position of being a woman in a male-dominated field for most of my life. My prison work is really interesting. It's in a women's prison but I didn't intend it to be that way. Had I known it was a women's prison, I wouldn't have gone in the beginning I thought I was going to a men's prison. I've always been more comfortable around men and always been involved in a lot of things with men. So my situation in aikido was kind of classic for me. In fact, in some ways I'm sort of an anti-feminist. I really relate much more to men and see much more of their side. The whole feminist movement completely gets on my nerves. But there was a point, you know, where I was really interested because I wanted to understand about being a woman in aikido.

Mary Heiny was around then, but her art was so much like the guys'. When I first saw Mary in the early '70s, mid-'70s, when she came back from Japan, I was very impressed by her, but boy, did she look like a guy. There are some women around who do great aikido, but the tradeoff is they've become guys to do it. I'm not interested in that. When she would throw Stan Pranin his head would bounce on the mat. Mary was unbelievably powerful.

I didn't see Mary for a number of years after that. And then a few years ago I intuitively went to a seminar. And she completely blew my mind. She had made a total switch. I feel that she has reclaimed herself as a woman and is now teaching an aikido that is awesome to me. But it was only three or four years ago that I discovered her. Now she represents to me the one woman who has made that leap toward mastery as a woman. But I'm not in the dilemma anymore. I have other things I'm in a dilemma about, but it's not about being a woman in the art. That was my big dilemma for two years. And interestingly, Mary wasn't in my field of vision as a woman model at that time, which she is now, because we also share a very strong Tibetan Buddhist practice. She's absolutely great, she's phenomenal. She represents so much of the essence of bringing the principles of aikido into life. She really talks about space a lot. She's not talking about twisting somebody's wrist or any of that; she's talking about how you lead your life.

And that's what my own training, particularly my time with Sao-tome Sensei, has led me to: aikido is about how to lead your life. I remember hearing "the purpose of aikido is to protect the attacker." As the Buddhists say, that really stopped my mind. I love that as a concept. To me, aikido is really the study of my own fear and aggression. In aikido you put yourself in a position where you can flush all of that out. So does meditation, but it's a little different. It feels like fear and aggression are what stand in the way of my being able to have the kind of mind that protects the attacker. My heroes are Gandhi, Martin Luther King, Mother Theresa and O-Sensei. I feel all of them were so unified they were not distracted by their fear and their aggression. They were able to really follow their goals. I want to develop the kind of kindness and compassion those people exhibited, and it feels like that will naturally surface once I can come to terms with my fear and aggression. I feel kindness and compassion are a natural part of our being, but our fear and aggression get in the way. So I want to continue to study fear and aggression at a very deep level so I can come to a more complete awareness of them, because as I become more aware, I can start to find ways to accept them and incorporate them.

In aikido training it seems like we have to spend years establishing some kind of foundation so we can look at our fear and aggression. Without a strong foundation, you don't have a platform from which to observe yourself. You can't tolerate it. Nobody can. So when I teach I place a lot of emphasis on getting the students to stabilize themselves, and that comes through learning form and learning how to be grounded, learning what I call "base." You have to get relaxed enough to stay put, just "keep your seat," as the Buddhists would say. It feels to me that if we can start to do that, if we can stay put and tolerate our discomfort, we can start to examine it. And then through the examination, insight, and understanding will come.

The discomfort we feel on the mat usually comes from the approval-control thing. We're so run by approval and control; we want to feel like we look good or we do it well. And we want the control;

we want to think that we're controlling our partner, but we rarely experience moments of genuine openness and interest. If this person is attacking you, how many of us are genuinely open and interested? Most of us are trying to do something to the person. My understanding of O-Sensei and these other people is that they weren't doing, they were being. But it takes a tremendous amount of training to be there and to relax. And then if you can, the process will unfold itself. I've seen over and over again that the system will handle skillfully whatever happens. But it's like the Tao says—everybody understands it, nobody can do it. It's a worthy endeavor, though, for all of us to continue to learn how to be there, how to be open, be relaxed, be alert and allow the situation to unfold. To me it's the difference between an intuitive response, which you can't think about, and thinking about what you're going to do: if you've been able to think about it, it's too late.

The Buddhists talk about "don't-know mind": If you don't know then there's room for something to be born. If you already know it, there's no space. Nothing can come up. If you come into a situation with pre-conceived ideas, then nothing can be born, nothing can arise, no spontaneous, creative events can occur. But if you're open and you have some training, then you can watch and allow the system to respond at a much more intuitive level. That's beautiful. And I believe for the most part that the response will be benevolent, that goodness is innate in us.

What I'm talking about occurs at an advanced level of training. With my own advanced students I talk a lot about "the atomic view," that they have to practice being the nucleus while the *uke* is the electron. The nucleus holds the space so the electron can do whatever it needs to do. In the best-case scenario, if you want to be crazy, I'll hold the space for you, you can be crazy. Terry talked about O-Sensei. He said, "When I met him I was homicidal and suicidal." Terry said O-Sensei was the only person who could contain that. To me that's the greatest gift we give each other, total acceptance. You want to be suicidal, you want to be homicidal? Absolutely, I'll hold the space for you. I'll welcome you into my territory; I'll allow you to be there, and the situation can unfold. Not: I'm going to take you into the space and change you and make you a nice guy. I don't think that was the intention. The intention on O-Sensei's part was, "I'll accept you and I'll meet you and I'll match you." And he had the strength to accept even that tremendous negativity that Terry brought when he started. What a healing that was for Terry!

Actually, I teach this stuff right from the beginning and it's the theme of what I call "conscious embodiment classes," which is an aspect of a teaching that I've developed that's not formal aikido. There are no falls; anybody can do it. I have a tape and a book out about it. But even in aikido I talk about it, although in formal aikido a lot of what I emphasize in the basics and most beginning classes is form because form is important as a reference point. Once everybody has learned the forms a little bit, then they have a reference point from which they can start to examine those things. But if you try to give them philosophy *and* form, people are completely overwhelmed. They can't do it all. We really learn at the most one or two things at a time. If you try to show them ten things, they can't do it. So in aikido I try to give the students form as a reference point, get them to relax and learn how to move their bodies. Once they can do that, we start to be more interested in the space they're holding, the quality that's in the space, the level of attitude that they're taking, all of those things. But without the form you can't examine those other things.

Then of course, following a lot of Ikeda's principles, I encourage students to just relax and do a thousand repetitions. Gradually their aikido will improve. Just like with the old tortoise and the hare, the tortoise won the race. We're such a hare kind of culture. Everybody rushing around, trying to hurry up. I always say that even after twenty-some years in the art I consider myself a true beginner. And the more I dig, the more there is to discover. It's like a geological experience. And all martial arts and spiritual practices teach the same basic principles. There's a unity in everything of that caliber, and in all of them, there's a geological process of discovery and development. I don't think we ever get to the place where we've got "it."

We can get a certain level of experience. But if we hang in, a yet deeper level of experience will occur, endlessly. My understanding is that even in the last few weeks of his training O-Sensei was saying, "I've so much to learn. I still have to train and practice." And I really think that's very much my feeling, that it is endless and great.

In the Conscious Embodiment classes, nobody gets a certificate. I always say you can teach the work any time you want. The only credential you need is that it helps you. I have a video that I made that people can use, and it has a little training segment at the end where it talks about the principles that I teach. It's meant to be available to anybody who can walk. I wanted to make it available to people who would not or could not for some reason ever come to a martial art. I wanted them to have some of the principles and some of the teachings and some of the trainings that are so incredibly valuable in aikido.

Conscious Embodiment is derived primarily from aikido, but I do bring in a lot of other influences from Buddhism, meditation practice, and bits and pieces of everything that has touched me and helped me to find my way along the path. Sometimes I describe what we do like this: Something will happen in aikido that will happen in two seconds. We'll take that and spend two hours on it in Conscious Embodiment. In aikido these remarkable moments occur but you haven't got time to sit down and discuss them or go deeply into them. You have to throw the person again or get up and be thrown again. I started doing these classes because I wanted to have an environment where we could stop and explore some of these remarkable moments that were occurring and go over and over them and somehow find out what's going on there. So, we do a series of warm-ups that are a little bit similar to aikido warm-ups, a lot of breathing and centering. I work primarily with two intentional states; I'd say that's the most essential part of the work. The first intentional state is called "dropped attention" and it's simply a meditation-type state where you collect and focus your awareness within. The idea is to develop the ability to focus on yourself and not someone else, and to focus on yourself in a positive way. And then people use a quality, described in just one word. I take one for a whole year, a quality like "kindness," "softness," "openness," "aliveness," "courage," all those kinds of things. And I have them ask a question: If there was more kindness in my being, what would that be like?" And we wonder. In so doing we try to develop that kind of "don't-know" mind.

That's called basic practice, developing "dropped attention." That's the foundation, the reference point, being able to get yourself back into center, where you're connected to yourself first. We spend a great deal of time in interactive exercises—I hold you, I move you, I push you. No throwing, no falling. You practice just staying with yourself. Don't think about me, even if I push you or pull you or hold you. Just be able to concentrate on yourself. That's the beginning. I always joke that "we need to have a self to come back to." Most people, when they come back to themselves, come back to guilt or confusion or monkey mind. Through basic practice we can develop a self to come back to. That leads the way to "open attention," which is what we talked about before with the idea of the atom where I'm the nucleus and you're the electron. Ideally you can be as rude as you want and I'll hold a space for you. That's the thing that Terry did. He was so weird, nobody could be weirder than Terry. So you could come and be with Terry and be as weird as you wanted and Terry would just be there with you.

So that's our goal: to hold the space. I always say that in a relationship the most beautiful thing is I'll hold a space for you, you hold a space for me. We'll hold a space for each other. What I call "ellipted attention" is the codependent state. An ellipse has two centers, you and me, whereas in the atomic view there's just one center. And then there's a space which I'll generously welcome you into. The idea is that I want to develop myself to be deeper and stronger so I can tolerate you no matter how weird you are. I accept you, that's the training. If I can't hold the space for you, if your behavior throws me off center, then the training is to disengage from the person and come back to yourself. Don't try to change them, ever. That's basic. Your options are either stabilize a space for yourself or stabilize a space for them, but don't try to change them. As a concept it's not a problem. Doing it is the problem. And the better people get, the more pressure that we'll put on them to see if they can steady their concentration even when people are acting up or being inappropriate. I mean, if you're a nice guy, it's easy to hold a space for you. But if you're a jerk, can I hold the space for you? Just like aikido. Ikeda Sensei has a saying: "*Uke* is never wrong." That's such an incredibly powerful concept. "*Uke* is never wrong." So whatever it is, it's a workable situation. That's the goal. And if *uke's* an asshole, good.

As I said, I have a book and video out. They're both called *The Intuitive Body*. My next book is inspired by my work at the prison. I want to do a book on—and this is interesting for aikido, too— "what is freedom?" I'll be interviewing women in a prison, elderly people in their nineties, teenagers, rich people, homeless people. I want to get their views on what freedom is. And then I want to see if I can pull together my understanding of what O-Sensei, Gandhi, Martin Luther King and Mother Theresa had to say about freedom. Not to answer the question, mind you, but to put out some ideas. I hope to get people to ask themselves, "What is freedom?"

Gandhi was just extraordinary. I really think that he was an ultimate *aikidoka,* Gandhi. He and O-Sensei were very similar. Gandhi was reputed to have gone to visit some of the northern tribes where the men are very fierce. Gandhi saw a group of these men, big bearded guys carrying guns. He went up to them and stood there in his loincloth and said, "Don't be afraid." They said, "We're not afraid." And he said, "Well, if you're not afraid, why do you have guns?" Ghandi added, "I'm not afraid. I don't have a gun." He said, "Be like me. Be courageous. Put your gun down." Really, really amazing. What he and O-Sensei said are almost identical.

I teach conscious embodiment in the federal women's prison where I work. We're not allowed to teach aikido to the prisoners. I began working there after I was invited to teach a workshop in a federal prison by a woman doctor who studies aikido with us. I always say "yes" when people invite me, and prison sounded very attractive. It wasn't until we were driving there that I found out it was a women's prison. I said, "Oh no! Nine hundred women? Not my idea of a good time. Nine hundred men, no problem." I relate to men, I understand them, and before the last few years I felt like I couldn't understand women. So I went there just to do the one workshop.

There were women from all different countries and everywhere you can imagine. One woman was a Soviet spy. There were black women from the street, Latino women from South America who didn't speak English very well, women from Africa, women from almost every country of the world. There are women who have done nothing worse than selling homeopathic remedies and women who have murdered people. Everybody's in there together because they don't yet have maximum, medium and minimum security prisons the way they do with men. And there are so few federal women's prisons that the prisoners are from all over the world. Seventy percent of the women are in prison for conspiracy. It's all because of the war on drugs. Grandmothers are in there because their nieces and nephews were dealing out of their houses and they got twenty-year conspiracy charges. It's not the Yuppie population. Some of these women have never heard the word "codependent" in their life; they don't know what you're talking about. They're amazing beings. That's why I kept going back.

Eventually I helped establish a holistic program for the prisoners. I'm the director. It's been going on for about three years now. I personally go there and I teach two meditation, two yoga, two conscious embodiment classes—I call them "conflict resolution" classes—and a pre-release class. And then I see a number of people individually for counseling. I'm way into it. I'd like to see a holistic health program in every prison in the United States because prison for the most part is about punishment even though there is something about rehabilitation in the mission statement for the federal system. And as you know, the prison system is extremely corrupt, so even if a person is not a criminal when they go in, they will be a criminal when they come out. Not everyone can or will be rehabilitated, but there are a number who will take it if it's offered.

Some of these women who've been in the program for three years are just amazing to me. They have really taken it seriously. They meditate and do yoga regularly. I've assigned Gandhi's writings to all of them and Mother Theresa's. They're really turning their lives around, big-time. It's very, very impressive to feel their dedication. It's just beautiful. I feel honored and thrilled to be part of this. These women have lost everything. They really know something about being at the bottom. So they don't have the kind of stuff that you have to get through dealing with most other people. It's pretty straightforward there: they're pissed off, they're angry, they're afraid, period. It's very, very powerful and rewarding, and for whatever non-linear reason, I've been drawn there. I feel like I've "found my bliss" as Joseph Campbell says. I get up at 4:30 in the morning Tuesdays, leave the prison at four in the afternoon, come right back, teach an aikido class and get home at nine at night. I'm tired but I'm not burned out and I'm not exhausted. I don't even take lunch at the prison most of the time, I just work all day long, straight through.

It makes me think of Mother Theresa. The reason Mother Theresa's so inspiring to me is that these women in her group work twelve-hour days, 365 days a year. They eat food that most of us would think you couldn't survive on. They own nothing. They work in the worst kind of impoverished, diseased areas, yet they're happy, healthy, glowing. Now look at that and then look at your Yuppie executives who work six hours a day, who have fancy stuff, who are exhausted and all have "the Yuppie disease," chronic fatigue syndrome. What's the difference? To me it's that these people have found that giving is receiving and that there's so much energy when we can find what we're supposed to be doing. It's so wonderful. And I feel like I've been given this great gift. I've found out, at least for now, where my heart is supposed to be. I feel like I have so much energy for it. I don't get burned out, I don't get tired. I feel very fortunate. I make almost no money at it. Most of my income comes from conscious embodiment classes, counseling and workshops.

All of this has happened because of aikido. Aikido really is an amazing art. It is such a great opportunity for people to observe their fear and aggression, if they're allowed to do that. But all too often in aikido we say, "Let's be harmonious, let's be loving, let's be nice," while underneath is all of this unexamined fear and aggression. For many of us, how we feel about ourselves is completely run by how your *uke* falls. It's real interesting; people really check themselves out. How do you feel when your *uke* slaps hard or they don't slap hard? It's just unbelievable to inquire into the level that we judge ourselves by outside circumstances. It's such a powerful thing to recognize that. It's a tremendous opportunity to see that our well-being is dependent upon how the other person reacts. Aikido has this possibility for us to really study ourselves deeply and to study our fear and aggression. I can't emphasize enough how important I think it is and I think it's a place that's not often taken advantage of in aikido.

You know that saying: "It's wisdom to know others; it's enlightenment to know yourself." Instead of just getting good at doing the technique to someone else, we can use that incoming energy as a way to really observe ourselves so truthfully that we begin to see how we cover up, how we avoid, how we dominate under the auspices of harmony, under the auspices of "throw." Too often the philosophy's about harmony, blending and taking care of your partner, and not about self-observation, not about seeing the degree to which we, after all these years, still react with fear and aggression. And having seen it, the next stage is to make space for that. If you're my attacker, ultimately in this virtual practice, you represent me. Can I accept that part of myself? Can I take that part of myself in, represented by you? Can I let it come in and be there, or am I going to take control over myself, dominate myself and make myself be there? The important part is to see that it's so. I am that way; I am aggressive because I'm afraid, and these kinds of situations trigger my fear. Then I need to know myself thoroughly and truthfully and really accept myself in a most compassionate way. I hope that in the future people will be able to study aikido in that way, that there will be places where it's emphasized as a means of self-examination, as a recognition of our own aggression.

Right now I wish that sort of thing were occurring more. In schools where the teachers have some psychological background that possibility certainly grows. The problem is that it tends sometimes in those cases to get real soft and wimpy. It doesn't have to be that way; you can have a very strong psychological look at yourself, really observe yourself and train really strong. But it tends to be either strong training with no clear observation of self, or psychological training that's wimpy. I'm interested in more of a combination. Let's come in really strong, but let's observe, instead of trying to control or dominate or even be beautiful or graceful. Beauty and grace will happen; they occur as an intuitive response. But they're not the goal to me. The goal is to see the truth. That's the thing that I feel the most sad and inspired about—sad because I feel it's not being taken advantage of as it could be, and inspired that aikido is one of the few realms I've ever experienced in all of my work and spiritual forays where that possibility exists. Aikido is potentially a very powerful arena for spiritual development. And you can have fun, too!

12

DANIELLE EVANS

With the build of a life-long athlete, a bright smile and beautiful prematurely gray hair, Danielle Evans is a strikingly handsome and likable woman. The head of a dojo in Monterey, California, she is a contemporary of George Leonard, Richard Heckler and Wendy Palmer.

Evans began her practice of aikido as a student of Stan Pranin, the editor of Aiki News. *Shortly after getting her black belt, she was suddenly thrust into the position of being a teacher when Pranin left for Japan. In the following interview she speaks candidly of the difficulties she encountered as an inexperienced teacher and as a woman in a field dominated by men. And she elaborates on how two well-known psychological syndromes affect aikido: co-dependency and "the victim cycle."*

What makes Evans an Innovator is her involvement with Model Mugging, a successful self-defense course designed originally for women. Model Mugging started out as a sixteen-hour course where women learned how to deal effectively with violent attacks. But when Evans became an instructor of the program, she soon began to apply the aikido metaphor to the course and Model Mugging began to focus on psychological growth and change in its participants as well as on physical effectiveness. For Evans, the aim of aikido is not attack or even to change the attack or the attacker but to "move in without judgment" to control the situation. She sees this approach as a means of breaking the "victim cycle" out of which much physical abuse grows. Encouraged by her success with women, Evans also began teaching Model

Mugging to men. The men experience exactly the same situations as the women and are encouraged to look at how they too participate in the victim cycle. In a number of ways the issues which emerge for men are the same ones Dobson speaks of in describing his work with Robert Bly.

first got interested in aikido when I was living in Ohio in about 1972. I read an article in *Atlantic Monthly* which talked about a kind of energy that was beyond just regular physical energy and it mentioned t'ai chi and aikido. At that time I was in the Accelerated National Program with ATT and was very interested in the humanistic side of management. I was also involved in the women's movement in Cleveland, helped found Cleveland Women's Counseling, and taught classes called "Our Bodies, Our Selves," which were based on the book by the same name. I was interested in the human growth potential movement and in my own personal growth. So I wasn't drawn to aikido because I was interested in self-defense. I was really interested in doing something that was very physical and involved dealing with attacks but that had a healing aspect to it. And from the article, aikido seemed to fit that bill. So I thought that if I ever went any place where they had aikido, I'd study it. Actually I think there was aikido in Cleveland at that time, I just didn't know about it. Within a year I went to Monterey, California, for a few months. My plan was to go teach skiing in Colorado afterwards. But when I got there in September I found out that an aikido group had just started in July with Stan Pranin, the editor of *Aiki News*. So I joined them. I never did make it to Colorado.

Stan was a real flamboyant teacher. He was really into a lot of fast movement, and the way he put it across and the kind of specialness that he attached to it were attractive to me. He portrayed what we were doing as being better than what other people were doing in aikido, and that got everybody really jazzed. He said that we were just this incredible group. Because of that we were all attracted and we felt that we must really be doing something great. But he almost never talked about the non-physical side of aikido:

he talked about it more mechanically. If you follow *Aiki News,* you know that he is very interested in the technical side of aikido and how it developed from Daito-Ryu. At that time he didn't seem to be interested in anything that smacked of philosophy. Which may explain why, although I heard people talk about the healing aspects of aikido, I couldn't see clearly where the healing actually was. The movements were supposed to be in harmony with the joints, but beyond that, it wasn't very clear how aikido could be healing. It may sound strange that I found his teaching so attractive given my own interest in the spiritual side of aikido, but Stan really did make practice very exciting and attractive.

There weren't very many women in aikido then. I remember one time Stan was showing us movies in the dojo of aikido in Japan. And when a woman came on the screen in a *hakama,* one of the students blurted out, "You mean there are women black belts in Japan?"—like it was a real shock even to conceive of it. In fact she probably wasn't. But the idea of a woman black belt was just real shocking to some people. Actually there weren't that many people in aikido, period. Stan was a *sandan* and Doran Sensei and Bill Witt and Nadeau Sensei and all those people were *sandan.* That was the highest rank around on the West Coast. There weren't a lot of *shihan.* Kanai Sensei was in Boston, Akira Tohei was in Chicago. Koichi Tohei had still not broken away to form Ki Society when I first started. In fact, the first exam I took covered the eight basic techniques as defined by Tohei Sensei.

It was a real exciting period. There was a real kind of freshness and aliveness in the air; aikido was something new. There was really a lot of enthusiasm around aikido in Santa Cruz. Linda Hultgren was at U.C. Santa Cruz; she was a *shodan* and had just come back from Shingu. And Bob Frager was there. That spring Saito Sensei went to Palo Alto and Stanford University. We all trained with him. There was a lot of excitement around it.

After I had only been training for twenty-six days, Stan gave the first test in our dojo. The way he explained it to us was the ranking would start with tenth *kyu* and people would be ranked at different levels. I took the test just for the experience of it. Mary Heiny, Dick Ravoir and Linda Hultgren were just back from Shingu, and they trained there that night and helped judge the exams. Two of us were promoted to fourth *kyu* and all of the others, who were all men, were in these other ranks, like fifth *kyu*, sixth *kyu*, seventh *kyu*. I almost didn't get the fourth *kyu* because I was living with Dennis Evans, who I later married, and Stan felt really funny giving me a fourth *kyu* and Dennis a fifth *kyu*. But Mary was there and stepped in and supported my promotion. Anyway, there was a big uproar: half the class quit because of the way the *kyus* fell out.

That was when I started instructing. After I got my fourth *kyu* I talked to Mary Heiny and said, "Please, is there any way you can teach here in Monterey?" And she said, "Well, actually I'm going to be settling in Santa Cruz but I could come down on Saturdays and teach." And I said, "I'll set up a class for you for women." I set the class up that way because there was such a dearth of role models for women. It was a time when there were very few women black belts in aikido. Linda was a black belt and Mary was the highest-ranking woman in the United States and she was a *sandan*. And Betsy Hill had taken her exam. But there weren't a lot of women role models, so it was good to be together and be visible to each other. And I was really hungry to train with Mary. Mary was real supportive of it, and we also trained with Linda. So we set up a class called "Women in Action Aikido" and Mary came down on Saturdays. But in the first class, Mary announced that I would meet with the same group of women twice a week and go over what Mary had taught on Saturdays. So I actually started teaching as a blue belt. A number of people got started in that class, including Pat Hendricks, who trained there for a year and a half.

Meanwhile I continued to train; we trained seven days a week. I was training four hours a day for a couple of years. Stan considered me a special student. In fact, I remember his talking to me about becoming a world-class *aikidoka*. And then just before I was to take my *shodan* exam, we had a falling out. He said I couldn't train in the dojo and stuff like that. A lot of people came to my assistance: Jack

Wada and Mary Heiny and other people countered what Stan had said. So I went ahead and took the exam with the support of all these people, two years and ten months after I started training, and thought that now I was going to be *sempai* [senior student] and help out Stan. The exams were held quarterly up in the Bay Area. I took it in San Francisco at the same time as Richard Heckler and Wendy Palmer. George Leonard had taken his the quarter before that. The day after my exam Stan announced that he was leaving and that we had forty-eight hours to buy the mats. So then I went from being *sempai* in the dojo to being the only black belt in the dojo. And because I had believed and gone along with what Stan had said about being special, the falling out and his leaving were really hard for me: it really affected my confidence.

I officially took over the dojo after Stan left, but I had Jack Wada from San Jose and Linda Hultgren from Santa Cruz come and teach regularly because although I'd trained a lot in the two years and ten months before then, my aikido was very immature. Then a year later Dennis and another person took their black belt exams. But I didn't even think about taking another exam for about five years—I just didn't have much confidence.

It wasn't just my issues with Stan that affected my confidence. There's one teacher in the Bay Area whose way of relating to women students is very sexual; he always brings in sexual innuendo and even makes direct passes at his female students. I've tried to relate to him as a student, but the way that he would always bring sex into the equation was really difficult and confusing for me. This is an important issue for many women: many women come to aikido wanting to find self-esteem and instead there is too often a kind of "power over" situation. Teachers are in a position of responsibility and power; they get to be father figures, and the kind of relationships that develop between male teachers and female students can be really confusing for a lot of women. I've never gotten into a sexual relationship with that person, but the whole thing has been erosive of my confidence as a martial artist. For example, a few years after I got my black belt, he made the comment that "I would have passed you on your *shodan* exam based on your ass alone." To be out there in an area that's dominated by men and then to have somebody who is really an authority and a really good teacher be relating to me and valuing me because of the shape of my ass rather than because of the way that I do aikido is really tough.

It has been helpful for me to be able to talk to other women about it—I've gotten a lot of support that way. Like one of the things I do is talk to Linda Hultgren a lot, who also runs a dojo. And I used to communicate a lot with Mary. It has been great that we've supported each other and never wanted to go against each other. But you know, I've learned a lot from it. It has been really good for me philosophically to learn to never see the men in aikido, or anyone else I've had difficulties with, as enemies, to know that even with that energy coming towards me, I can still connect up with my center and relate in a powerful way with that individual and not be adversarial. So I'm grateful actually for the challenges that all that has provided. But when I was younger, when I was more immature with it, it did erode my confidence: I was looking for affirmation about being a good *aikidoka* from the outside, from my teachers. And if they related their caring about me or their interest in me to my body rather than to how I did aikido, then it made me wonder, it made me question myself.

Being a woman instructor in a traditionally male arena has been very interesting. I often feel the effects of my being a woman with my students. A lot of military men come in and they go a number of different ways, depending on their background. You know, male instructors sometimes have difficulty establishing clear boundaries. Part of the problem I've experienced with this one male instructor I was telling you about concerns boundaries. It's an abuse of power, but because of his position and his own damage he doesn't see it. It's just like he keeps coming from that place all the time. But I've been able to keep real clear boundaries with my students, so that if students see me as attractive and try to relate to me in a way that they're used to relating to women—which would be to be patronizing or be sexually advancing—I've just been real caring of their process and done aikido with it, you know, never ignoring it or turning my back on it but just staying with it and keeping it clear.

And then there have been situations where I'll grab a student's wrist in class and I can feel in his body that this person is just not going to stay because it's just too charged for him. Even if they've had other martial arts training, a lot of men have never seen a woman instructor and to have an attractive woman instructor is just too much. Men have definitely left because of that. It's not like they've said, "Hey, you know, I just can't handle this," because I don't even think that they're consciously aware of it. But I pick up on it.

And then I've had other people who just stay with it and work with it. Julio Toribo is a really good example. When he came into the dojo he was a *shodan* in karate. And he said, "Who's the head of the dojo?" And I think he first talked to Dennis and Dennis said, "Well, my wife is. And she's just had a baby." Julio's first view of me was that while I would be teaching aikido Colin, my son, would cry and since Colin was nursing on demand, I'd get off the mat. So I'd demonstrate something, I'd get off the mat, I'd nurse him and I'd get back on the mat and teach some more. I kept on saying, "Okay, aikido's about making human beings one family and we've got a family dojo," but it was pretty strange for some people. Julio had just never seen anything like that. I mean, women and martial arts were like the difference between the moon and the sun; they may be up in the same heavens, but they don't travel together. But little by little he started changing, and working together in Model Mugging has only accelerated the process. Now we work as equals and we've created a real effective way of working on any issues we have.

There are some more general gender-related issues I've had to deal with in myself or that I've seen in other women. For example, Stan treating me as someone special was appealing to a place in me that wants to be chosen or needs to be special. Many women experience the same need or desire. I mean, it's real common for women to want to be chosen or be special. It's the Cinderella syndrome. Of course, men experience the same thing but I think it manifests differently. With men it comes out as wanting to be rescuers. And tied to the waiting to be chosen and the wanting to be taken care of, women will take personally any pain done to them. That's something that women need to work with: their feelings of maybe being "one down" or of being in a victim cycle, being the oppressed one. If there's somebody who's rough in the dojo or if there's somebody who comes in with an ego, women are more used to maybe getting angry about it or feeling victimized by it.

A man might also react as a victim, but the way he will do it is to get competitive and to show off and to be "one up over." A lot of women have the sense that that's not the answer. Part of the reason is that they haven't had much success at it in their lives. But what women will do is they'll disappear. They'll draw inward or disappear in the form of avoiding training with certain people who they feel uncomfortable with, whereas a man will avoid training with someone he can't throw hard enough or who he feels too challenged by. Women will disappear in the context of working in the dojo: rather than extending out and being present, they kind of draw in. I've had a lot of conversations with women about this, black belts, too.

I can think of an example of this kind of thing: there was somebody in the dojo who arranged a demo and he asked a number of us to be involved in the demo. Well, the way that he arranged it really showed him off as a martial artist. There were a couple of us, another woman black belt and myself, who were upset by this. It was such a downer feeling invisible and being there to support this person as a martial artist instead of being there to make a general presentation about aikido. My inclination was to withdraw and pull back and feel hurt or think of ways of getting revenge, like ways to put this other person down. "Okay, the next class I'm going to say this and this." But the way I resolved it was I thought about it, meditated about it and took a few days to process it. And what I came out with was, "Oh, what I need to do is I need to put myself out of there. Not in a kind of way that's better than someone else. I don't want to focus on and give my power to this person out here, but it's not time to disappear. I need to connect up with my center and be out there in another way." And so I thought of some things that involved the whole dojo in a public way and that were really supportive of every-body in the whole dojo. And then I felt fine. It was a learning expe-rience in that way. So that's what I mean by disappearing.

I don't mean to imply that women have special weaknesses or even special strengths. I think people's fear manifests differently, and women disappearing or waiting to be chosen are the ways that they commonly victimize themselves. With men it just looks differ-ent, that's all. People come in with their stuff and everybody has "stuff." And some of the stuff that has allowed people to survive the best is the stuff that has to be let go of the most, like disappearing or being real out there physically. I think it can be particularly tough for people who are really coordinated and really good at sports. Very often they come in and they learn aikido really fast and their teacher keeps pushing them on through, saying, "That's really good, that's really good" but never really helping them deal with their "stuff." I see people being reinforced all the time for things that I think are great athletics, but I don't think that by itself gives them the oppor-tunity to move on emotionally and spiritually. There's a real danger for physically competent, charismatic people who are reinforced for their charisma and who get followers based on their charisma. Too often they stay in the same spot. That's really hard to watch.

You see, that's what they've developed to survive all their lives and boy, it's being fed here. That's something I have to deal with. One of the things that attracted me to aikido was that I had this basic belief from what I had read that you couldn't perform in it, that you needed to be real and in the moment with it. Part of my survival had been to be a good performer. I've got a lot of presence. I can be out there in a way where people respond to me as if I'm competent. But underneath that I had a lot of insecurities. So I was hoping aikido would help me deal with that. But I had to struggle with that issue in aikido, too. People still responded to me as if I knew what I was doing! And it always left me with this kind of feel-ing of "Well, somebody's going to find out." It's a terrible, terrible position to be in. It's one of the worst. So aikido has been a chal-lenge for me in that way because I've had to keep on being real, and sometimes it meant just showing my lack of confidence in something and saying, "Hey, it's okay to learn from someone who is lower ranked. I'm grateful for this opportunity," and not having it mean that I'm less.

Another issue that comes out in aikido and that affects both men and women is the whole codependency thing. There is more than just the art itself that drives people to practice aikido and makes them enthusiastic. That certainly was true of me and the people I started with. You know, people would make comments about being addicted to aikido. In fact, I still hear people say that or things like "aikido's the only good addiction." And in having had much more experience with codependency and with working with people, I know that there are no "good addictions." Aikido can be for people a way to alter how they experience reality, and in a negative sense: if there's something that's really uncomfortable for them to look at in their lives, aikido can become a way of not having to look at that. I've seen how that can affect families, which addictions do. Anything can become addictive and I feel that aikido can do that. Not that that has to happen. I think it varies from dojo to dojo and it varies with the individual. But I feel personally that we live in an addictive society and that it manifests in a lot of different ways. We come with a propensity for altering our state of reality in a way that helps us avoid painful issues. If somebody comes to aikido and has a teacher or leader who can keep them focused on what their feelings really are, on what their reality really is, then aikido will not be addictive. But that requires that the teacher has actually done enough work himself or herself that he or she can provide that kind of leadership. If the teacher is into power it can lead into something that I consider an addictive, unhealthy atmosphere.

I don't know how prevalent that is. In fact, I feel that overall aikido is evolving beyond where O-Sensei left it. But I also feel that there are some places where that is not happening. Unfortunately, even some of O-Sensei's students don't seem to be following what O-Sensei wrote down. I once sat through a three-hour talk with one of the best-known of O-Sensei's *deshi* where he was saying he has the one true aikido and if you want what true aikido is you have to get it from him. I hear the fear in there and the competition and I don't hear some of the things that strike me as being what aikido is really about. But I support aikido wherever it's happening, even when it's practiced as a kind of power-over thing or even if it's being taught like jujitsu or even if there's no philosophy being taught. As long as people are doing it they're going to connect up with other people or they're going to read something or they're going to join AA or they're going to join CODA or they're going to get into something else, and with their new knowledge they're going to begin re-examining what they're doing in aikido, and that will contribute even more to the growth and evolution of aikido. The whole thing operates in spirals and so it's going to affect the whole process. I see aikido as an opportunity. I feel that it affects the way that we conduct ourselves on our planet, and as a consequence it affects the level of violence or peace.

This is what I feel is happening: in the United States there are a lot of us who are under many other influences and things are changing really fast. I feel that there are a lot of ways that people are learning from aikido. Take the philosophy of Model Mugging, for example. That's something I have developed and expanded on under the influence of my aikido background, even though somebody who teaches aikido all the time might look at it and think, "I don't like that because it's violent." But it actually contains a lot of the messages about choosing not to be a victim that I see in O-Sensei's writing. I guess what I'm thinking is that if even just a few people catch the current of what can actually be done with The Way and how that can be manifested, aikido will continue to grow in importance. I believe we're living in a time and a place where this can happen because the West, and in particular the United States, allows for that kind of development to take place.

I think my involvement in Model Mugging is a good example of what I'm talking about. I'm one of the founders of Model Mugging along with Matt Thomas, Julio Toribo, Sheryl Doran and Mark Morrison. I got started in Model Mugging in this way: about 1983 I had

301

just come back from a year's sabbatical with Dennis. I was gone nine months from the dojo. It was the only time I had stopped training for an extended period and when we got back we held a black belt meeting and talked about what we could do with the dojo, and among other things, we talked about self-defense. I had never believed in self-defense courses because I thought they were inadequate. Someone can walk on the mat and in one day be profoundly affected by aikido, but to be physically effective takes a longer period of time. It takes less time now for some people because of the good teachers, but basically it takes a long time to learn to defend yourself well. So I didn't believe in self-defense courses. But we had heard rumors about this course called Model Mugging because aikido people were involved in it in the Bay Area.

So we decided that Julio and I would go and investigate it. And the way we did it was that I took the course and he observed it. And so for eight weeks we went up to Palo Alto, it was the only place that it was being taught. Sheryl Doran taught it and we were really impressed with it. It was a sixteen-hour self-defense course for women where the participants actually got mugged and learned how to deal with it. The "model muggers" were and are men trained to act the role of muggers and who wear protective clothing so the women can hit them as hard as they need to. It was really effective physically.

We brought it to Monterey right away. The first thing that happened was Julio and I needed to work together as a team. There were no well-working female and male instructor teams. And so we needed to work out our own conflicts and develop a format that allowed us to always deal with situations where feelings of ego and other "stuff" came up so that we could support each other. From the very outset we knew the answer wasn't to be judgmental or to attack each other but rather to support and move in. That's basically the aikido model, and that's what went into the teaching and that's what was passed on to the students.

It wasn't taught that way at first—at first it was basically us experts teaching these victims how to get out of bad situations, which is a common way that self-defense courses are taught. But as soon as we started working with it, we started really developing it so that even a year later it was an entirely different course and two years later it was a twenty-four-hour course. And the difference in it was the result of identifying that what inspired us was not that somebody could deliver better than forty foot pounds of power to knock somebody out, but the transformation that the participants went through. If somebody is attacked and then goes in for vengeance, attacks the attacker, they become a victim needing a victim. They can survive an attack but they're thinking, "Okay, so now I can destroy all those assholes," and they keep the cycle going. If they feel that way at the end of the course, they still walk out with fear: they actually expect attack, they expect fear. You can see it in anybody who does a lot of fighting. They're really fearful and they'll move from learning open hand techniques to learning how to use a knife to having a Magnum .357. They operate from fear. But if you can really work with someone before they get in extremely challenged situations, get them to start focusing on themselves, on how they've felt victimized, and on how they can choose not to be a victim, then the action they take may be exactly the same—they may knock out the attacker—but what they're focusing on is not being the victim in a victim cycle. That's where the healing occurs.

For the first few years we only worked with women. And we focused on breaking the cycle of violence, which I describe as "a victim needing a victim," and that's not just my own description.

O-Sensei talked about it, too. When somebody attacks, they've already lost. By their very attacking, they've indicated their disconnection from the universe, so in that sense they're a victim. They want to victimize someone else so they can feel okay. And the emphasis in breaking a cycle of violence is not to focus on the attacker. But the more that we did it, the more that I realized, "Hey, this is something that we're all involved in. This choosing not to be a victim is something that we're all dealing with." So I had a staff retreat with the men and women who were doing the teaching and asked them to describe their choosing not to be a victim. And for the men it came a lot to "Well, I was a wimp as a kid but once I got to be a black belt, I was no longer a victim" or "When I got to be a corporal in the army" or "When I got to be head of this office, that's when . . . ." Somehow something had happened and you got a badge and you were no longer a victim and you became a non-victim. But the more we worked with it, the more we saw that it was something that you have to do on a daily basis, probably moment to moment. In anything that happens, you can either perceive yourself as a victim—either one-up-over or one-under in the victim cycle—or you can make a choice not to be a victim. And that's really what we're doing in aikido. Our focus is on choosing not to be a victim; it's not on trying to change the attacker. It's on joining the attack and the attacker.

It was in doing this intense personal work with the staff and particularly with the men that I started really understanding the victim cycle. Actually I call it "the victim ladder." What we've learned is to try to get to a higher and higher rung and as long as we have somebody on a rung down lower than ourselves we feel okay. Even all the way up to the most powerful person in the world, if their sense of themselves depends on anybody else being on the lower rungs, they're still on the victim ladder. And the only thing you can do to break the cycle is to make your sense of yourself not depend on being better than anybody else.

As the result of these talks with the staff, I decided to start doing men's seminars. The men's seminars are run a lot like the women's in that the men actually get mugged. And there's a lot of processing. It's a real intensive twenty-four hours. They start at three in the afternoon and do a lot of processing and stuff and really get into what their feelings are, what their history is. They fill out a questionnaire ahead of time that indicates some of the history and they learn some techniques, and the next day they go through several muggings. Mary and Tom Elliot teach it together, and Julio and I teach it together. It's extremely powerful because in that twenty-four-hour period they go through a lot. Like the women, they're terrified when they get attacked, and they are able to face their fear

304

and get the feeling of what it is to choose not to be a victim. But they also experience a bonding and a new sense of trust with the other men that's new for them.

When I started doing men's seminars I was so struck with the realization that the very core of the pain and the grief that men carry has to do with their feeling of separation of man from man, and that women have been drawn into that. Women have been treated almost like one of the aspects that can help you get "one up over" on another man: Historically speaking, there's property, there's physical expertise and there are women. But the very core of all this was this sadness, this grief, this pain that men carry from their childhood. It has something to do with being little boys and relating to their dads and with the sense of being betrayed by other men and boys as they've grown up. I really saw the cycle being broken for the men in these seminars when they began to share what their fear and grief were about, when they were honest about it and they didn't just say, "Things are cool and I'm okay." In most cases when men start to face their fears, they "pump up over" like in the army or football, in a kind of blind denial of any of the real feelings that come up. And when they really brought up what their feelings were and developed a kind of trust with this small group of men and could actually act out scenarios, some of which had really happened and some of which were imagined or symbolic, they realized that what they really wanted was for their shame to attack them so that they could really set boundaries and deal with the shame in their lives. They wanted the mugger to be somebody attacking them who's really saying, "You're really not worth it; you can't make it sexually; you're not strong enough; you're a wimp" and to actually deal with the feelings that come up for them.

As the camaraderie builds, a lot of the men will say things like, "This is the first group of men I've ever been able to really talk to and trust." At that point I try to steer them away from or guide the other kind of comments that come up about "and there are all these other guys out there." We do whole ceremonies that tie in the fact that their small circle is part of a whole larger circle. Just like we do in aikido, they say, "No, there's really not any separation." That's the only way that we can move in the way that we do. But it's just incredible the feelings that come up. And when I first experienced this, it struck me in my gut like an earthquake, an earth-moving thing. When I looked at these men I realized that the violence really came from their feeling of separation and isolation from other men, which expresses itself as having to be on guard, not trusting, being better than ... that whole thing. But that's where the healing needs to occur so that a man can walk out, and even if another man thinks that there needs to be separation, even to the point of attacking, a man can walk around feeling within himself a sense of connection. That's what's necessary to connect up with anything else. Otherwise it's just a joke. Even in aikido which has a philosophy of connection, you see people fighting and competing and needing to be better than. You see that kind of thing on an aikido mat just as much as you would in judo, and judo is an organized competition. It comes from that feeling of separation. To end that separation it takes someone to realize, "Okay, even though this person is feeling that way, I can still move in a caring way." That's not the way we grow up, but that is where the healing can take place. So I love teaching these men's seminars because I feel that it's one important step. They really confirm our belief in what we are doing.

Now Model Mugging is everywhere. We developed the instructors' training course and for a number of years, anybody who taught model mugging, we taught. That's not the case anymore, and I do know that there are places where the philosophy is different. It's oriented more toward learning to defend yourself and less on the transformations than can occur, on breaking the victim cycle. But I still think it's beneficial: I know that at least people are learning a self-defense method that will stick with them and that they'll learn how to knock attackers out. But the course is so much more powerful when the emphasis is on the personal transformations that take place and on breaking the victim cycle.

I get so moved at the end of courses. The changes that happen to people are just amazing. For example, there was a woman in one course I taught. It was after the fourth class in which they're mugged by someone who is acting as if they're on drugs. This means that the women don't deliver just one knockout blow, they have to deliver a whole bunch and they have to stay in there a long time. They lose their breath, they get into an anaerobic state and it's really scary. Some of them are reminded of past victimizations. Some of them feel that they're going to die, and some of them actually have the gift of getting down to the bottom place in which their whole being is crying out to have that person stop. They actually want the attacker to take care of them in that way, which is something a lot of women who were abused as children experience because the attackers were people who took care of them. So they get down to that point and that's when it clicks that they need to stop the whole thing, and it's the first time in their lives they can even do that. They realize that they are the ones who need to act on their own behalf. That's all we talk about. It's not that this person is their dad and they've finally kicked the shit out of him, it's that they've acted on their own behalf.

And so in this one class I taught, we were talking about how difficult this fourth class was and about how they got really scared and they weren't sure about their confidence and this woman said, "You know what I got? I was down there and I realized that this person might rape me and might even kill me, but I realized all along that even if that happened, I wasn't a victim." That's making a perceptual change. That's realizing that our being a victim doesn't depend on whether we're attacked or whether we're mugged or whatever's happening. This woman can go out in her life and she may never actually be attacked, and I pray that she never is, but now she can put her realizations into practice in her daily life and realize that she can choose not to be a victim and that it doesn't mean attacking someone else.

As a mother it affects me with my son. It means that when he does something that a boy will do that pushes my buttons and makes me feel victimized or angry or hurt—like "How could he say that or do that?" it means that I'm able to stop and know that my choosing not to be a victim is to realize that he's the child, that I'm feeling from my child space and that that's about my history; that I'm okay and my job here is to parent and that rather than attack him—and you see it all the time, parents attacking their children verbally or emotionally—that I can parent him, just be with him in it. And that breaks the cycle of violence because it's my son who'll carry on what I start.

I feel strongly that Model Mugging is an extension of my aikido training. Aikido is really based on the perceptual change that breaks the victim cycle. Instead of wanting power over someone, instead of beating out someone or beating their attack, you let go of the attack and deal with the other person's center. That's the very core of aikido. Instead of power over, aikido offers empowerment. Power over has to do with externals, power over something on the outside. That's different from empowerment, which involves an internal perception that isn't dependent on being better than something on the outside. There always has to be something on the outside that power is relative to, whereas empowerment is something that always comes from the inside. I think that although aikido offers opportunities to practice in a kind of way that involves competition and power over, at the very core it gives us an opportunity to say no, if I'm going to be true, I have to go in with no judgment, no competition, nothing about "against," I cannot attack the attacker. If I'm going to be clear in my spirit, I can't even think about the attacker as separate, which means that I have to really come from a centered place.

And it's cyclical: Model Mugging made me look at my aikido practice. And what I learned then added to what I do in Model Mugging. It's a spiral. So when I teach people aikido, when I practice aikido, I really practice with a mind set and a state of connecting up with my own center and going into the attack without judgment. The attack's not really the most important thing for me to deal with. I need to connect up with my center. That allows me to experience someone else's center and to move in without judgment. In fact, it's the only thing that gives me the right to move in. And that's when I can really be one with that person.

13

KOICHI BARRISH

Koichi Barrish is a charming, robust man of medium height, with a full beard, short-cropped hair and a sunny smile. He has generated a good bit of controversy in the aikido community. Around 1989 reports started circulating about a martial artist who claimed to be a high-ranking aikido instructor but who was virtually unknown. It was said that he conducted Shinto ceremonies. In demonstrations, Barrish's students fell over with the lightest of touches. Sometimes it seemed that Barrish had done nothing at all to cause them to fall. Some people thought he might be a charlatan, but others who had met him were impressed with his ability. Although no one was certain of where Barrish had received his training, he himself has consistently aligned himself with the art of O-Sensei and has in fact received many invitations to teach in "mainline" aikido schools.

As it turns out, Barrish has not practiced a great deal of mainline aikido. Instead, most of his training has been in a traditional form of aiki-jujitsu. For nine years he studied with a man named Ideta in Los Angeles from whom he formally inherited the art he had learned, Ideta Ryu. Barrish justifies his claim to be teaching "aikido" by pointing out that he feels a strong connection to O-Sensei. Like O-Sensei, his primary interest is in misogi, *"purification." He has received training in some of the Shinto ascetic practices O-Sensei performed daily, notably* chinkon, *a practice which combines breathing with chanting, vigorous physical movements and visualizations. Borrowing an idea from*

Rupert Sheldrake*, Barrish also talks about the inspiration he has gained from the powerful "morphogenetic" field O-Sensei created. According to Barrish, anyone who "tunes" himself properly can hook up to that field. Because of all this and because Barrish has allowed his spiritual interests to transform his physical art, he feels that he is no longer practicing or teaching aiki-jitsu but aikido.

Barrish teaches in Everett, Washington. His dojo contains an authentic Shinto shrine designed and built by an American trained in Japan to be a temple carpenter.

My training was very interesting. I trained with a fellow named Ideta Sensei, who adopted me and made me head of his family and *soke* [successor] of his family art. His family was from Kuomoto, Japan. His training was quite severe. My teacher's art was really aiki-jitsu; he was not from O-Sensei's line. I have practiced mainline aikido, primarily Ki Society Aikido, though very little.

Ideta Sensei was an interesting man, a classic kind of instructor, very traditional. During the whole time of my apprenticeship I wasn't able to ask a question in class. I would get in trouble if I moved my eyes the wrong way. It was that kind of real, real traditional upbringing. Needless to say, he wasn't a very popular instructor. He would have most people in tears very quickly. His English was very poor and he sometimes misunderstood things that were going on around him.

I met him in the community center near where I lived in West L.A. when I was just a kid. There were periods when our time together was really intense for a year or so and then he would disappear for a while. When he stopped coming, a lot of other people would come; I'd be teaching class for him. And then it would get filled up. We'd be somewhere over a Japanese market in West L.A. training—that kind of thing. We'd get a full class. And when he came back he'd yell at everybody and they would all leave and then it would be him and me again.

---

*Sheldrake, R. *A New Science of Life*. London: Paladin, 1981.

All told, I trained with Ideta Sensei for just over nine years. That's not very many years, but it was pretty intense. He wanted me to live with him and be *uchi deshi,* but I was just a little too American for that, so that never happened. But we spent a lot of time together, ate a lot of meals together, prepared food together.

When I inherited his art through *doto,* through succession, my teacher felt that I would go in directions that he couldn't imagine, that he couldn't follow, that he couldn't go, but he had total confidence in me, regardless of where I was headed. He felt really good about it. He gave me his name, Ideta, which was by far the most important thing to him in his life. Actually, when he met me he was not a young man and he had long since given up the idea of transmitting. So it was a real special thing for him to be able to pass on his name and to feel good about it. I think at the time I inherited I had my own place in Santa Monica, which was on Fourth Street in Ocean Park. My teacher came to me and said that he wanted to pass on the name to me and pass on the family art. We did this ceremony and that was that. We ate sushi on that day. I remember the day. I just don't remember the year. I remember the day.

He was a very special man. What he did and what he said were exactly the same. His feelings about *budo,* his feelings about nature, his feelings about people were integrated, and his abilities in terms of *budo* were completely integrated; he was phenomenally powerful and of course he always knew what was going to happen long before it happened. His art was very fiery, really quite explosive, *atemi* [striking]-oriented. His father's art hadn't been so atemi-oriented,* but that was my teacher's very favorite thing. The type of *atemi* he used dealt with *tsubo,* pressure points. The bottom line feeling was a sense of "one strike, one killing." But his whole art was very integrated.

I don't really like to talk about other *aikidoka,* but there are people who do really beautiful karate movement and they do really

---

Atemi-oriented: Ideta Sensei's art emphasized the use of strikes *(atemi)* to anatomically weak points such as the ribs.

beautiful *aikikai*-style aikido movement. Each aspect is really beautiful, but the integration is maybe not so complete. There's a really beautiful reverse punch followed by a beautiful *irimi nage,* but there isn't so much the sense of if *atemi* is made here how does the body move? If you strike a strong person and they recoil or "echo" off that strike, where do they go? And what is the psychology of it, the energetic organization, the physiological organization? What is the organization of somebody who knows about the rough and tumble? How do they respond to *atemi?* How do they fold and come back? In any real discussion of *atemi* I think that's very important. Sometimes with other *aikidoka* "the echo" of the *atemi* is not being utilized. You see a really beautiful, precise karate movement and then entering, *irimi nage, kokyu nage,* but you do not see so much the sense of blending, the integration of the qualities of movement.

It's convenient, having done more severe training—it does give you a nice bottom line, having a good working understanding of that real pragmatic nature. But I don't think severe training is necessary. Somebody has to do it along the line and then it's tricky how it's transmitted. But if the lines are clear and it's happening I don't think severe training is really necessary.

There does have to be a certain physicality to the training, though. We can't just drift off into la-la land. That won't work. I think that's a real fine line. Hard training in the dojo is not really a practice fight anyway. It's not like someone's really trying to hurt you. There's a fine line. You really have to go back and forth; it's really difficult to walk that line in such a way that the people we're training with really get the stuff.

The levels of intensity in training are very interesting. Even within the same dojo there are people training at different levels of intensity. There are the more hobbyist *aikidoka* [aikido practitioners] and that's fine too. Their life is really enriched, really enhanced by the experience. And then there are the people who are really remaking themselves, almost rebuilding themselves. At a certain point for those people, pressure has to be applied. There are many different kinds of training in the same dojo.

In my own training I am primarily interested in *misogi*, "purification." Actually, I've been interested in it for quite some time. When I lived in Southern California I used to go up into the high Sierra, outside of Yosemite, and do purification practice there. That was not part of my training with my teacher, though. We used to go out into salt water a lot, but we didn't do much of what I would call *misogi* practice together.

I believe that *misogi* practice is very pragmatic as well as spiritual. The answer to many practice problems, like getting beyond *kata*-training [form training] is really in *ki*, in *musubi* [connection]. You extend beyond the radius of the interaction between you and the environment. When you're clear and extend beyond that radius, everything else is inside. I don't know how to describe it, though it's easy to demonstrate. The ability to perceive movement prior to movement happening can also be seen as the result of *misogi*. If you're really clear, if you're really centered, if you're really hooked up, it's really easy to perceive movements in the energy body, and any movement in the physical body is preceded by movement in the energy body.

With *misogi* practice, training is so enlivening that practicality begins to come in. It's a really interesting subject. One of the guys in the dojo who I have a lot of fun with is also from Los Angeles, from a different part: he's from East L.A. He grew up as a gang member; he did some hard federal time and he has also been a boxing coach. Most of his peer group, from when he was a young man, is either dead or in prison. At any rate, he's a guy who pretty thoroughly explored the nature of physical conflict between people. And when we do *waza* he can appreciate what's going on from a level that practically nobody else can in a given class, because he has that understanding. He knows how people move. Because he survived, you know he knows how. He has a physically demanding job, and he's a big man so he can appreciate aikido in a way that a lot of people can't. He can appreciate the real, incredible pragmatic practicality of it. Within the last year someone came punching at him and he did a touchless throw. Someone swung at him; he entered and never touched the guy. The guy bounced back a considerable distance and slid on his butt and was disinclined to continue. But the experience for him was so funny because instead of just dropping him, he was so amazed that he didn't have to touch him. He was so amazed at the feelings he had after the confrontation, in contrast to other feelings where he had successfully smacked people. He felt great. He didn't touch him and he didn't have to hurt him. I mean, the guy who attacked him was bruised, but it was not really anything serious. He was really very thrilled about it. We wrote a story about it for our newsletter.

People's reaction to aikido is interesting. Sometimes there will be people who come in and take a peek and say, "Oh, this doesn't look very practical." But if a high-ranking karate practitioner comes in, they always seem to really like it. They can really appreciate the body dynamics, the energetics, the physicality . . . also that sense of timing and flow.

Of course there's more to training than *misogi*. There are all the physical issues like angles, timing, continuous entry, that kind of stuff. And then there's *musubi*, "connection" of which there are two kinds. There's the connection between human beings, that's *yoko musubi*. If someone were to attack you, that's a very sincere connection. The vertical part is simply the heaven-earth connection or human being and divine, *tante musubi*. When those two things are in place, that's the formation of the aiki cross. And from that place, technique manifests.

Anyway, several years after I inherited my teacher's art I moved up here to Washington state. I had been interested in the more pragmatic aspects of aikido for a long time, but after I moved here I got less and less interested in those aspects. I think I started calling my art "aikido" after I moved here; generally we use that term though we also sometimes use the name I inherited, Ideta Ryu.

I heard that Hikitsuchi Sensei said that all sincere sound is *kotodama*,* and I think in the same sense really sincere movement is

---

*Kotodama—the Japanese science of "sound-spirit," based on the idea that certain "pure" sounds have spiritual and healing power.

aikido. That's why I decided to use the word "aikido" even though my teacher was not from O-Sensei's line. One of the things I think is so special about O-Sensei is I feel he created a kind of morphogenetic field, a field of consciousness. If you go to a church and everybody sings a particular song, there's a real special feeling. Part of it is just the *musubi* of the situation, your voice is moving with other people's voices, there's that group consciousness. But also, beyond that, if it's a song that has been sung for a few centuries, the repetition of that song has almost built up a field of consciousness, a morphogenetic field about that particular act that you can kind of tap into while doing that act. I'm sure lots of people in the martial arts have had experiences like maybe training outside in the rain somewhere, doing *suburi* [basic weapons movement] in the rain, feeling somehow psychically or energetically linked to all the centuries of people who have been perfecting their *suburi* on a particular kind of day in a particular kind of weather. I think the thing that's so spectacular about O-Sensei is that through the sincerity of his beliefs, his life-long search, over a long lifetime he created a very powerful morphogenetic field. Maybe if somebody were interested they could tune their receptor to learn directly from that field. I think the information is certainly there and certainly continuing to evolve.

What's fascinating too is O-Sensei continues to affect a lot of people not involved in aikido, not involved in physical training. There are a lot of people who perhaps hear of him or who haven't even heard of him but have had psychic experiences of him. It's very interesting—a lot of people not involved in the training are deeply affected by O-Sensei. Psychic people come into the dojo, and see a picture of O-Sensei and react strongly. It's not at all uncommon. Frager Sensei always says that one time when he was with O-Sensei toward his death O-Sensei said, "When you practice aikido, I will be there." There's something going on. There really is. We could call that again a morphogenetic field, a field of consciousness, but there's something there that we can certainly receive inspiration, even information from. And there also exist technologies for tuning, centuries-old, millennia-old, very exact technologies for tuning the receiver.

One of those tuning practices is *chinkon,* which O-Sensei practiced every day. I've practiced *chinkon* for a few years. *Chinkon* practice is kind of hard to get information on. O-Sensei, I believe, learned from Onisaburo Deguchi, the leader of Omoto-kyo. It's very hard for people, even Shinto priests, to learn. I was really very lucky to learn it and then to learn enough to be certified to teach it. One of the priests at Tsubaki Grand Shrine had to spend eight years at Isenokami Ginjen, and a woman who worked at the shrine had to spend four years there. Over a period of a month or so the priests at the Grand Shrine introduced me to various levels of practice. I've been there to deepen my practice a couple of times since then. It's a very powerful tuning practice. Before that, I practiced *mitamashizumei misogi harai* daily for many years. People in the Ki Society call it "misogi breathing," but the real name of that exercise is "mitamashizumei." That and my *kotodama* practice I've been doing for lots of years.

When I lived in Los Angeles, most of the chanting I did I learned from my teacher. It was a mixture of Shinto and Buddhist chanting. Then I learned some chanting practice from a man named Shokai Kanai, who now is Nichi bishop in Tokyo. Again, that's a mixture of Buddhism and Shinto. And I learned a lot about chanting practice from Jack Wada, who learned from Hikitsuchi Sensei. Then when I went to study Shinto in Japan, I learned the chanting practices that I use these days. I haven't been practicing "sound" *kotodama.* In a sense, it's almost like *otodama.* There's *kotodama* and *otodama. Kotodama* is "word," *otodama* is "sound." "Sound" I've practiced for many, many years. There's some really specific, really involved chanting practices, that for instance are practiced at Subaki Shrine that are very, very old, some of the original practices. I studied those there. They're the ones that I use these days.

I've been interested in Shinto forever. I've been very drawn to the practice since the early '70s, really drawn. I practiced *misogi* whenever I had the chance and I practiced *mitamashizumei* daily. And my diet was essentially macrobiotic. So I've been involved with a kind of tuning process for a lot of years. In fact, I had already built a shrine even before I was invited to study in Japan. We had a small shrine in our dojo and then we built a large shrine, really kind of made a big deal out of it, really made that the heart of the dojo— for me anyway, not necessarily for the people who train there. Some of them are only vaguely aware of it, and I don't really try to draw people into the practice at all. There's not a really wide appeal. But we built a big shrine, and through another *aikidoka* some of the people from Subaki saw a picture of our shrine and were really impressed by it. So because of that I was invited to go and study more formally at Subaki Shrine in Japan. I went over in the mid-80s and then became even more involved in the practice, in some ways more formally, then later built the shrine that we have now. I wasn't there long, though I go a couple of times a year.

I had some really amazing experiences there though I don't know if I can talk about that. When I was staying at the shrine, I would wake up at two or three in the morning. It was almost like I got a "call" of some kind. And then I would go out on the mountainside, maybe during a storm, and receive specific information about aikido practice or something like that. I had episodes of automatic movement, answers to certain questions; maybe I had a question about an angle and then I would find my body moving in a way that explained a certain cut. I had some really interesting experiences. My training to a really large degree comes from experiences such as that, realizations about the nature of technique that I want to pursue.

A lot of what I inherited from my instructor was really worthwhile and pragmatic information, for example, about moving to the side instead of back, *kokyu rokyu* [breath power] and timing. A lot of it was important, and it has formed kind of a matrix for the knowledge that I've received since. But the most important knowledge is knowledge that didn't come from quite such a traditional root. I don't want to make any claims. My ambition is just to have a small shrine in the country, do that kind of shrine practice every day, and do *misogi* every day and have people to do aikido with.

Most of the training in our dojo is just physical aikido training.

We do have the regular *misogi* training, *misogi* meaning "purification." A lot of people have become interested in certain aspects of the diet, things of that nature. And there are some people who are interested in *chinkon* practice. A lot of people come from other places to study *chinkon*, to study those things for a while and go back to wherever it is that they are.

We have a corporate entity, the Aiki Institute. And then we have the Aikido Shinden, the group connected mainly with the shrine. A lot of people are connected to that. One way to read the characters for "shinden" would be "hall." But "shinden" can also be interpreted as a place under one roof where people come together to have experience of another dimension.

I don't take any money, I'm an amateur. I was professional for many years but I regained my amateur standing some years back. I do healing as a means of making money. I practice a couple of different healing systems. I'm well versed in a number of forms of acupuncture, for example.

Our dues are not high here. I suppose I could charge more, but then we wouldn't be able to have what we have. Recently we were given a $150,000 piece of land and we have something like $85,000 cash in the building fund and we just built a shrine. [Barrish's dojo is non-profit.] We built the shrine last year, which was like a $30,000 thing, and now we still have $85,000 and the land. We couldn't do that if I took a salary. And also I've done a lot of workshops. I've been invited to a lot of different places, pretty much all mainline aikido places. There are even USAF [United States Aikido Federation] dojos where I'm welcome.

There are some personality cults out there. That's one of the reasons I don't take a salary. I really wanted to distance myself from that. On a lot of different levels I wanted to distance myself from that stuff. My personal training is a couple of thousand *suburi* every day, a couple of hours of *chinkon*. My everyday training is really about my personal purification. Also I didn't want to be involved in the finances of the dojo or connected to any other of the dojo's finances. I don't even sign checks for our dojo. I don't have a checkbook, I never touch the dues. I don't deal with it. I just want to go to the dojo and train every day.

The most valuable thing for an instructor to have is a beginner's mind and to have sincerity in your training, sincerity in your own personal search. I personally have been real careful about how I behave as an instructor because I've seen some folks go bad, I've seen some difficulties. That's why I'm so careful with my own personal daily *misogi*. I just want to stay right with the universe, if you will. That constant purification and tuning makes it simpler not to become involved in things that get in the way or that get in the way for somebody else. Sure it's tempting to sleep with women students, but it will always mess up their training. That's a pretty nasty bit of karma to mess up somebody else's training.

It's gone great for the most part. I've been invited lots of places and traveled quite a bit and met lots of wonderful people, had a really good time. I've been to Russia a number of times as you might have heard. I had done an aikido demonstration for the Byakushin-kukai, the Society of Prayer for Peace, which is actually a kind of new Shinto group. They're headquartered in Japan and have branches all over the world. The organization's founder was a very close friend of O-Sensei's. They were really great buddies. So the Society has a real connection to aikido. They're quite connected with Doshu in Japan. And I think Waka Sensei comes at least once a month to their dojo. Anyway, when they did their first international, outside-of-Japan big world-peace prayer in Los Angeles—I guess this was in '86, '85, somewhere in there—I was invited to come down and do an aikido demonstration. And I did some other things in conjunction with them. So I think it was through that that this woman came and said that people within the Soviet Union were asking for aikido. And they asked if I would come.

I agreed and we put together about thirty people, some of our friends from California and various more traditional *aikidoka*, and we all went in 1987. The first night of training it was just bizarre because it was pre-glasnost and perestroika and all that. The first night of training it was just a few people in some bizarre little hall.

319

We had to go quietly, run through the city, enter quietly through the side of the building, it was just bizarre! By the time we were ready to leave the Soviet Union a few weeks later, we had hundreds of people training with us. It was great! Hundreds! Two hundred fifty people on the mat, that kind of thing. In fact, we had a big thing that was going to be at the Olympic Village. The KGB canceled it, though. It was our last day. We had television coverage and a lot of newspaper coverage, a lot of things were going on, we had a lot of support from people who were very, very moved by the aikido they saw. We were canceled and within two hours we had secured another hall on the outskirts somewhere and we still had close to 300 people there that night. Somehow they had found us and we had this really special training. Then we didn't hear from our Soviet friends again for a year or two. When we heard from them next there were about 500 people training, a huge group in Leningrad, groups all over. I don't know the number of groups but they all consider themselves attached to us. There are a lot of really wonderful, very sincere *aikidoka* there. A lot of people have been so moved by aikido that it has become the driving passion in their lives. Some physicists I know have become so obsessed with aikido that they want to do nothing else but aikido. There's a lot of those folks there. There's a real sincerity about their practice that I really like.

EPILOGUE

As mentioned in the Introduction, the interviews in this book illustrate several broad historical trends in aikido in America today and how they have been reflected in the lives of the thirteen featured instructors: the early fascination with the still-living Founder, the not always harmonious meeting and blending of two cultures, the prominent role of Koichi Tohei, the gradual growth in popularity of the art, the interest in how aikido can be applied to everyday life and non-martial disciplines, the struggle of women to find a place in a traditionally male-dominated arena, etc. In addition to these themes, the interviews also explore several other important issues of great concern to aikido practitioners:

1. Was O-Sensei a unique, one-of-a-kind person? Or is it possible for anyone with the right training or attitude to achieve the same magical qualities he exhibited on a regular basis?

2. How important is it to Americanize aikido? How far can we go in removing the Japanese elements without harming the art?

3. Is it possible to attain a deep understanding of the principles of aikido without prolonged intense physical training? If the answer is no, how can aikido be anything more than a limited esoteric art?

4. How can aikido metaphors be applied to other disciplines? Could doing so lead to a watering down of the martial side of aikido?

5. Is aikido training a way to access another dimension of energy?

6. How effective is aikido as a way to break the cycles of negative violence and abuse?

7. How can aikido be practiced as a spiritual discipline?

We hope that our book has given you a sense of the richness of the art and why people have chosen to devote their lives to studying and promoting it. We also hope that our book will inspire further explorations of the history of this wonderful art and of the themes and questions mentioned above.

If you do not practice aikido yourself but would like to investigate it, we suggest you call the periodical *Aikido Today* (909-624-7770) and ask for the name of the dojo nearest you. If you are lucky enough to live near one of the individuals whose interviews you have read, please consult the next page for the address of his/her school and phone number to call.

HOW TO CONTACT SOME OF THE PEOPLE
FEATURED IN THIS BOOK

Robert Nadeau teaches at several locations in the Bay Area, notably at Aikido of Mountain View, 293 Sleeper Ave., Mountain View, CA 94040. (415) 961-0724.

Robert Frager teaches at the Institute of Transpersonal Psychology, 744 San Antonio Road, Palo Alto, CA 94303. (415) 493-4430.

Mary Heiny teaches at seminars given throughout the United States. Consult the Aikido periodical, *Aikido Today Magazine* c/o Arete Press, 1420 Claremont Blvd., Ste 204C, Claremont, CA 91711. (909) 624-7770.

Rod Kobayashi teaches at the headquarters of Aikido Institute of America (Seidokan Aikido), 2235 Hyperion Avenue, Los Angeles, CA 90027. (213) 667-2428.

Frank Doran teaches at Aikido West, 3164 Bay Road, Redwood City, CA 94063. (415) 366-9106.

George Simcox teaches at Virginia Ki Society, 5631 Cornish Way, Alexandria, Virginia 22310. 703-573-8843.

George Leonard, Richard Heckler and Wendy Palmer teach at Aikido of Tamalpais, 76 E. Blithedale Avenue, Mill Valley, CA 94941. (415) 383-9474.

Tom Crum can be reached through Aiki Works Inc., PO Box 7845, Aspen, CO 81612. (303) 925-7099.

Danielle Evans teaches at Aikido of Monterey, 1251 10th Street, Monterey, CA 93940. (408) 375-8106.

Koichi Barrish teaches at Kannagara Dojo, 17720 State Road 92, Granite Falls, WA (206) 691-6389.

SUGGESTED READING LIST

Books by or about the People Featured in This Book:

Crum, Thomas. *The Magic of Conflict*. New York: Touchstone, 1987.

Crum, Thomas. *Your Conflict Cookbook*. Aspen: Aiki Works, Inc., 1985.

Dobson, Terry, and Miller, Victor. *Aikido in Everyday Life: Giving In to Get Your Way*. Berkeley: North Atlantic Books, 1993.

Dobson, Terry. *It's a Lot Like Dancing*. Berkeley: Frog, Ltd., 1993.

Heckler, Richard. *Aikido and the New Warrior*. Berkeley: North Atlantic Books, 1985.

Heckler, Richard. *The Anatomy of Change: A Way to Move Through Life's Transitions*. Berkeley: North Atlantic Books, 1993

Heckler, Richard. *In Search of the Warrior Spirit: Teaching Awareness Disciplines to the Green Berets*. Berkeley: North Atlantic Books, 1990.

Leonard George. *The Ultimate Athlete: Revisioning Sports, Physical Education and the Body*. Berkeley: North Atlantic Books, 1990.

Leonard George. *The Silent Pulse*. New York: Viking Penguin, 1992.

Leonard George. *Mastery: The Keys to Long-Term Success and Fulfillment*. New York: NAL-Dutton, 1992.

Palmer, Wendy. *The Intuitive Body: Aikido As a Clairsentient Practice*. Berkeley: North Atlantic Books, 1994.

Books about Aikido and Morihei Ueshiba

Reed, William. *Ki: A Practical Guide for Westerners*. Tokyo: Japan Publications, 1986.

Saotome, Mitsugi. *Aikido and the Harmony of Nature*. Boston: Shambhala, 1993.

Stevens, John. *Abundant Peace: The Biography of Morihei Ueshiba, Founder of Aikido*. Boston: Shambhala, 1987. Originally published by Kodansha.

Stevens, John. *The Essence of Aikido: Spiritual Teachings of Morihei Ueshiba.* Tokyo: Kodansha, 1993.

Tohei, Koichi. *Aikido in Daily Life.* Tokyo: Japan Publications, 1978.

Ueshiba, Kisshomaru. *The Spirit of Aikido.* Tokyo: Kodansha, 1984.

Ueshiba, Morihei. *Budo: The Teachings of Morihei Ueshiba, the Founder of Aikido.* Tokyo: Kodansha, 1991.

Books Primarily about the Technical Side of Aikido

Saito, Morihiro. *Traditional Aikido.* 5 vols. Tokyo: Minato Research and Publishing, 1974.

Saotome, Mitsugi. *The Principles of Aikido.* Boston: Shambhala, 1987.

Shioda, Gozo. *Dynamic Aikido.* Tokyo: Kodansha, 1968.

Stevens, John and Shirata, Renzuko. *Aikido: The Way of Harmony.* Boston: Shambhala, 1986.

Tohei, Koichi. *This is Aikido.* Tokyo: Japan Publications, 1968. (revised, 1975)

Ueshiba, Kisshomaru. *Aikido.* Tokyo: Hozansha, 1985.

Yamada, Yoshimitsu. *The New Aikido Complete.* Secaucus, New Jersey: Lyle Stuart, 1981.

GLOSSARY OF TERMS

aikidoka: Practitioners of aikido.

aikijutsu/aikijujutsu: Any of those martial arts based on the principle of aiki.

aiki-taiso: Basic solo movement practices performed at the beginning of class.

atemi: Strikes to anatomically weak points.

bokken: Wooden sword.

budo: Martial ways or paths.

bujutsu: Martial arts.

bushido: The Way of the Warrior.

chinkon: A Shinto spiritual exercise, combining physical movements with breathing, chanting, and visualizations.

dan: Grade. Refers to the rank of black belt holders.

deshi: Student, disciple.

do: Path or way. Refers to a discipline intended to lead to self: perfection.

Doshu: Leader of the way. Refers to the current head of World Aikido, Kisshomaru Ueshiba, O-Sensei's son.

doto: Succession.

gasshuku: Special intensive training session.

genki: Eager or enthusiastic.

geta: Traditional Japanese sandals.

gi: Training uniform.

hakama: Traditional pants-like skirt worn by aikido practitioners.

hanmi: Stance.

hanmi handachi: Refers to techniques performed where the defender (*nage*) is seated (in *seiza*) and the attacker or attackers (*uke*) are standing.

hara: Belly, "center."

ikkyo: Joint control technique number one.

ikkyu: First level. The highest level below black belt.

irimi nage: Entering throw.

Izanagi/Izanami: male and female deities who created Japan.

jutsu: Art. Refers to disciplines where technical competence is of foremost importance.

jiyu waza: Free techniques. Refers to a practice in which *nage* can use any technique he/she wishes, in contrast to normal basic practice in which students practice only one specified technique.

jo: Wooden staff.

jujutsu: "Supple" art. The martial ancestor of judo.

kata: Form.

kiai: Yell which often accompanies a strike or throw.

ki no nagere: Ki flow practice. *Nage* moves before he/she is grabbed and performs the technique while in motion. Contrasted to basic or static practice in which *nage* allows him/herself to be grabbed and starts the technique from a static position.

kokyu dosa: Seated practice to develop *kokyu rokyu.*

kokyu rokyu: Breath power. Refers to the power generated when one moves in a centered, unified way.

kote gashi: A wrist technique.

koto: Japanese musical instrument.

Kotodama: "Language of the Spirit." Belief system in which sounds have spiritual significance.

kyu: The name for all levels below black belt rank.

misogi: Purification.

musubi: Connection.

nage: Thrower. The one who executes the technique.

nidan: Second-degree black-belt holder.

nikkyo: Joint control technique number two.

nisei: Second generation Japanese-American.

randori: Practice in which *nage* deals with multiple attackers.

ronin: Masterless samurai.

samurai: Warrior.

sandan: Third degree black-belt holder.

sankyo: Joint control technique number three.

seiza: Position in which one sits in a kneeling position.

sempai: Senior student.

sensei: Teacher.

shiho nage: "Four-corners throw."

Shinto: Japanese polytheistic religion.

shomen uchi: Strike to the top of the head.

shugyo: Austere training.

suburi: Basic individual striking practice with a weapon.

suwariwaza: Techniques performed where both *uke* and *nage* are in *seiza.*

shihan: Master instructor.

shodan: First-degree black belt holder.

soke: Head of traditional family martial art.

t'ai chi ch'uan: Chinese internal martial art. Similar in movement philosophy to aikido.

tatami: Straw mats.

tenkan: Turn, turning.

tsubo: Pressure points.

tsuki: Thrust.

uchi deshi: Live-in student.

uke: Attacker. The one who takes the fall.

ukemi: The art of falling.

yudansha: Black belt holder.

yokomen uchi: Blow to the side of the head.

waza: Techniques.